Accepting the Radical
You Can NOT be Fixed

Ronna Smithrim & Christopher Oliphant

2014

Accepting the Radical:

You Can NOT be Fixed

Ronna Smithrim & Christopher Oliphant

First Edition   October 2011

Second Edition   April 2014

ISBN 978-1-9082931-0-7

© Ronna Smithrim & Christopher Oliphant 2011 - 2014

Ronna Smithrim & Christopher Oliphant have asserted their rights under the Copyright, Designs and Patents act 1988 to be identified as the joint authors of this work.

All rights reserved in all media. This book may not be copied, stored, transmitted or reproduced in any format or medium without specific prior permission from the author.

Published by:

CGW Publishing
B 1502
PO Box 15113
Birmingham
B2 2NJ
United Kingdom

www.cgwpublishing.com

mail@cgwpublishing.com

This book is dedicated to our many clients, with special thanks to the ones whose stories are included within.

This being human is a guest house
Every morning a new arrival.
A joy, a depression, a meanness,
some momentary awareness comes
as an unexpected visitor.
Welcome and entertain them all!
Even if they are a crowd of sorrows,
who violently sweep your house
empty of its furniture,
still, treat each guest honourably.
He may be clearing you out
for some new delight.
The dark thought, the shame, the malice.
meet them at the door laughing and invite them in.
Be grateful for whatever comes.
because each has been sent
as a guide from beyond.

Rumi

Contents

1 Introduction 1
    Theme 1: The Wheel 6
    Systems 10
    Archetypes 11
    Theme Two: Maturity 13
    Theme Three: Self-Discovery 14
    Theme Four: Self-Acceptance 14
    Theme Five: Principles 15
    Theme Six: Responsibility 15
    Theme Seven: Observer 16
    Stories 17

2 The Wheel 21
    Event 22
    Feel & Accept 23
    Discover 26
    Integrate & Accept 29
    Plan 32
    Act & Accept 35
    The Wheel 37

- 3 Maturity ... 39
  - Maturity: Event ... 46
  - Maturity: Feel & Accept ... 48
  - Maturity: Discover ... 51
  - Maturity: Integrate & Accept ... 53
  - Maturity: Plan ... 56
  - Maturity: Act & Accept ... 58
  - Maturity ... 60
- 4 Self-Discovery ... 63
  - Systems Discovery ... 68
  - Critical Thinking ... 70
  - Projection ... 74
  - Attachment ... 76
  - Self-Discovery: Event ... 79
  - Self-Discovery: Feel & Accept ... 80
  - Self-Discovery: Discover ... 81
  - Self-Discovery: Integrate & Accept ... 83
  - Self-Discovery: Plan ... 84
  - Self-Discovery: Act & Accept ... 85
  - Self-Discovery ... 87
- 5 Self-Acceptance ... 89
  - Self-Acceptance: Event ... 94
  - Self-Acceptance: Feel & Accept ... 95
  - Self-Acceptance: Discover ... 97
  - Self-Acceptance: Integrate & Accept ... 99
  - Self-Acceptance: Plan ... 101
  - Self-Acceptance: Act & Accept ... 103
  - Self-Acceptance ... 105

6 Principles 107
    Principles: Event 113
    Principles: Feel & Accept 115
    Principles: Discover 117
    Principles: Integrate & Accept 119
    Principles: Plan 121
    Principles: Act & Accept 124
    Principles 126

7 Responsibility 129
    Responsibility: Event 138
    Responsibility: Feel & Accept 140
    Responsibility: Discover 141
    Responsibility: Integrate & Accept 143
    Responsibility: Plan 145
    Responsibility: Act & Accept 147
    Responsibility 149

8 Observer 151
    Observer: Event 155
    Observer: Feel & Accept 157
    Observer: Discover 159
    Observer: Integrate & Accept 160
    Observer: Plan 162
    Observer: Act & Accept 163
    Observer 166

9 Linda: The Wheel 169

10 Yvonne: Maturity 203

11 Mac: Self-Discovery 233

12 Anthony: Self-Acceptance..259

13 Amanda: Principles...281

14 Tara: Responsibility..309

15 Kathy: The Observer..337

16 Conclusion..361

17 Summary...373

    The Wheel...374

    Systems...377

    Archetypes..378

    Maturity...380

    Self-Discovery..380

    Self-Acceptance...381

    Principles..381

    Responsibility..382

    Observer...382

18 About the Authors...385

    Ronna Smithrim..386

    Christopher Oliphant..388

19 Bibliography..391

20 Contacting the Authors...395

1 Introduction

Years ago I was told that I needed to love myself. This sounded like a good idea, so I asked what practising self-love involved and how I could make it concrete in my life. These questions seemed straightforward and important, but no one seemed to have the answers. What followed for my wife and me was the journey that eventually resulted in this book: the journey to discover the meaning of self-love in grounded, concrete and practical terms.

Our search for clarity took us down many different paths. We read, meditated and debated and listened to our thoughts, feelings and intuitions. When we explored love as a feeling, we noticed that it came and went like all other feelings. Could something so transitory really be so important to our lives? We explored love as intention: when we made a choice about an action that had an impact on us, we would always choose actions that were healthy, gentle and kind. This worked as well as a New Year's resolution; it started out well, but we couldn't sustain it. The stress of trying to maintain these intentions and the sense of guilt that arose when we failed just didn't feel like self-love.

We attended workshops on self-love and spirituality. We listened as the leaders of these workshops said, 'God is love', 'The universe is love' and 'All is love.' But we were still left asking, 'What do these phrases mean?' No one could provide us with an explanation.

Our research into self-love eventually ground to a halt. In the meantime we continued our work as therapists, helping clients who came to us with their personal issues. Therapy requires us to be with our clients fully without judging them; we work to accept them for all of who they are. It was after a few weeks of therapy sessions that we realised how this attitude to judgment held the key to our understanding of self-love. Practising self-love means seeing ALL of who you are without judgement – not labelling any part of yourself as good or bad, positive or negative, right or wrong.

We began to focus more deliberately on acceptance in both our personal and professional lives. When we were sitting in a café in Thailand some months later, someone asked about what we did and the premise of our work. My wife thought for a while and replied, "Acceptance... Radical acceptance.'

Newcomers to Radical Acceptance often ask us the same set of questions. One of the most common questions is, 'How can I accept behaviours that are clearly hurtful to me and other people?' The answer lies in seeing how acceptance of who you are is just a step on a longer path. Once you've accepted yourself, you can go on to make behavioural choices that honour your life's motivating principles. When I accepted myself as a liar, an addict and an angry person, I was better able to make choices about my lying, using and angry actions. These parts of myself had previously driven my behaviour from deep within my subconscious mind, but now they were out of the shadows and I could make choices about them for the very first time. I was able to deal with my behaviour much more gently and compassionately than if I'd simply tried to force myself into change.

Another common concern is that acceptance turns you into a doormat, accepting everything and letting everyone walk all over you. Acceptance as we teach it involves responding to life's events. When we began to act in this way – consciously planning our actions from a place of acceptance – we found that we were responding with much greater clarity and often obtaining much better results than if we'd responded in the heat of the moment. Our choices were now more compassionate, incorporating more love for both others and ourselves.

Many people also ask us how Radical Acceptance deals with change. We reply by saying that you can't change who you are, and wanting to do so takes you out of self-love and into self-rejection. The alternative to changing who you are is accepting who you are. This idea may need a little further explanation. I recently read a book, 'Warrior Pose', by Brad Willis. It's about a news reporter who was driven, ambitious and obsessed with his work. He then became seriously ill and was only given two years to live. It was at this point that he discovered yoga, and the book described how yoga had transformed his life and taken him on an incredible journey of healing. It was clear to me that yoga hadn't transformed the man's life at all; he was still the same driven, ambitious and obsessed person he'd always been. When he took up yoga he didn't just do a few stretches, but rather a daily session that was twelve hours long. He then went on to found a yoga school and write the book that I'd picked up. His drive, ambition and obsession hadn't changed, but how he expressed himself had. Yoga also wasn't responsible for his healing, which had actually happened because he'd come to terms with who he really was. He was a fanatic at heart, and yoga allowed him to express his nature in a way that he'd never managed as a news reporter. The book was an excellent example of Radical Acceptance's fundamentals, and the author's path had led him to a much greater state of self-love.

Radical Acceptance has the power to give you a degree of control over your life that endless years of 'fix' therapy could never touch. Trying to fix yourself is pointless because you simply can't fix who you are. You can change how you express yourself like the man who discovered yoga, but your core, fundamental personality will always remain the same. You already know this at some level, despite your inner protests that it can't be true.

Attempting to fix, transform, transcend, heal or cure is to step out of love. Radical Acceptance helps you to discover who you are and how to love all of this person. It invites you to say a big 'Yes!' to the wondrous, messed up and powerful human being that is the beautiful you.

* * *

We'd like to pause at this point to introduce ourselves: we're Ronna Smithrim and Christopher Oliphant, the creators of Radical Acceptance. We're teachers and therapists who have been married for the past 23 years and have five children. We both became practising psychotherapists soon after we met. Our training didn't come from the hallowed halls of an educational institution, but rather from our work on our own lives and our experiences with an ever-increasing number of clients.

We've taught Radical Acceptance to groups around the world and have finally produced this book in response to constant pressure from our clients and students. Our experience tells us that its contents won't be for everyone: Radical Acceptance is a multi-faceted approach to personal growth work which can be both demanding and painful, opening up doors in your life that will lead to challenging and sometimes even shattering places.

As you read the book, you'll see that Radical Acceptance takes many existing tools and re-orients them to facilitate acceptance – and through acceptance, a deep state of self-love. There are seven themes, or major aspects, to the program. These themes are interconnected and complementary, and explanations of them make up the book's central section. After the themes have been covered, stories from our clients' experiences show how the themes can be applied in real-world situations. The rest of this chapter gives a brief overview of each of the seven themes, an explanation of some important terms and more information on the stories and how they're useful for gaining a fuller understanding of Radical Acceptance.

Theme 1: The Wheel

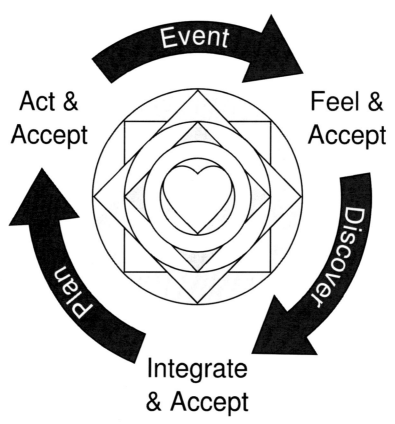

The Radical Acceptance Wheel invites you to gain a deeper understanding of yourself by looking at how you respond to life. It's only from a place of knowing and understanding who you are that there can be genuine self-acceptance and, through acceptance, self-love. Your deeper understanding will also give you the power to choose to respond life's events in new, more creative and more constructive ways.

The Radical Acceptance Wheel begins when you react to a life event with an emotional response. We refer to events as being 'charged' whenever they're reacted to in this way. Imagine that someone lies to you, for instance. The lying is really what's termed a 'neutral' event – it's just something that's happened. If you respond to the lie by getting angry, tearful or afraid, then your emotional response means that the event holds a 'charge' for you. This is where the Wheel comes in. Its six spokes use the charge from the event as energy to propel you through Radical Acceptance's other themes and into a more complete state of self-love.

The Wheel's six spokes will be covered in much more detail later on, but the following descriptions offer a brief overview:

Event

Events are happening all the time. Most events are unimportant and so are simply ignored. Other events grab our attention, triggering off something in our psyche that 'charges' these events with an emotional response. These events are what Radical Acceptance is interested in. We start from a premise that all events are neutral and go on to suggest that charged events are really just invitations from our subconscious minds to take a deeper look within.

Feel and Accept

You know that an event isn't neutral when you feel or think obsessively about it. That's right: every time you feel happy, sad, angry, powerful, fearful or excited, the event that caused this response isn't neutral. If you're a thinker rather than a feeler, you'll notice the charge through your thoughts – you'll find yourself thinking about the event repeatedly and imagining how it might have gone differently. The event's charge is the invitation to go on a journey of self-exploration. To begin this journey you must be able to step back from your emotional response, being aware of the feeling without becoming caught up in it. This is only possible when you fully feel and accept the feeling instead of judging it as being either positive or negative.

Discover

Radical Acceptance uses a variety of tools to explore your psyche, opening up the door on your unconscious world. Each tool is driven by your response to an event and will help you to discover parts of yourself that have been forgotten, suppressed or rejected. These discoveries aren't flaws which needing fixing: they're integral parts of who you are. These are the parts of you that have been rejected and discarded. Changing this rejection into acceptance is the cornerstone of self-love.

Integrate and Accept

Once a discovery has been made, Radical Acceptance prompts you to accept what you find no matter how awful it may first appear. This means seeing the gift in the discovery and being grateful for what you may once have despised. This step also recognizes that integrating and accepting what was once rejected is a process, and we teach you tools to help with deepening this integration and acceptance over time. There will be discoveries for which integration and acceptance are lifelong processes that you never manage to complete. For other discoveries, the same processes of integration and acceptance will be far shorter and more solid.

Plan

When you've integrated and accepted a discovery, the next step is to plan a response to the original event. If the event was someone lying to you, this event now needs some kind of response – even if the response is a decision to do nothing. It's time to stand back and plan an appropriate answer; time to analyse your options and consider the potential consequences that are associated with the choices that you could make. Responding in this considered manner is more likely to lead you into actions that honour both you and any other people involved.

Act & Accept

Whatever response you choose, the next step is to act on your plan. Sometimes doing this will be easy, and at other times it'll be more difficult. Some responses will also be internal to you – such as choosing to forgive someone – while other actions will be external. If your response is external and likely to affect others, you'll need to remember that other people's responses to your actions belong to them and not you. The acceptance part of the Act & Accept spoke is equally important as it invites you to accept the consequences of your actions and not blame others for them.

Completing the Wheel's final three spokes ensures that you respond to the original event carefully and with integrity. The alternative is a reaction that's caught up in the heat of feelings and doesn't involve any planning. Such actions often lead to regret and self-criticism. Using the Wheel is more work and takes more time but its benefits are clear: greater self-awareness, greater self-acceptance and actions that honour you. This is self-love made real.

Two terms that are used throughout this book need to be defined before we explore the six remaining themes. These terms are 'Systems' and 'Archetypes'.

Systems

Systems are one of the cornerstones of Radical Acceptance. Their short definition is: rules made by you as a child to make sense of your world. These rules then become subconscious, firmly held beliefs that direct much of what you do and lead to undesired results.

A young child experiences many painful and traumatic events. Some of this trauma may come from the extremes of sexual and physical abuse, but it's most often from events that appear less traumatic to adults. Potential sources include parents, teachers, other children, siblings and the child's extended family. The child's psyche needs to develop a way of managing the pain associated with such trauma – but without the ability to understand the reasons behind what's happened, he or she compensates by believing that the problem lies within. The child creates a belief that gives order to the chaos by making the reason for the chaos the child. Over time, this belief then becomes enforced and deeply engrained within the child's psyche. Radical Acceptance calls these ingrained beliefs 'Systems'.

In life as an adult, all thoughts, feelings and events go through the Systems that you developed as a child. This gives Systems a powerful impact on your life. You'll generally have two or three major Systems. These are the foundations of your personality, and understanding the concept of Systems gives you important insights into why you make the choices that you do as an adult.

Systems guide and direct behaviour from deep within the subconscious. They need to keep re-creating the childhood experiences which formed them for reasons we can only speculate on, and in doing this they direct your actions into dysfunctional patterns. As such, while you can't see a System directly, you can see its influence through your actions; a System is discovered by assessing how what you do contradicts either your stated goals or who you see yourself to be. You may see yourself as an open and loving person but then have trouble maintaining close relationships. This issue is often caused by a System that says, 'I'm unlovable' – a result of a child's interpretation of the universal limit on how much attention parents can give to their children. This System will drive unconscious behaviours such as pushing loved ones away when you consciously want deeper, more intimate relationships. Noticing this contradiction is the key to unveiling the System.

As with other parts of your personality, Systems can't be fixed and they also won't go away. Once you can make your System conscious, however, you can start making some sense out of what drives your behaviour. You can then ultimately begin to make new choices as a result of this new knowledge. Instead of rejecting your Systems and being self-critical when they act in your life, accepting your Systems is a huge step away from self-rejection and into self-love.

Archetypes

Another cornerstone of Radical Acceptance is archetypes. The term 'archetype' was originally introduced by the psychologist Carl Jung, a student of Sigmund Freud. Jung suggested as early as 1919 that the human psyche is structured in a way that helps us to interpret our experiences of life. This structuring is inherent to being human but is also personal and based on our individual histories. Jung suggested that there are many archetypes, but this book focuses on the three that are most important to Radical Acceptance: the Child, the Adult and the Observer.

The Child archetype is the one that everyone encounters first in life. This archetype doesn't grow or mature but remains as a child – even when you've physically grown. It's the Child that accumulates all of your hurts and traumas. The Child can lead to dysfunctional choices if it's left to run your life without the supervision of the Adult archetype. The Adult archetype generally develops later in life as you physically and emotionally mature and begin to leave adolescence behind. The Adult is the one that thinks about the world and is mature and responsible. He or she acts based on principles. The Adult acts even when an action hurts others, costs you money or makes you look bad. It's the ability to do what you know is appropriate even when everyone around you is saying otherwise.

The Child remains with you even once you've developed the Adult. In fact, there will be areas of your life for which the Child is in charge regardless of how old you become. You may be an adult financially, for instance, but your personal relationships may be run by the Child. Alternatively, you may be an adult when it comes to professional relationships, but then in your role as a parent you may act like a child – inappropriately trying to be friends with your children.

The Observer archetype also develops later on in life, but only in those people who do the necessary personal growth work. It comes into play when we learn to step back from life and notice what's going on. The Observer is fully aware of all feelings but doesn't act upon them. While the Child wants to react immediately and the Adult wants to think things through before acting, the Observer just watches what's going on. Calling on your Observer gives you the space and time to then call on either the Child or the Adult depending on the situation. The role of the Observer is to stand back, see with awareness and know that all is neutral.

Each of the three archetypes has gifts to offer and can also cause problems. All of the archetypes are available to us at any time. Each has its time and place and each can be inappropriate at the wrong time and place. What many do not realize is that you have a choice: you can choose which archetype to put in charge. How you relate to your archetypes is an indication of your degree of self-acceptance. If you make the Child archetype 'bad' and the Adult archetype 'good' then you've rejected a vital part of being human and being you. This is self-rejection and not self-love. Equally, always indulging the Child and his or her wants leads you to reject the needs of the Adult. Self-love is to say yes to the Child, Adult and Observer and call on each one when appropriate.

Now that these two terms have been defined, let's continue looking at Radical Acceptance's themes.

Theme Two: Maturity

Maturity is the second theme of Radical Acceptance. It's defined as: honouring and respecting both the Child and Adult archetypes and being in charge of which one is appropriate in any given situation. Most people focus entirely on the Child in their lives; our culture of instant gratification and overindulgence encourages the inner wounded Child over the rational, tempered Adult that develops with age and experience. Once you've accepted the role that your Child plays in your life, you can then work on developing a strong Adult to act as an alternative choice in any situation – limiting the Child, taking charge of your life and moving both archetypes into balance.

As loving parents, we're called to act on behalf of our children in situations where there's potential danger or their health is at risk. We don't let our children play with sharp knives, for example, and we ensure that they eat a healthy diet. On the other hand, we also let them have fun and make age-appropriate decisions. We ultimately strike a balance between our children's needs and their health and well-being. The Maturity theme calls on us to find a similar balance in our own lives by honouring the Child and Adult archetypes. Just as parents find balance out of their love for their children, Radical Acceptance calls on you to find inner balance out of your love for yourself.

Theme Three: Self-Discovery

The self-discovery theme focuses on making you more aware of who you are, continually inviting you to go deeper into your subconscious mind. This process is vital to making the discoveries that play a key role in the Radical Acceptance Wheel – ultimately giving you some real insight into who you are and why you act in the ways that you do. You won't find things to fix or a roadmap to change, but you will make discoveries; you'll gain invaluable insights into your inner world and glimpses of the forces that motivate your behaviour. These are the discoveries that – when combined with Theme Four – play a huge role in making self-love a reality.

Theme Four: Self-Acceptance

Once you've discovered hidden aspects of your personality, the next step in Radical Acceptance involves accepting that your discoveries are both real and useful parts of who you are. Doing so allows you to be totally honest with yourself – freeing up significant amounts of energy that you'd otherwise use for repressing these unwanted personality traits. The self-acceptance process also helps you to see and accept others for who and what they are. Once you stop judging yourself, you'll be able to see the world around you with much more clarity and compassion. Increasing self-acceptance involves moving away from self-rejection and toward self-love.

Theme Five: Principles

Radical Acceptance defines principles as 'intentions to guide how I behave and a plan for when I miss'. These intentions and plans can cover anything from how you'll treat others to how you'll treat yourself. Principles offer a clear outline for what to do in any number of situations both before events occur and in response to them. By spending time working out in detail what principles you want to live by, you can increase your chances of living a life that develops in accordance with your goals. Living by principles gives you a sense of integrity and being able to count on yourself. Of course there will be times when you'll fail to act in accordance with your principles. Having a plan in place enables you to respond to situations, but also acknowledges that you're human and will sometimes miss the mark. Accepting this potential for error allows you to be gentler on yourself when you do miss. This gentler approach incorporates much more self-love than is available through attempting to be super-human and acting in planned ways every time.

Theme Six: Responsibility

Responsibility is the broadest theme in Radical Acceptance and takes something from each of the other themes. Its definition is split into two parts because of this breadth. The first part states that 'everything you do comes as a result of choices that you've made'. This means accepting that you're the only one who decides what actions you take. It might be tempting to pass blame for your actions onto others, but responsibility is about accepting that the choices for your actions are entirely your own. The second part of the definition states that 'the consequences of your actions are yours to accept'. This means that you're responsible for what happens as a result of your actions – including how others' reactions to your choices affect your life.

As stated in Theme Five, being responsible does not mean always making the right choices. Knowing it was you who made your choices is not fuel to be self-critical. The focus here is on looking inward for the forces that shaped your choices instead of looking outward. Look inward with acceptance and kindness, as the rewards for doing this are far greater than the benefits that are available from blaming anyone else.

Theme Seven: Observer

The Observer theme covers the third archetype introduced in this book – the archetype that notices all thoughts, feelings, behaviours and events without engaging in them in any way. When you develop this archetype, you'll be able to set aside your attachment to the emotions in your life that are associated with the Child and the Adult. You'll instead come to experience life from a more objective perspective. Developing this archetype doesn't lead to detachment or apathy, but actually enables you to experience life more fully. The Observer enables you to feel your feelings in their purest forms and make the most rational decisions on this basis. The Observer can therefore be said to be the purest form of self-love.

These themes are not linear and no single theme is more important than the others. All of the themes work best together, with each complementing and supporting the rest.

Stories

There are stories used throughout the book to demonstrate Radical Acceptance in action. In the seven chapters that cover the seven themes there's an ongoing story about the lives of George and Judy. These two people are entirely fictional, although many of the incidents described have been drawn from our clients' lives.

Chapters nine through fifteen each feature a story that's focused on one of the seven themes. These stories are based on, and sometimes partially written by, real people – clients we have worked with over a number of years and who have made major transformations as a result of the work that they have done in applying Radical Acceptance to their lives. These stories show the movement that these people made from self-rejection toward self-love. While the people are real, their names, details and some of the events described have been changed for reasons of confidentiality – although we've reproduced their basic issues and personality traits as far as possible.

The stories are also written in a somewhat-peculiar form – a combination of the third person and first-person plural. When we refer to something that both of us did, we've used words like 'us' and 'we'. When just one of us was involved, we're identified by name. This isn't a conventional style, but it has given us flexibility in explaining complex dynamics in print. We've also kept the swearing down to a minimum, although it has been included when we've felt that it's appropriate.

To Linda, Yvonne, Mac, Anthony, Amanda, Tara and Kathy, we wish to offer our heart-felt thanks for allowing us to share so much of your lives' journeys in these pages. We also wish to thank the many others who have been parts of our lives and work.

* * *

A final word about the two of us. To label us 'unconventional' is an understatement. Calling people to see and accept all of who they are is our driving force. Issues such as being nice and orthodox take a distant second place. There may be times when you find things that we say or do in some of the stories unsettling, but always know that they're done with love and respect for the clients in an effort to break their patterns of avoidance and denial. Confrontation is sometimes the only way to call them forth to see and accept all of who they are. It's our special version of tough love, inviting them into a full expression of self-love.

We now invite you to stop trying to fix who you are and instead love all of who you are – to accept all of the glory that is you by doing the work of Radical Acceptance. This won't be easy, as the tendency to fix is a fundamental structure in our culture. Changing your approach to personal growth takes time, patience and real effort. Nevertheless, the material provided here will enable you to make real and profound changes in your life. Seeing life from a place of self-love fundamentally changes your relationship with yourself, life events and the people who move in and out of your life. These changes will in turn begin a cascade of further changes that will have a profound and transforming effect on the way you live.

2 The Wheel

The six spokes of the Radical Acceptance Wheel are the basis for all future work. Using our feelings to open the door to our inner world starts the personal growth journey and drives the deepening of all of the Radical Acceptance themes.

Event

Everything starts with events. Simply put, these are the things which happen in our lives: from wedding days and divorces right down to visiting the hairdresser and cleaning the kitchen. By themselves, these things are all neutral – it's our feelings which make them good or bad, right or wrong, positive or negative. These 'charges', and not the events themselves, are what Radical Acceptance focuses on.

Why is it so important to recognise that all events are neutral? When you do this, you begin to appreciate that your responses belong to you, and not to the events themselves. Consider, for example, how a tragic event might leave one person feeling sad, another angry, another fearful, another happy and another numb. Similarly, the same event might make a single person feel differently at different points in time. Responses come about as events are filtered through each individual's perceptions, histories, personalities, Systems and beliefs. When you recognise this, you recognise how much control you have over how you react to the feelings which arise from the events in your life.

Events come at the start of the Radical Acceptance Wheel because they're what trigger reactions. These reactions, or charges, then go on to drive the rest of the Wheel, providing opportunities for elements of personal growth such as maturity, self-discovery, self-acceptance, the development of principles, responsibility and the development of the Observer archetype. In other words, when you accept that events are neutral and that you're in control of how you act in response to them, you set the Radical Acceptance Wheel and all of its possibilities in motion.

George and Judy were employees at a small family business – George managed the office, and Judy was in charge of the marketing. The company had been started by an older couple who, over a number of years, had turned a good idea into a successful enterprise. The couple were nice people, but could sometimes be difficult to work for: they had put a lot of effort into making the business viable during its early stages, and were reluctant to give up any control now that it was doing well.

One afternoon, George came back from lunch to find Judy sitting at her desk in tears. Another of her marketing ideas had been rejected by the owners, and she took this to mean that her input to the company wasn't respected. George did his best to reassure her, reminding Judy that, as the owners, they were allowed to choose the ideas that they wanted. This didn't help, however. In a sad tone, Judy looked up at him and said, "Of course you support them – you always do. No matter how bad the idea, you go with what they say. You just hate conflict." Without another word, George went back to his office.

For the rest of the day, he buried himself in work, but was short with his colleagues whenever they came in to see him. Before Judy left for the evening, she came to his office and apologised for what she'd said earlier on. George reassured her that it didn't matter, but Judy wasn't convinced. When she asked him why he'd been different with everyone since her words, he seemed genuinely puzzled: "I'm really not angry," he said, "I've just got a lot to do."

Feel & Accept

The variety of feelings which humans can experience in response to events is virtually endless; we're capable of experiencing everything from love, passion, happiness and excitement to hate, anger, sorrow, fear and shame. What this stage of Radical Acceptance focuses on is saying 'yes' to each one of these feelings.

When you accept your feelings, you change how you experience them. This is one of the strange aspects of Radical Acceptance: accepting grief, happiness, anger, passion, fear, excitement or any other emotional response changes your experience of that feeling. One change, for example, is that you'll become the feeler of the feeling instead of allowing the feeling to consume you. Now, instead of making judgements about whether any feeling is either 'good' or 'bad', you'll start to see each emotion as a gift which can help you to learn more about yourself. This allows every feeling to become a teacher and a healer. In contrast, if you choose to reject your feelings, they're likely to become your tormentors: driving you to act in ways that later lead to regret.

Rejecting a feeling is the process of labelling it as 'bad' or 'negative'. In the West, some of us may have heard statements from our parents such as 'big boys don't cry' and 'good girls don't get angry'. When we hear these messages as children, we're inclined to reject our grief and anger – to deny that we even feel these emotions. However, rejected feelings never go away. Instead, they enter our subconscious minds and find destructive ways of expressing themselves in the future. For women who believe that 'good girls don't get angry', for instance, years of rejected anger can easily turn into depression. Similarly for men who internalise the 'boys don't cry' message, feelings of grief often turn into an inability to feel anything except degrees of anger, ranging from annoyance right through to violent rage.

The way in which feelings are rejected varies from person to person and from situation to situation, but knowing some of the most common methods can help you to identify the process of rejection within yourself. Repression is a method used by many people – hiding from yourself that you're feeling the 'bad' feeling at all. If, for example, a certain emotion was labelled as negative when you were a child, then you might have decided that it was safer to just never feel it. The emotion never really disappears, though – it just goes 'underground'. Repression can happen during adulthood, as well. This is particularly evident in the Spirituality Movement, where it's often seen as 'unspiritual' to feel fear or anger. Spiritual followers pretend that they no longer experience these 'negative' feelings in an effort to achieve their spiritual goals. The emotions never go, however – they just get pushed into the subconscious, from where they continue to express themselves in damaging ways.

Another common method of rejecting a feeling is re-labelling. This involves feeling one feeling but labelling it as something different. If you received the 'good girls don't get angry' message and are uncomfortable with anger, for example, then you might unconsciously choose to label it as grief – which is what often leads women to cry when angry. This pattern is somewhat more common among women than men, but is not exclusive to them. For men who hear the 'boys don't cry' message, it's equally easy to convert hidden grief into anger or indifference. Striking out or withdrawing in anger is often a man's response to feeling sadness or pain. By taking these diversionary courses of action, a 'bad' feeling becomes something more acceptable.

So, does this mean that it's necessary to feel fear, anger, sadness and all of those other 'bad' emotions? Absolutely. You don't need to like them, of course, but you do need to recognise that it's okay to feel them, and that accepting them – instead of judging and rejecting them - can help you to learn more about yourself.

When you accept your feelings, you make yourself conscious of them, and this allows them to become your teachers and healers. The process can be difficult with emotions such as depression, rage, fear and grief, but the work is always worth the benefits: you'll be able to respond differently to feelings in the future and, as described in the next section, your acceptance can also be used to discover hidden truths about yourself.

> Both George and Judy reacted emotionally to events: Judy felt sad when her ideas were rejected by the people she worked for, George denied that he felt anything after Judy's comments, even though his behaviour suggested otherwise. In reality, all either of them felt was anger – Judy relabelled her anger as sadness, and George repressed his into what he thought was nothing. The people around them could see how the events had made them angry, but to George and Judy, it was easier to pretend otherwise.

The Wheel

Later that week, we met George and Judy at a Radical Acceptance workshop we were running for company executives and managers. As part of the programme, we first explained the basics of the Radical Acceptance idea, and then asked each person in the group to describe a recent event from their lives which had carried a charge.

When we got to Judy, she mentioned the event from earlier in the week. We asked how this had made her feel, and she explained how she felt saddened when her ideas weren't respected by her employers. We then asked her colleagues how they'd interpreted her reaction to the rejection and they agreed that she'd seemed angry, not sad. After taking a few moments to consider this judgement, Judy agreed: "You're right – I was angry, and in fact, I still am. I want to do something exciting with this company's marketing, but every time I come up with an idea, it gets rejected. It makes me really, really angry."

Next it was George's turn. He talked about Judy's comments from the same morning, but again emphasised that he wasn't angry. Coughing suddenly broke out across the room, and George looked up in surprise. We laughed, and suggested that his co-workers might be in disagreement.

After looking down for a while, he looked up again, turned to Judy, and said: "They're right, I am angry. You had no right to speak to me like that."

Discover

Once you've said 'yes' to all of your feelings, it's time to start learning from them – to discover how your past influences your present and how your mindset can colour events. The answers to these discoveries lie in your subconscious, which is the part of your psyche that holds repressed and forgotten memories, instinctual urges and your Systems. These things affect many different aspects of our lives, and by discovering them, we can learn how to work with them rather than fighting against them.

There are many different tools available for opening up the subconscious mind, and which one we choose depends on the event itself and the reaction which we experience to it. The most commonly-used tool is projection, which was first developed in the 1890s by the leading psychiatrist Sigmund Freud and then furthered by his student, Carl Jung. Briefly, projection involves someone denying one of their personal attributes, pushing it into their subconscious, and then judging this attribute when they see it in others. The judgement is often felt as anger or envy, although it can express itself through any feeling – from happiness and love to sadness and hate. As such, if you get angry because someone lies to you, then it's because you too are a liar, but have pushed the fact that you're a liar into your subconscious. You won't lie in quite the same way as the other person, but you will have your own personal lying behaviours. For most of the time, these will be invisible to you: only by recognizing your anger as a clue will the hidden attribute become clear.

Another frequently-used tool is identifying Systems. This is best applied in response to repetitive patterns in your life, and involves looking for discrepancies between what you say and what you do. Many people, for example, say that they want more intimacy in their lives. However, they also unconsciously take steps to block this intimacy from coming to them. A System is often behind these actions. It may say, for example, that "I am unlovable" – which could be the result of coming from a critical and judgemental family. This 'unlovable' System will unconsciously work to repeat behaviours that block you from intimacy. You might hide your real feelings from your partner, for example, under the guise of protecting them – really blocking intimacy, as intimacy is the sharing of your inner world with another. When you recognise what the System is doing, you can begin to work with it instead of fighting it.

A third powerful tool is critical thinking. This is well-suited to addressing feelings of shame and inadequacy, and involves you thoroughly examining your thoughts. You won't need to think critically about everything that enters your head; you think thousands of thoughts each day, and most are quickly discarded. The ones which you really need to assess are the ones which stick with you - the ones which feed your Systems; thoughts such as "I'm no good" or "I'm bad/stupid/ugly". These are the thoughts which are given all kinds of importance and seen as the 'truth'.

Critical thinking invites you to assess these thoughts rationally. Are you really no good? Are you truly bad/stupid/ugly? Such thoughts will almost always have little to no basis in reality. Instead of seeing them as important, discard them exactly as you already do with most of your thoughts. Alternatively, recognise that the repetitive or charged thought is feeding one of your Systems, and deal with the System rather than focusing on the thought. Either way, take what is valid and discard the rest: there's no need to waste time dwelling on false thoughts.

When we address the theme of self-discovery, we'll cover these and other tools in more detail. Until then, it's important to appreciate how it's possible to use the charge from an event to get answers from your subconscious. Then, when you know why you react like you do, you'll be able to integrate these discoveries into your life.

> As they admitted their feelings of anger to the group, both Judy and George had blamed someone else for it - Judy the owners, and George Judy. In Radical Acceptance, blaming others is often a sign of a hidden personal issue. If these issues can be discovered and resolved, they can help us to see things differently. It was time to do some searching into our participants' subconscious minds.
>
> George went first. We started by asking him to describe how Judy had appeared to him that morning. He described her as insensitive: "I would never speak to another person like that. She's so insensitive and often lashes out," he added. From here, we moved the discussion on to 'projection' - the idea that when we respond to things which other people do, it's normally because those actions reflect an unconscious aspect of ourselves. The next logical step, then, was to ask George how he was insensitive himself. He initially denied that he was, but when we asked for the opinions of other people in the group, he found it hard to deny; many of the others said that he'd often dismiss them without listening to what they said. Although his insensitivity wasn't the same as Judy's, it was there.

After this revelation, we moved on to Judy – who was now a little worried about what we could discover about her life. To shake things up, we didn't talk about projection this time, but asked her to describe her first memory of being treated without respect. Almost immediately, she talked about her father: he was often away from home during her childhood, and she resented her failed attempts to get his attention. To make sense of this experience, we told the group about 'Systems' – that when Judy was small, her experiences may have led her to create a rule which stated 'I'm not worthy of respect'. This would then have followed her into her adult life, affecting the decisions she makes today. After considering what this meant, she had to agree. It all made sense, after all: it was this System which made her repeatedly put forward marketing ideas which were likely to be rejected. Her lack of self-respect meant that she couldn't express her creativity within the guidelines set by the owners.

Integrate & Accept

Once you've discovered a secret from your unconscious, you'll need to integrate it into your being to make use of it. Before you can do this, however, you have to accept that what you've discovered is an important, vital, gift-giving part of who you are. This has to be done without judgements or conditions: if you discover that you're lazy, for example, then you can't say, "I accept my laziness, except when it costs me my job". This isn't acceptance. Instead, Radical Acceptance invites you to say, "I accept being lazy, and won't try to fix my laziness. I love myself as a lazy person, even when my laziness costs me something important".

If this sounds insane, then it's because it is. Fortunately, it's insanity that works. If you choose to only accept part of your laziness, then you have to continue hiding the rest of it. This unaccepted part then carries on tormenting you. If you accept all of it, however, then you can get a full impression of how you're already being lazy – the Systems involved, and the choices and behaviours which you're already subconsciously making. It's important to remember that acceptance isn't permission, though. It's not about saying, "I accept that I'm lazy, so I'll just stop working", but is rather about saying, "I see how I'm choosing to be lazy. Do I want to continue making these choices?" Acceptance lets you see the choices you're already making – and for the first time gives you the choice to act differently.

This is the beauty of Radical Acceptance. The more you accept yourself, the more areas of your life in which you'll have a choice. When you discover and accept that you're a control freak, for instance, you can choose whether or not to act in a controlling manner. When you know that you're an addict, you can decide whether or not you want to stop acting on your addiction (interestingly, this is also the basis of first of the 'Twelve Steps'). The list goes on and on: once you accept a rejected part of yourself, you'll be able to choose your behaviour in that area.

For some discoveries, the process of integration can take months or even years, and will often be a layered process which involves several trips around the Radical Acceptance Wheel. For other discoveries, the process will work much faster. To help things along, it's possible to use the Scoring Tool. If you discover a System which says that you're not worthy of love, for example, begin to make a note of everything you do which supports that System. When you downplay a compliment, write down a 1 out of 10. If you find yourself actively pushing away someone who's trying to be closer, write down an 8 out of 10. By making yourself aware of what you're doing, you'll be able to constantly take steps to make new choices.

When you've made it this far on the Radical Acceptance Wheel, most of the energy from the original event will have been discharged. In other words, you won't feel such an intense need to react, and you'll also have learnt more about yourself. However, this isn't the place to stop. If you miss the final two steps, you'll fail to act on the original event – and all events call for a response, even if that response is a decision to do nothing. To take things forward, you'll need to plan your next move.

After lunch, the group got back together, and we returned to George and Judy to see how they were coping with their revelations.

George was the first to admit that he was struggling. As he saw things, if he accepted that he was insensitive, he would have to question his sensitivity as a husband and a father. In fact, he'd have to question every aspect of his life. We recognised that acceptance would be a difficult process, of course, and that it would probably take a lot of time to accept fully – but it perhaps wasn't quite as difficult as he imagined, as he didn't have to change anything he did as a result of the acceptance. In fact, we pointed out that his job required a degree of toughness, and so insensitivity could sometimes be a professional advantage. All he had to do was recognise within himself that he was an insensitive person. If he could manage this, then he'd be left with a more honest perception of himself and his emotions.

By the time we turned to Judy, she was already set on change: "When I look back at the past year, I wonder how the owners put up with me. As soon as they set a direction, I'd always head off in the opposite one! It must have driven them crazy. I'm going to change. I'm going to stop fighting for respect and just respect myself". This was a valiant commitment, but as we pointed out to her, it was overly ambitious: the System was in place, and it wasn't going to disappear just because she'd discovered it. Changing her behaviour was something to work toward, but actually managing it would be a slow process. For it to begin, she needed to accept that her System of 'unworthiness' was working to sabotage her efforts. Once she'd accepted this aspect of herself, she could begin to work with her System instead of fighting against it.

Plan

In Radical Acceptance, planning your response to an event is crucial. What's more, taking time over this step will increase your chances of making a decision which is appropriate to your situation and goals. To simplify the process, it helps to first answer three questions before acting. The first of these is, "What outcome do I want to achieve?"

Outcome-based planning will probably be a huge shift away from how you currently plan, as at present you most likely focus on rules and morals when making your decisions. In contrast, outcome-based planning pays attention to what you want to achieve. This type of planning isn't permission to act in any way that you desire, though: illegal acts will have legal outcomes; hurtful acts will alienate you from others; lazy acts won't help you to meet your targets.

Outcome-based planning starts with setting out what you want and then considering possible consequences from your various options. Consider both your short-term and long-term goals. If you partner makes you angry, for example, your short-term goal may be to punish them. Your long-term goal, however, will probably be to have a loving relationship. Consider both of these goals when deciding on how to respond, and avoid just making the choice which seems easiest at the time. Remember: in many cases, the easier choice won't be the best one.

Related to this consideration of outcomes is the second question: "What are the potential consequences of my action?" Consequences are similar to outcomes, as both come about as a result of an action and, like outcomes, every action has consequences. However, outcomes are focused on the goal, while consequences are concerned with the side effects. For example, speaking sharply to another person has the outcome of communicating your frustration, and the consequence of the other person distancing themselves from you. Planning must take equal consideration of both the outcomes and consequences of every potential action, trying to find the optimal balance between the two.

The last question to ask is, "Is the planned action consistent with who I am?" This question is important, as is it allows you to set realistic, achievable targets for the changes you want to make. If your goal is to get healthier through exercise, for instance, and you're a lazy person by nature, then planning an ambitious exercise regime is most likely going to result in failure. If you incorporate your laziness into your plan, however, then you can compensate for it – perhaps by asking a partner to encourage you or by starting off on an easier program before making things more difficult over time. There are always ways to achieve your goals once you've accepted who you are. If you drop the judgements that you make about yourself and only factor the truth into your plans, then you'll greatly increase your likelihood of finding success on a regular basis.

Planning is about looking ahead – considering outcomes, consequences and who you are as a person. Once you've found what appears to be your best option for what you want to achieve, the only thing left to do is to put your plan into effect. It's now time to act.

After listening to Judy's discoveries, George began to feel sorry for her. "I'm really sorry for being angry with you," he said, "I now see why you spoke to me like you did." We challenged him on this: how did his understanding make Judy's comments okay? Similarly, even if he wasn't angry any more, how did this close the event? Judy had spoken angrily to him, and he needed to decide on a response. Initially, he didn't have any answers to these questions.

While George took some time to consider his response, we moved back to Judy. Now that we'd shown her that she probably couldn't change her System of seeking respect, what could she do? She first suggested going back and redoing her work to put it in line with the owners' demands. This was a good idea, but didn't address her deeper issues. When we asked further, she explained that her father was dead; how could she resolve any issues which came from her relationship with him? This wasn't a problem, of course, as her father wasn't really dead – at least, not in Judy's memory. To really make progress, Judy needed to work on her system and how it affected her. She needed to see the gifts it offered – gifts such as inspiring her to be the best she could be, and driving her to earn the respect of others.

George had now done some thinking, and had realised that he was still angry. He wanted to express this by being verbally angry with Judy, but realised that this would damage their relationship. Overall, he wanted to get on better with his co-workers. He was stumped: he didn't want to apologise for feeling angry, and also didn't want to alienate Judy. Our suggestion fell between the two: as a compromise, he could tell Judy how he felt.

Act & Accept

The Act & Accept step brings us to the end of the Wheel – and, being a Wheel, also back to the starting point. So far, when an event has raised feelings, you've used those feelings to discover some aspect of your subconscious and then integrated and accepted what you've discovered. After that, you've planned your response to the event. Finally, it's time to act.

Sometimes actions are internal, such as deciding not to act or to cut cords (an idea talked about in the Responsibility theme). At other times, actions are external, such as speaking with someone or performing a task in response to the original event. Regardless of what you do, the Act and Accept step asks you to do it responsibly – acknowledging that the action you take is the result of a choice you've made and accepting any consequences which may result.

Acting also reveals how well you've planned. If the time comes to act and, for whatever reason, you can't follow through, then your planning was faulty. It may be that you planned on having more courage than you actually have; demanding a pay raise sounds much easier to do when you're not in front of your boss, for instance. Sometimes, a plan fails to consider who you are as a person. For example, if you joined a gym with the intention of working out regularly, then not having been for the last two weeks suggests that you didn't consider your laziness when planning. Planning can also fail to consider the realities of life. If you quit work with the intention of thinking positive thoughts and having the universe provide for all of your needs, then you're likely to discover pretty quickly that your landlord isn't very impressed at receiving good thoughts in lieu of rent.

The next part of acting is accepting the consequences of your actions. This can be as wonderful as accepting applause after a good performance, or as difficult as losing a friend after asking them to lean on you less often. A consequence could also be paying for an item which was broken in a store after a moment's carelessness. No matter what the consequence, it belongs to you.

If you don't like a consequence and find that it leaves you feeling angry, sad, embarrassed, guilty or some other feeling, then realise how that feeling still belongs to you, just as the feelings from any event belong to you. Trying to avoid the emotional consequence speaks to a lack of responsibility. Avoidance can take the form of blame, excusing, rationalizing or hiding – any strategy which tries to shift responsibility away. One of the most common strategies of avoidance is saying, "I don't want to hurt their feelings". The response to this is simple: it's your feelings which you're trying to protect, not anyone else's. Take responsibility for your actions and accept their consequences – knowing that if another person gets angry in response, then that reaction belongs only to them.

Acting is where your plan moves from thought into reality. Given the unpredictability of people and life, expect the unexpected. Be open to learn even as you act.

> Now it was time for George and Judy to act on their plans. For George, this was a real challenge: he wasn't accustomed to feeling his feelings, let alone telling anyone else about them. Initially, his response was to talk about Judy: "You made me feel angry when you said those things". As we pointed out, this wasn't explaining his feelings, but talking about what she'd done. The solution was to create a statement which didn't use the words 'you' or 'Judy'.
>
> After several faltering starts, he made progress: "I felt hurt and reacted angrily when I was told that I had no original thoughts. This is probably because it's close to what I sometimes tell myself, which makes it hard to hear from others". The group congratulated him – this was a breakthrough, and he was visibly relieved.
>
> Next, it was Judy's turn. When we asked her about how she planned to work with her System, she first gave a long answer which sounded much more like a battle than acceptance. When we told her this, she was down-hearted. "I can't get anything right," she said. This was the perfect opportunity to change her pattern of thinking.
>
> As soon as she started to be self-critical, we asked her to rate how good she was at putting herself down – 1 for a small put-down, 10 for a big one. How good had she been a few moments ago? "For that one, I suppose an 8?", she said. "Excellent," we replied, "You did a great job! You

got an 8/10 at putting yourself down! Great job!" This wasn't sarcastic: by scoring her System, she could begin to see it in a new light. Also, the more she worked with her System and came to recognise it, the more she'd be able to make effective choices around it. We even asked her to give her internal put-down a name to help the process. Laughing, Judy said, "Agnes, I think, after my Great Aunt Agnes. I never heard a compliment come out of her mouth." Like George, she'd made a breakthrough. It would have to be consolidated with practice in the future, but it was a start.

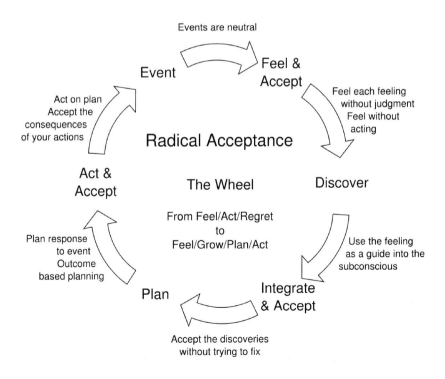

3 Maturity

According to Radical Acceptance, maturity is the transition from living a life run by your inner Child to a life in which you actively choose how you respond to events. When you are in charge, you can invite conscious input from both the Child and the Adult archetypes without either of them being in control. A life run exclusively by the Child tends to be a life of extremes, polarised toward either reactive drama or disconnection from the world in ways which the Adult would find foreign. In contrast, a life run by the Adult is reasoned and responsible, but can be heavy and dry without the balance provided by the Child. As such, becoming mature means seeing gifts in both the Child and the Adult archetypes – instead of just valuing one over the other.

The transition toward maturity is a painful, difficult journey: it's one of moving toward, but never fully arriving at, the mythical destination of 'full maturity'. People undertake this journey because they don't see an alternative. Tired of a life run by the Child and fed up with chaos, they want more say in how their lives unfold. They also want better personal and professional relationships and the ability to make new choices in the face of addictive behaviours such as substance abuse, over-eating, over-exercising, over-spending, laziness and workaholicism.

Given that the Child's emotional development stops at a very early age, it isn't hard to see how a life run by this archetype ends up being dysfunctional. The journey toward maturity offers an alternative: an alternative to walking around in an adult body with the emotional maturity of a child. The work begins when you discover an area of your life being run by the Child. When you first notice this dysfunction, the Child will get labelled as 'bad', and developing the Adult will start to seem like a solution. Over time, you'll come to learn the gifts of both the Child and the Adult, although since there isn't a destination, there will continue to be times when the Child takes over or when you lean too heavily on the Adult. If you stay vigilant, you will notice when the one or the other is back making the decisions and, with strength and discipline, you will then be able to take back control. Given the need to develop your Adult, this chapter will focus on moving from the Child to the Adult. Mastering the final stage of seeing the gifts in both will come with time and acceptance.

Before learning more about maturity, it's helpful to have some background knowledge on the human psyche. To assist with this process, imagine an orchestra. Any good orchestra has many different instruments, and guiding these different instruments is a conductor. The conductor holds a baton and calls on the musicians to either play or be silent, and to play either loudly or softly. With precision, a skilled conductor can orchestrate a beautiful symphony. What would happen, though, if the conductor left the podium and the lead violinist took on his role? Now all you'd hear would be the violins – who would then have to play their own music and the music from all the other instruments to keep the symphony going. The result would be a truly awful performance.

In the human psyche, there are archetypes instead of musical instruments – with each one having a role to play in the music of life. The word archetype was originally introduced by the psychologist Carl Jung, a student of Sigmund Freud. He suggested that the human psyche contains structures, or archetypes, which help us to interpret our experiences of life. While there are many archetypes, the two that are important at this stage of Radical Acceptance are the Child and Adult. The Child archetype is the one everyone encounters first in life, and is the archetype which determines our playful natures on the one hand while accumulating our hurts and traumas on the other. In contrast, the Adult archetype develops later and carries a more rational and reasoned approach to life. Just as a human child needs an adult to guide appropriate behaviour, the Child archetype needs the Adult archetype for the same reason; just as you wouldn't leave a child on their own to make important decisions, the Child archetype, when left to its own devices, leads to a dysfunctional life. Different from a human child, however, the Child archetype will not grow up: maturity is instead accomplished by adding the Adult archetype to the psyche.

Both the Child and the Adult have separate and distinct roles, and both also have times when they are appropriate or inappropriate. For example, if you go to a bank for a loan and present the Child, always wanting to play and have fun, then the loans officer may have some reservations about your ability to repay. Presenting the

Adult, however, and thereby showing the loans officer that you can be responsible, will greatly increase your chances of getting the loan. Conversely, a trip to the playground with your children will be a boring flop if the Adult is in charge. Instead of insisting that everyone sits quietly and just watches the swings and slide, letting your Child out will make the trip a great success.

Going back to the music metaphor, the archetype that seizes the podium most often is the Child. This archetype isn't equipped to handle adult life: despite an idealistic desire to create a safe and happy world, the Child is ultimately too self-centred and focused on wounds from the past. That the majority of people's lives are run by the Child is seen in our climbing rates of divorce, addiction and debt. How can you really know when your life is being run by the Child archetype, though?

Here's a short quiz to increase your awareness. Consider each statement carefully and honestly. When considering each statement, remember that it may be true in some areas of your life and not others. When you see something that applies to you, put a check mark next to it. If you find yourself struggling, it may help to write out your thoughts on a piece of paper or in your journal as you go along. When you're done, tally your score. The more check marks you have, the more your life is being dominated by the Child.

1. I want my life to be about being happy and having fun
2. I want my life to be fair
3. I struggle in asking for what I need
4. I have trouble apologizing – either I don't like to apologise or am constantly offering apologies
5. I struggle with feelings – either I feel too much or have trouble feeling much at all
6. There's a lot of drama in my life, and I often seem to move from crisis to crisis
7. I have trouble with anger – either I act too rashly and then have regrets or I rarely get angry
8. I lack patience, wanting things immediately
9. I have trouble with confidence – I am always worrying about what other people think of me
10. I have trouble with relationships – either I'm stuck in a dysfunctional relationship or I avoid making commitments
11. I have trouble with initiative – either I'm driven to achieve perfection or I just don't care enough to make the effort
12. I'm extremely self-critical and have low self-esteem
13. I have trouble with change – either I crave it or avoid it
14. I have trouble with my past – either I live in the past dwelling on my traumas, or I avoid my past by living in the future where everything will be okay
15. I make when/then statements such as "When I lose weight, then I will have the confidence to get a new job"

Now that you're aware of the Child's influence on your life, here's a deeper analysis of the differences between the Child and Adult, written with a focus on the problems that the Child creates – contrasted against the more appropriate choices made by the Adult. Presenting the Child as the 'problem' and the Adult as the 'solution' is a deliberate attempt to swing your pendulum away from the Child, knowing that it will eventually swing back to the centre as you gain more maturity. From the centre, you can honour input from both Child and Adult.

The Child sees the world either through rose-coloured glasses or with bitterness and resentment from past injustices. This allows the Child to construct fantasies according to their impression of how life should be. Neither of the views is an accurate representation of how life really is. In contrast, the Adult looks at the world from more of a distance, seeing all of its beauty and ugliness and recognising the presence of injustice, hunger and war alongside compassion, abundance and peace. Through the eyes of the Adult, it's possible to get a much more accurate impression of the world around you.

The Child lives either caught up in the drama of their feelings or by sacrificing their emotions for a dry intellectualism. The Adult takes a more balanced response to issues of head versus heart, seeking to feel every feeling fully without dramatizing or rationalizing. While feeling, the Adult steps back and thinks objectively about what it's experiencing before deciding on a response. If you take a more thinking-based approach to life, then the Adult prompts you to think critically, but also encourages you to check in with your feelings on a regular basis so that you never come to rely solely on rationality.

The Child often responds to life's events without thinking, following a reactive process which can be described as Feel-Act-Regret. When you opt for the Feel-Act-Regret process, you don't get a chance to weigh up the consequences which your actions may have. This lack of planning often leads to feelings of regret. Unlike the Child, the Adult makes choices according to a process of Feel-Grow-Plan-Act (the core elements of the Wheel). This method allows you time to fully consider what could result from any potential course of action. In general, this conscious approach leads to far more satisfying conclusions.

The Child sees life in absolutes, considering things to be right or wrong, black or white, good or bad. The Child's view of the world is concrete and rigid, simplifying the complexities of life into the absolutes of good versus evil. The Adult, however, sees the world in infinite shades of grey. Where the Child tries to apply a fixed rule regardless of the situation, the Adult knows that every action has a time and place. Instead of seeing events as right or wrong, the Adult determines what is appropriate or inappropriate to each situation. The actions themselves – like events – are neutral. Similarly, when the Adult is proved wrong, he or she will take an honest look at the situation, apologise, make amends and move on. In the same situation, the Child would become defensive, either certain that their opinion is correct or refusing to back down even in the knowledge that they're in the wrong.

The Child is focused on the destination, not the journey. In general, the destination is normally an idealised view of perfection which will somehow be achieved at some point in the future. This tendency often plays out through something called a 'when-then' system: when something has been accomplished, then the Child's world will be better. The Adult knows that life doesn't have a destination, as perfection is an unattainable goal. Instead, he or she accepts imperfection as a reflection of life, and rather than avoiding issues with 'when-then' thinking, accepts and addresses the issues at hand.

This list of the ways in which the Child and Adult differ is far from complete, and would be beyond the scope of this book. Take note of the above examples, though, and think about how letting the Child run your life unchallenged leads to dysfunction. In contrast, consider how the Adult archetype gives a perspective that can help you to avoid the pitfalls of the Child. Of course, the Adult should never be allowed free reign over your life either. Instead, Radical Acceptance calls on you to return to the podium and strive for a balance between both archetypes.

Maturity: Event

Dr. Jill Bolte Taylor, PhD, is a neuroanatomist – a specialist in the anatomy and function of the brain. She writes in her book, 'My Stroke of Insight', of the difference between the limbic (or emotional) part of the brain and the cortical (or thinking) part. As she explains, "The limbic system functions by placing an effect or an emotion on information… When we're newborns, these cells become wired together in response to sensory stimulation. It's interesting to note that although our limbic system functions throughout our lifetime, it doesn't mature. As a result, when our emotional 'buttons' are pushed, we retain the ability to react to incoming stimulation as though we were a two year old". She goes on to say that it is only through thinking that you can begin to "choose a more mature response" to the events in your life.

Restated in Radical Acceptance language, the events in our lives are neutral. It is you, based on your unconscious history, Systems and beliefs, who (albeit unconsciously) add the feeling element to some events. Maturity is the ability to know this and to stand back from any feelings which occur – seeing the Child on the podium and then taking the podium back, recapturing control of your life. Only when you've done this can you bring in the Adult to provide a more reasoned and responsible response.

George was so taken by the Radical Acceptance workshop that he decided to come and see us privately. He began his first session by announcing that since he was in touch with his anger, he wasn't going to sit back and take the crap that he'd been tolerating in the past. From there, he launched into a list of grievances, mostly about people at work.

There was one person he kept returning to in this list, a fellow employee who cracked his knuckles – something which George really hated. "Every day Albert comes into my office to discuss things, and every day he cracks his blasted knuckles. I want to toss him out of my office – via the window."

We asked him, "So he does this every day?"

"Yes!", George replied indignantly.

"Do you get upset because the sun rises?"

"No, of course not. Besides, what would be the point? It's going to happen anyway."

There was a long pause. Finally he said, "So you're telling me that Albert's knuckle cracking is as inevitable as the sun rising?"

"Yup".

He started to speak a few times, each time stopping before he got anywhere. "This acceptance is much harder than it looks."

"Yup", we smiled.

Maturity: Feel & Accept

In terms of Radical Acceptance, it's important to become aware of your feelings and have the maturity to not act on them – at least to not act on them immediately. Actions made in the heat of the moment are reactive, and come from unconscious habits rather than conscious choices. Action in response to events is important, of course, but the issue is whether you act in the heat of the feeling or whether you first step back and think about what you really want to do. As pointed out in the previous section, feeling is automatic. Thinking isn't.

Stepping back from your emotions takes discipline and maturity, as it's the Child archetype that reacts and the Adult who takes the step back.

Rejecting your feelings is another potential problem, as this is another attempt by the Child to manage your emotions. When you believe that a feeling is bad or unsafe or pretend that it isn't there at all, you get the illusion of safety. Feelings which aren't felt, though, don't go away – they're just pushed into the subconscious from where they can influence your actions in powerful and destructive ways. To avoid this issue, feel your feelings without reacting to them, using them for growth before you decide how to respond.

Very few people just feel their feelings. Most let the Child move them straight into acting, and so a feeling of anger becomes yelling, a feeling of grief becomes tears, a feeling of happiness becomes laughter, and a feeling of love becomes compassion. As soon as the feeling becomes an action, you've moved away from simply feeling the feeling.

Feeling a feeling means just allowing it to be – being aware of how it feels in your body and how it feels in your thoughts. The feeling invites you to be aware of its energy and to stay with it. This can be comfortable or uncomfortable, and might bring up pleasant or unpleasant memories from your past. Sitting in the feeling won't happen if the Child is in charge. You may have to fight to take back the podium in the midst of strong feelings, but you'll get better at the process as you practice and gain maturity.

Staying with your feelings allows you to use them as your teachers – revealing your unconscious beliefs and unhealed events. Most importantly, though, it also gives you time to think about how you want to respond to events – stopping you from reacting quickly and then later regretting your actions. Actions made without regard for consequences are common in playgrounds and school yards, but they're not always beneficial in the adult world.

Radical Acceptance encourages you to break up the Feel-Act-Regret process by taking responsibility and calling upon the Adult to use the Feel-Grow-Plan-Act alternative. This latter process, as the difference in its name implies, leads to more effective actions and fewer feelings of regret.

> George continued, "So you're telling me that I shouldn't get angry when Albert cracks his knuckles?"
> We laughed and said, "You getting angry is as inevitable as Albert cracking his knuckles and the sun rising."
> George growled in frustration. "I don't want to be angry all the time."
> "Why not?" we asked.
> "Because when I'm angry I say and do things which hurt others. I can see that now."
> "How are being angry and doing hurtful things connected?"
> George gave us the same reaction we usually get when we ask this question: his eyes glazed over and he looked totally confused. "How are they connected?" he replied, "Simple, I get angry and hurtful words come out."
> "Yes, that's what happens when you let your Child run the show. What if you took over and asked your Adult? What if you made the choice instead of just letting your Child choose?"
> We could see him pondering this, still looking very confused. After a while, we took pity on him and said, "Having a feeling and acting on a feeling are two very different things. Yes, your Child wants to strike out when angry, but your Adult can show more restraint. I imagine you already show restraint, actually."

Still looking confused, he asked, "I do?"

"Sure. Think of wanting to throw Albert out of the 23rd story window. Did you do it?"

"No."

"When you want to throttle your children, do you?"

"Of course not!"

"If you didn't do those things when angry, how is you saying angry words any different? Feeling and acting are different, but first you have to be in touch with your anger and stay in charge of your life."

"I don't like feeling this way."

"We don't remember saying anything about liking it. We're simply pointing out that the anger isn't new – you're just accepting it now. In the past you denied your anger and justified your angry actions. Now you can feel and accept your anger, giving you more choices – including the choice to not act on what you feel. On a good day, you'll even be successful in your efforts. On a bad day you won't, and will instead need to go back and apologise for those things which you did in anger."

He digested this for a while, and then asked, "So if I don't act on my anger, what do I do with it?"

We smiled and replied, "Now that is an excellent question – one that's asked by the Adult."

Maturity: Discover

This step focuses on using your feelings as a guide into your unconscious. One of the tools used for this process (and one which is also covered in detail in the next theme) is the Projection Tool – a tool which helps you see how you're similar to the people that you judge. When you're angry and judgemental of someone else's behaviour, this tool can use those feelings to reveal an aspect of your subconscious which you'd previously disowned.

If you tell people "What you judge in others is what you're really judging in yourself", most will agree. However, when you point out a specific judgement to those same people, you'll often get fierce denials. Show them that they're a liar when they tell you how they hate someone else's lies, for instance, and they'll do their best to convince you otherwise. Why? It's because when you put someone in that position, their Child takes the podium – and that Child lives in fear of their 'bad', 'negative' or 'dark' side being seen. The Child also has their very sense of identity tied up in the fantasy of who they believe themselves to be. If the discovery from the Projection Tool is accepted, a reality will be exposed which the Child has worked to hide. Doing this work when the Child is in charge is not going to be very productive. Only when you call upon the Adult can you really put it into practice.

Being able to use the Projection Tool is crucial to the Discover step; its ability to reflect back hidden parts of you is invaluable for the journey of personal growth. However, stepping back and using the tool can only be done if you have the maturity to be in charge of your life and to call upon the Adult while the Child is screaming, "No!"

George had now realised that he didn't have to act on his anger – but what else could he do with it? We said, "Let's return to Albert. When he's cracking his knuckles, what's he being? Describe him in one word."
George thought for a moment and said, "Annoying."
"How?"
"He doesn't care about how his actions affect others."
"One word."
"Inconsiderate."
We paused and asked, "So how are you inconsiderate?"
This is where the Child is most likely to fight against the Radical Acceptance work. The Child will deny any similarities. George was no exception. "I'm not inconsiderate!", he yelled. "After all, I haven't thrown that jerk out the window yet! I haven't even asked him to stop! It's not me being inconsiderate here."
"What about the inconsiderate things you've done over the years, though? The things that are separate from this situation."
We watched as the inner struggle between Child and Adult played out in him. His Child made one last attempt, "But I wasn't inconsiderate all of the time."
We smiled and waited. Sure enough, the Adult won out; it was like all his bravado disappeared and a core inner strength appeared. "You're right. I'm not always the most considerate husband and father."

Maturity: Integrate & Accept

When the Child discovers some unpleasant aspect of his or her subconscious, the first question asked is, "How do I fix it?" There is often the feeling that who you are isn't good enough, that if you could just stop being needy or bitchy or insensitive, then everything would be better and you'd be happy. Even more importantly to the Child is what's asked next: "How do I fix it now?" To address these desires, the Self Help Movement, with some notable exceptions, has produced countless books, tapes and lecturers with strategies for instant fixes. An example of an instant fix would be the claim that to change some aspect of yourself, all you have to do is change your thinking. It sounds good and appeals to the Child, but it doesn't work. The old thinking patterns are not simply going to go away: under stress, they will return.

Radical Acceptance offers a much less popular teaching: what you discover can't be fixed – only accepted. Once accepted, you can begin to change the choices you make with respect to an issue. Through these new choices, you can ultimately alter your behaviour. The discovery remains in place, however, and when the Child is on the podium, the old patterns are likely to return. The Child won't agree with this teaching on discoveries, and will instead want to argue that everything that you uncover can be permanently fixed – somehow. The Adult archetype, in contrast, will see that the teaching is true and so will work to make acceptance a part of your life.

Once you've accepted your discoveries, the next step is to integrate them – to accept them as vital, important parts of who you are. This process can take significant time and effort, as it can be difficult to say yes to parts of yourself which you've despised for a long while. In other words, integration requires the patience and discipline of the Adult and the maturity to call upon the Adult in the first place – when all the Child wants to do is to fix, and to fix now.

Here's an example. If the Projection Tool reveals that you're similar to a person who lies, then the Child will initially want to deny being a liar at all. After you've brought in the balanced objectivity of the Adult, the Child will begrudgingly accept the discovery, but then immediately want to fix the situation. The Child might encourage the belief that liars are unlovable – after all, who could love a liar? Attempting to fix is preferable to the Child, as leaving the discovery unfixed seems terrifying: it might mean that they're 'bad' and even unlovable.

At this point, you need to reassume your role as the conductor. Do you let the Child stay in charge, or do you call in the Adult and say, "Yes, I'm a liar and I accept being a liar; I don't need to fix that." The second option, acceptance, means that you won't have to hide your lying from yourself any more, and can instead freely choose whether or not to lie in any given situation.

To put this into context, imagine that your five year-old daughter comes to you one morning with breakfast in bed. Instead of an appetising meal, she's actually prepared cold toast, thick with butter and cold, overly-sugared tea. When she asks, "Is it good? I made it myself," you lie and say, "It's delicious, thank-you for making me breakfast." Now, some may suggest that this is only a 'white lie' and so it doesn't matter, but to Radical Acceptance, a lie is a lie is a lie. Trying to minimise or rationalise the lie shows us that the child is in charge. In contrast, the Adult response is, "I chose to lie because it was more important to show my daughter my love than to tell the truth about the breakfast." Accepting that you're a liar allows you to consciously choose when and how you lie.

When you next notice yourself trying to fix, know that the Child is on the podium and so it's time to reassert yourself. Once you've retaken your rightful position as the conductor, bring in the Adult to help integrate and accept.

Having seen how he too could be inconsiderate, George added, "I'm just as bad as Albert."

"Being inconsiderate is bad?" we asked.

His Child promptly returned, "Sure, it hurts other people. Thanks for pointing this out. From now on I'm going to be much more considerate."

"You define being inconsiderate as annoying people. So, you're never going to annoy anyone again?"

"Not intentionally."

"You work in finance, so you must get requests for projects which make no financial sense."

He laughed and said, "Do I ever."

"Well, saying no to those applicants must annoy them, right? It probably even makes them angry."

"Sure it does," George replied suspiciously. He could sense there was a trick here, but couldn't see it yet.

"So now, given that you'll no longer cause others annoyance, you'll have to say yes to their requests. It'll be the same when your daughter asks if she can go to an all-ages club when she's only twelve. If you don't want to annoy her, you'll have to give your permission."

He could now see the trap. "I see," he responded sullenly.

We continued, "Being inconsiderate is a problem in some circumstances, but it's the appropriate response in others. Stop making it bad — just accept it as part of who you are and make choices about when to use it and when to leave it aside."

We watched as George took control and brought the Adult and Child into internal alignment. He soon smiled and said, "I can do that." Shaking his head, he then added, "Far more than I could stop being inconsiderate."

Maturity: Plan

At the beginning of this chapter, it was stressed that maturity is not about replacing the Child with the Adult. Instead, it's about being in control of which archetype is present at any given moment – recognizing that both archetypes have a role to play, but that each one only works well when it's in balance with the other. Nowhere is this more important than in the Plan step. When it comes to planning, the Child has real fears and concerns which have to be factored in so that the next step, Act & Accept, can be carried out successfully. If the Child is ignored in your plans, it will hide away in your subconscious – ready to reappear with vengeance later on to sabotage any actions which you try to put in place.

As an example of the balance, imagine that you see one of your colleagues taking home office supplies. After working through the stages of Radical Acceptance, you come to the Plan step. The Adult suggests reporting the employee to the company because that's the right thing to do. However, when considering the consequences of this decision, the Child is afraid of being disliked by the offending employee and being criticised by co-workers. The Child also isn't keen to be known as a tattle-tale. These are real concerns and need to be taken into account; the Adult may be okay with being ostracised by the other employees, but the Child likes having a friendly work environment. In fact, the Child may wisely point out to the Adult that alienating co-workers will lead to a less efficient working environment. Working together, the Child and Adult may decide to speak privately to their co-worker, warning them that if they're caught by management, the theft could result in disciplinary action. This meets the need of the Adult to act and the fears of the Child in being the one to report the employee.

Ultimately, your choices are always your own to make. In that situation above, what would you choose to do?

Having discovered and accepted that he was an inconsiderate jerk, George smiled and said, "So, we're done here for today?"

"No, you still have the matter of Albert and his knuckle cracking. Events need a response, and it's now time to think about what your response will be."

He looked confused. "I've accepted Albert as being inconsiderate and I accept that I'm also inconsiderate. From now on, I just won't let his knuckle cracking bother me."

Chris cracked his knuckles, and we watched George cringe. "It seems that knuckle cracking still bothers you."

"I guess so. But if I accept Albert, then I have to accept his knuckle cracking – don't I?"

"Have you ever thought about asking him to stop?"

"Telling him he's an inconsiderate jerk may not be good for office relations." We immediately identified the Child.

He thought for some time, and then said, "I really don't like confrontation. It's easier to be angry with him than it is to ask him to stop. At least, that's what my Child thinks."

"How can you speak with Albert and still honour your Child? How can you get inner agreement between your Child and Adult?"

"How about the Child and Adult do it together? That way the Child won't have to feel like he's acting all on his own."

"An excellent idea." We then spent some time working out some strategies he could use. He left nervously – but with confidence in his plan.

Maturity

Maturity: Act & Accept

If planning requires a balance of both the Child and the Adult, then acting requires more of the Adult – the archetype which is more strongly associated with courage. In contrast, the Child is normally either too afraid to act or has a tendency to act recklessly. If you want your carefully-planned responses to be effective, then the Adult is usually the archetype of choice.

On a wider note, regardless of what action you need to take, only you can decide which archetype is best able to lead in each specific circumstance. While much of the time the Adult is the appropriate choice, there are times when it makes more sense to call upon the Child. Let's say, for instance, that your partner is feeling down and you've worked out a plan which involves play to help cheer them up. This is a time when calling on the Child makes more sense. Just be certain that you ultimately stay in control of the podium, though: don't let the Child take things too far. As the conductor, you are the one who decides how much play there should be, how it intense it should be, and when it should stop. When you get this right, you'll make the time of play a beautiful symphony of fun and safety.

Even harder than acting is accepting the consequences of your actions – whether these consequences are a speeding ticket for driving too fast or taking responsibility for a vase which you've broken. The Adult needs to take the lead here, as the Child will come up with endless excuses for why he or she isn't responsible for what took place. The Adult, however, calmly accepts responsibility and deals with any consequences which result.

Returning to the example of the co-worker taking office supplies, imagine when you speak to them privately that their response is to be critical and to share the private conversation with other workers. While the criticizing and sharing is the choice of the supply-taking co-worker, the resulting alienation at work is the consequence of your actions. If the Child is on the podium, then you may strike back, escalating the dispute. If you are on the podium and call upon the Adult, however, then your response will be more level-headed. Instead of blaming or accusing, you might now return to work, treating your co-workers with respect and letting the whole incident just blow over.

On the other end of the spectrum, the Child may also lead you into accepting responsibility for consequences which are not the result of your actions. This could be apologizing for the weather or cleaning up a mess which someone else created.

Maturity isn't a destination, but is instead the ongoing process of being aware of when an archetype has taken the podium, and then taking back the podium and calling on the appropriate archetype at the appropriate time.

> It wasn't until two weeks later that we learned how George's discussion with Albert had gone. "It took me three days before I was able to speak with him. The first day I just wanted to see how I'd react to his knuckle cracking. It didn't bother me nearly as much as it used to – it was as if I was only upset by the cracking, and not all the other baggage that used to go along with it. I thought I could live with it. By day two I knew that wasn't going to work. It was funny: I didn't judge him, but the cracking was still annoying. It was interesting to see the split between judging and tolerating something so clearly. I could see his actions as neutral and my dislike as neutral as well.
>
> "So on day three I decided to broach the subject. I was nervous, but I kept remembering our session and the promise made between my Child and Adult to have the conversation together. The funny thing was, it turned out to be no big deal. He admitted it was a habit – one which he was trying to break – and that I wasn't the only one who'd complained to him about it. He admitted he'd forget sometimes and asked me to remind him. All that energy I'd wasted for nothing!"
>
> "Not for nothing," we said. "You learned about yourself from the experience. You now know how you can sometimes be inconsiderate – and you also know that whether you're considerate or inconsiderate is a choice which depends on you. In other words, you've matured."

Maturity

4 Self-Discovery

The second theme of Radical Acceptance is about becoming more aware of who you are – bringing the subconscious into the conscious. It's not about acting on what you find, though, as this will come in later chapters. Freud was the first modern advocate of the idea of the subconscious. Through his work and that of many who have followed him, it's become apparent that much of what goes on in our lives happens without conscious awareness. This is an effective coping mechanism and has helped humankind to develop as it has – firstly by making many of our decisions without our having to stop and think about everything that we do, and secondly by giving us a place in which to hide things that we find ourselves unwilling or unable to deal with.

The subconscious is not always friendly, however, and can sometimes have a destructive effect on our lives: it can make decisions which we wouldn't consciously choose for ourselves and can also allow forgotten traumatic events to leak out from their hiding places and into our everyday lives. This chapter will help you to reduce such issues by making conscious what is hidden in your subconscious. Once you know more about what's really going on in your psyche, you'll be able to deal with it appropriately – a process which we'll explore more thoroughly in the rest of the book.

What's inside your subconscious? The full list is extensive, but it's possible to identify several core categories. These are:

1. Memories
2. Instincts
3. Beliefs
4. Character Traits
5. Systems
6. Archetypes

The first category, memories, is made up of everything which we've experienced in our lives but have since forgotten. Some of these lost events will have had a significant effect on who we are without our realising it: eating a spoiled food which made you ill, for example, may have put you off that food ever since. If you take the time to remember the food poisoning incident (bring it from the subconscious into the conscious mind), then you can rationally address your behaviour and choose to try the food again. You may even find that you quite like a taste that you'd previously rejected.

Instincts are urges which all humans have had since the days of our ancient ancestors. A well-known example of an instinct is the 'fight or flight' reflex – a subconscious process designed to help us respond in threatening situations. In the modern world, this instinct is also the source of stress – caused when a low-level threat, such as the worry of losing your job, keeps the instinct running for long periods of time. A workaholic is an example of a person's life being ruled by this subconscious urge. There are many other instincts which can affect our daily lives including protecting those we love, sexuality, belonging to a group and more. Left unconscious, these can play out in ways that we may later regret. When a fundamentalist Christian minister's sexual instinct is constantly repressed, for example, it may be less than surprising to discover him in a hotel room with a prostitute. Bringing instincts into the conscious mind allows you to see them and then make choices about how to include them in your life in healthy ways.

Beliefs are ideas which you hold to be true. These can range from ideas about the world around you to thoughts about divinity, life and death. Once you assess what you believe and bring these ideas into your conscious mind, you can examine them for what they're really worth – either treating them as facts, discarding them as false or just leaving them as 'unknowns'. An example of this latter category is the question of fate. Is your life directed by fate? There are persuasive arguments both for and against. Since there is no way of conclusively proving that either position as true, the answer must remain an 'unknown'.

If you leave all of your beliefs in your subconscious, then you never get the opportunity to evaluate them as facts, fictions or unknowns – which can cause you to treat all of your beliefs as facts, leading to poor decisions in your life. The dangers of such poor decisions can be seen in the bubonic plague which swept through Europe at the end of the 14th century. At the time, many people believed that cats were responsible for spreading the disease and so started to kill them. In fact, fleas on rats carried the virus, so killing the cats meant that there were more rats to act as carriers! This is a classic case of superstitious ignorance, which is exactly what every unconscious and unquestioned belief is as well.

What about conscious beliefs? How are they tied to the subconscious? Conscious beliefs are ideas that can either be shown to be false or that are not provable, but which people still cling to as a way of protecting their subconscious minds. As an example, consider the Flat-Earth Society – a group of people who believe the Earth to be flat. To continue holding this belief, these people have to contort facts to fit their position and fail to seriously consider opposing arguments. Why do these people believe what they do and how does the belief protect their subconscious? It would be impossible to know for sure. Maybe they hold on to the idea that life was simpler and better back when this belief was common, and unconsciously feel incapable of dealing with modern life. Whatever the belief, it's important to them to hold on to their beliefs without questioning them.

Conversely, however, making a belief conscious and then questioning it allows you to act on facts rather than on superstition. This prevents you from relying on subconscious material to support your ideas.

Character traits are the aspects of your personality which define you as a person. Some of us are quite emotional, for example, while others take a more stoical attitude to life. Other examples include people who are controlling versus those who prefer to follow, hard workers versus lazy people, and frugal people versus spendthrifts. No matter what the trait, these aspects are what make up your unique personality. A common mistake with character traits is to see them as either present in all of your life or not present at all. If you've been angry at a liar and so pause to consider the Projection Tool, for example, then your Child may look selectively to areas of your where you don't lie – or where your lying is 'justified'. It may say, for instance, "I don't lie to my partner" while ignoring the lies told on your last tax return. In reality, no character trait extends across all areas of your life –

but this doesn't mean that they're not vital parts of the person you are.

You'll already be aware of some of your character traits, while others will live in your subconscious. Of the ones you know or discover, you'll consider some to be positive and others negative. Despite your opinions, however, Radical Acceptance says that all traits are just traits: instead of being either positive or negative, they just 'are'. As an example from your physical traits, you are a certain height. You can consider your height to be positive or negative, but doing so won't change it. How tall you are is a fact, and as such, no amount of pride or worry will alter this. The same is true for personality traits. They exist as they are, and no amount of worry or work will change them. All that self-discovery aims to do is to make any subconscious character traits conscious, allowing you to make choices about how you express them in your life. Accepting your character traits will give you more options in the choices you make when events occur.

Systems (rules created as a child to make sense of their world) and archetypes (psyche structures that influence perceptions and actions) have both been covered elsewhere and need no further expansion at this point.

* * *

The subconscious is huge, and so trying to make sense of it is daunting. The vast expanse of our past is simply far too big to start trying to work on without some help. How does Radical Acceptance aid in the process? The key lies in your response to events. If an event isn't neutral, then there's a subconscious discovery to be made. In other words, your feelings are the keys to the hidden world of the psyche. Actually uncovering what's hidden, though, can be complicated. To make things easier, many tools have been developed for bringing the subconscious into the conscious. Radical Acceptance makes use of some of the most common of these tools.

When you're reading about the tools, remember that the focus is on becoming aware, and this alone. The tools don't tell you what to do with your discoveries, as this will come in later chapters. Also remember that the tools can all be interchanged and are in no way fixed. Use the ones which work for you, and adapt them to suit your circumstances as you see fit.

The following table lists the tools, when they may best be used, and what kinds of discoveries they may lead to:

Tool	Event Response	Unconscious Issues
Systems Discovery	Betrayal, confusion, stuck or locked into repetitive patterns of behaviour	Systems
Critical Thinking	Inadequacy, over-confidence, shame, excessive pride, fear or excitement	Systems, beliefs, memories, archetypes
Projection Discovery	Judging another (either positively or negatively)	Character traits, memories, systems, instincts
Attachment	Like, dislike, love, hatred, happiness, sadness, desires or aversions	Memories, systems, beliefs

Systems Discovery

As we've covered elsewhere, understanding the idea of a System is quite simple: it's a rule made as a child to make sense of your world. Actually discovering these Systems and how they affect us later in life is more challenging.

In many ways, Systems are really similar to the wind. If you stand inside on a windy day, you'll know that it's windy outside because the leaves on the trees are moving. You can't see the wind directly, but you can infer that it's there from what it does to the world around it. The same is true for a System: you can't see it directly, but you'll know that it's there from the effect which it has on your life. One of the key clues to look for is repeated patterns. These might be feelings of grief after repeated betrayals in your life, confusion after saying one thing yet repeatedly doing another, or frustration with yourself over patterns of behaviour that just won't go away. For instance, you might repeatedly choose partners who have affairs – leaving you feeling betrayed, hurt and angry. You say to yourself and others, "The next person I allow into my life will be different; they won't betray me", and lo and behold, the next person does exactly the same. You then go into therapy and discover low self-esteem, finally think that you've solved the issue – and then the same thing happens yet again. Until you can discover the System behind your repeated actions and begin to accept the impact of how your System operates, you won't be able to make new choices about your behaviour.

A very common System is one which says 'I'm unlovable'. People who want love and intimacy sometimes never seem to get it – or when they do, they only get it for limited periods of time. This leads to confusion and a sense of being trapped in a repetitive pattern – and when relationships end, the feeling of betrayal. Why do we keep falling for people who can't give us the love we seek? The answer is simple: if we didn't, our System would be threatened. This keeps us unconsciously looking for people who will reject us, and can even force us to leave a relationship that could have otherwise given us what we wanted. This latter point is particularly evident in addiction recovery groups, where, if an addicted person gets help, their non-addicted partner leaves. Why do they leave? The non-addicted partner had a System which unconsciously required them to be in a dysfunctional relationship.

To discover your Systems, you'll need to look for contradictions between what you say you want and what you do – between your longings and what you actually get. If you claim to want love, success, more down-time or less stress but are actually finding unsuccessful relationships, failure, a workaholic lifestyle or more stress, then you've found a glimpse of the repetitive patterns driven by your Systems. When you make conscious the Systems which drive many of your actions, you'll better understand why you do the things that you do.

Critical Thinking

Your mind is incredibly powerful. Our Western culture, however, promotes very sloppy minds which are only rarely encouraged to think. Even in our universities it's best not to think too much – just regurgitate what's expected so you get the grades that you need to graduate. If you stop and consider the power of your mind, though, then you'll see how incredible it is: one good thought can make your day, while a single 'I'm so stupid' thought can ruin a week. Similarly, thinking critical thoughts about another race, religion, gender or sexual orientation can make you feel 'better' than them, while comparing yourself to more successful people can leave you feeling like a failure. The same is true of comments from other people. A compliment can give you a lift, while an insult can have the opposite effect. The Critical Thinking tool encourages you to identify your thoughts and ask 'Is this thought true?' – or alternatively to think about comments from someone else and ask the same question, especially for those comments that cause your mood to shift in a significant way.

As an example of the Critical Thinking tool in action, imagine that you're in a car showroom thinking about buying a new car. When you speak to a salesperson, he or she says: "I've got a great car for you. It has 400,000km on it and not all of the doors work, but it's an excellent car. It's currently on sale for $10,000. Pay me now and you can have it. You don't even have to take it out for a test drive – it's just that great." In all likelihood, you'd refuse this offer unless you found out more information. Instead of just handing over your cash, you'd want to see the car to judge if it was really worth the price that was asked. Now look at your internal world of thoughts and feelings. When you think 'I'm so stupid' (or whatever thought is appropriate to you) and don't consider this thought critically, you're effectively handing over $10,000 blindly. In other words, the Critical Thinking tool invites you to really think about your thoughts – to give them the same consideration you would if you were buying a car. Are you really stupid? Is your IQ really that low? Did you make it through school? What have you accomplished in your life? If you stop to consider these questions, you'll be able to see that it's the thought that's 'stupid', not you. Radical Acceptance invites you to use the Critical Thinking tool to see just how believing the 'I'm stupid' thought affects your wider life choices.

As with all Radical Acceptance tools, this tool begins by noticing your feelings – in this case feelings of inadequacy, over-confidence, shame or pride. When you've identified these feelings, try to remember the thoughts which accompanied them in as much detail as you can, even writing the thoughts down as you remember them – and without trying to explain them. From here, ask questions to assess how true the thoughts really are. Some might have a small grain of truth to them, but most will be total garbage. Now you can add another garbage thought by thinking, 'How stupid of me to believe those silly thoughts.' See this and smile. You weren't being stupid, you were just being human and will continue to be human. Because of your humanity, you'll continue to make these kinds of mistakes for as long as you live. The trick is to use your feelings to work with the mistakes as soon as possible, allowing you to move on with a clearer sense of direction.

Once you've identified any mistruths, you can also see how they're related to your subconscious mind. Firstly, the presence of mistruths points out your Systems. Here, the thoughts and feelings which really stick with you are the ones which are feeding your Systems. If you have an 'I'm ugly' System going, for example, then look for thoughts which say that you're too heavy or too thin or too tall or too short or any of the thousands of other possible criticisms of an appearance. Even world famous models can have these thoughts, as the thoughts themselves aren't based in truth – it's only your System which is making you feel that you're ugly.

Analysing the differences between your thoughts and reality will also expose your beliefs. If you believe that a certain skin colour makes a person less intelligent, for instance, then you might want to notice the doctors, lawyers and leaders of nations who come from all different races and religions. This will allow you to see that your beliefs about race and intelligence are connected.

Similarly, if you have thoughts around a gender, look around and see powerful men and women and gentle men and women. See both genders at work and at home – see lazy men and hard-working men, lazy women and hard-working women. Any attempt to generalise a gender speaks only of your beliefs, not of any reality. Watch out for beliefs which can be applied to yourself, as well: uncritically believing that men don't cry or that women don't get angry can cause you a lot of suffering.

As with all of the tools discussed in this chapter, seeing a belief or a System can lead to recalling the memories from childhood which fed them. These will be experiences which, when viewed from an adult's point of view, put the Systems and beliefs into perspective. To explain this further, if you believe that big boys and big girls don't cry, then reflecting on your childhood may highlight your tendency to be like one of your parents. You may have had a strong, angry mother and a gentler father. Your mother may also have been emotionally distant, so if you identified with your mother, then you may have taken on her attributes. Subconsciously, your mother's beliefs have become your own – even while you may consciously deny the similarities. This pattern is reflected in a quaint saying about therapy:, "After all the thousands of dollars I spent in therapy, I still turned out just like my mother". Acceptance means you can now say, "Yes, I'm just like my mother. Now what choices can I make?" Saying this doesn't mean that you'll suddenly start finding crying easy, of course – that's now a character trait. You can, however, start to see that there's value in all emotions.

Critical thinking can also reveal which archetype is in charge at a point in time. The Child is in charge when the thoughts contain key phrases such as:

1. It's not fair – the Adult knows that life isn't fair and doesn't need life to be fair.
2. Everyone does it – except everyone doesn't do it and, more importantly, even if everyone really did, that wouldn't necessarily increase the truth of the idea.
3. You should know that I... – this is the Child wanting another person to read the Child's mind, letting them off from the responsibility of conveying his or her own needs.
4. I won't apologise until they do – the Adult acts based on the right thing to do, not on whether or not they're getting what they want from another. This is a challenging one; the Child wants retribution or vindication. To apologise for your contribution to the problem and not receive anything back infuriates the Child, while the Adult quietly knows that you've done the appropriate thing.
5. I would never do that – the Child believes this to be true, whereas the Adult knows differently (see Projection for more on this topic).

The list goes on. Learn the favourite sayings of your Child and use Critical Thinking to be aware of when the Child is in charge.

Projection

The Projection Tool has been covered earlier, but it's repeated here in more detail as it's a powerful and demanding tool. 'Projection' is the notion that what you judge in other people is actually a judgement of yourself. You could be judging a character trait or an instinct, for instance. Revealing the character trait or instinct can also lead to discoveries of memories, beliefs and Systems. The Projection Discovery tool aims to reveal this unconscious link, bringing these discoveries into conscious awareness. When looking at judgements, remember that judging something as good and desirable is just as much of a judgement as making it bad or undesirable.

The tool is based around a series of questions to ask yourself. The first is: "What was the event which made you feel judgemental?" Describe it in as much detail as possible, letting your feelings really flow and writing down everything that comes into your head. Next, ask yourself: "How did I judge that person – in a single word?" You might need help from another person with this question. Try to be as descriptive in your answer as possible, making the judgement really clear. It often helps to start with a few words, and then narrow it down to one. Finally, ask: "How am I similar to the person I am judging?" It's important to note that you won't be identical, but similarities will exist. You'll need to draw on the Adult archetype to get the answers to this question, as the Child will want to deny any similarities that you think of – and the closer you get to finding real similarities, the harder the Child is likely to object. Be particularly cautious of Child rationalisations such as "But everyone does that...", "I'm not as bad as they are..." and "I only think it, whereas they do it". If you find yourself struggling, ask for help from someone that you really trust. Radical Acceptance requires brutal honesty, so really take all of these questions seriously; only by having the courage to go into the very deepest parts of your unconscious world will you be able to truly utilise this tool effectively.

Once the discovery is made, allow memories to surface which may have helped form the discovery, or memories that led to you to suppress it. Also have a look for beliefs that may have supported the suppression. Finally, see if the discovery is tied to a System. That's a lot to take from one tool, so here's an example to help make things clearer.

Someone lies to you and you become angry and judgemental. Remembering to use the Projection Tool, you pull out some paper and start writing. You begin by describing the lie and how you realised that you were being lied to. For this example, imagine that your partner told you that he or she had done a task which they had promised to do, but when you went to see the completed task, you realised it had not been done. Next you describe your judgements. You might begin by calling them a lazy, no-good, lying asshole. Then you begin to reduce the adjectives until you decide that the central judgement is that they're a liar.

Now it's time to see how you too are a liar. You won't tell the same lies as your partner did, but different ones. Your lies may be in a completely different area of your life, and you may not even tell overt lies. Maybe you lie by omission (failing to give all the information), diversion (asking another question) or through 'white lies' (lies you deem not to be 'real' lies). Maybe you only lie when it 'doesn't matter'. Maybe you lie to yourself. Regardless, if you're brutally honest with yourself, then you'll discover how you lie.

Having discovered how you're similar, you can now ask yourself what memories created your pattern of lying and why you felt the need to hide your lying from yourself. In this hypothetical situation, you might discover that you grew up trying to be 'good' to please your parents. That meant that you had to hide times when you weren't good and lied – and it also meant that you had to hide your lying from yourself. You may additionally discover a belief that lying is bad or that people who lie get punished. If you have a good look at these beliefs, you'll see that they're both incorrect. Lying has its place, and many lies are never even discovered, let alone punished.

Finally, have a look at the System which feeds this cycle. In the case of trying to be good, comparing what you say and what you do may suggest a System which says, "I'm not lovable for who I am, only for how I can please others." This System then drives the lies to try and make you look good, but also, as with all Systems, ensures that you never fully succeed; no matter how much you try and please other people, you'll always seem to disappoint them. As this example shows, it's possible to use judgement to learn about yourself, and also to let a discovery call forth memories and beliefs. Then, stepping back with all of this information, you can observe the workings of a System.

Attachment

Attachment is the desire for or aversion to any person, place, thing, thought or feeling. In its simplest form, desiring chocolate ice cream and hating lima beans are both examples of attachment. On a more complex level, what you are drawn to and what you reject can reveal a huge amount about the person you are. This latter aspect is especially prevalent when your attachments relate to a desire for love and happiness or an aversion to sadness and betrayal. These feelings in particular are what the Attachment Tool is best-suited for dealing with – both directly and for revealing the unconscious memories, Systems and beliefs which are at the root of these feelings. It can also assist you in seeing that many of your attachments are actually rooted in fantasies of the Child.

To work the attachment tool, you need to get your attachments to 'speak'. This idea of allowing an inner part of the psyche to 'speak' is actually a very useful tool. To apply it, you will need some paper. On this, you'll write as if you were writing a play. To start, identify the first character. In this case, as an example, make the first character your desire for happiness. The second character is you. Ask Attachment a direct question, and then begin to write the thoughts that emerge. It's important not to censor your thoughts: just write down what comes up. When the thoughts stop, move to yourself as the other character. Phrase the words in the first person so as to really take on the attachment's voice. Your dialogue can be short, or it can take several pages. Its results may just give a hint, or they could provide you with endless insight into your unconscious memories, beliefs, Systems and more.

As an example, imagine that you ask your partner if you can purchase the latest new cell phone. He or she says that the budget just won't support it at this point in time. You feel sad. Being well trained in Radical Acceptance, you realise that the sadness is a reaction and needs processing. You check with your notes and select the Attachment Tool, and then sit down and write the following.

You: Why are you so attached to getting this cell phone?

Attachment: I want to be happy. I crave happiness and I believe that the new phone will make me happy.

You: Happiness is not as important to me, and I'm concerned about the amount of money you spend to feel happy.

Attachment: I need to feel happy.

You: Oh, so it's not okay to feel sad?

Attachment: Of course not, why would I want to feel that? It reminds me too much of when I was a kid.

You: Tell me more about being a child.

Attachment: I remember feeling so sad; I didn't like it. Then, to make me feel better, my dad bought me new toys. I felt so much better.

You: And why did your father buy you things?

Attachment: He didn't like me to be sad. He felt sad when I felt sad.

You: So now you want to buy things so you feel better?

Attachment: Yes. I want to be happy because then I make other people happy and it's important that people are happy.

The example shows how giving attachment a voice has revealed some very important reasons why the attachment is so powerful in your life. It began by speaking of wanting to be happy. That brought up childhood memories. The dialogue then revealed that possessions made you happy. Finally, you made a most revealing discovery: that you needed to be happy so other people in your life would be happy. Now you can see a couple of beliefs. The first is that sadness is bad; it's not okay in your mind to be sad for you or for others. The next is that you're responsible for other people's happiness. Both of these beliefs have no basis in reality; they're fantasy. Life is both sad and happy – the idea that life should only be happy is the fantasy. The idea that you can be responsible for another person's happiness is also fantasy. With this realisation, you can challenge these beliefs. Going deeper, have a look for the underlying System. In this example, there may be a System that says, "I'm only lovable if I'm happy."

Working backwards, the System provides the foundation to the fantasies. The fantasies support the beliefs. The beliefs create the attachment, and the attachment then drives the behaviour. Remember, it's not a bad thing that attachment is trying to be happy by spending money – it's just noticed. The awareness in and of itself will not change or fix the problem, but it will give you choices the next time you're feeling sad and want to go and spend money.

These are only a few of the tools which are available for discovering what lies in the huge, untapped world of potential that is the subconscious. As you learn more and more, always feel free to try out any new tools which you come across. Remember: this theme of Radical Acceptance is all about being an explorer – breaking down boundaries and discovering key new knowledge in whatever way works best for you and the situation. What to do with what you find out will be discussed later on.

Self-Discovery: Event

Everything that happens in life can prompt you to make new discoveries. So long as you keep your mind open and stay aware of what's going on inside yourself, you can find out new things in any place and at any time.

As events occur, look out for what triggers the most energy – the events which cause you to have the strongest feelings. Notice each time a stray thought appears, especially those thoughts which are inconsistent with your principles. Remember events which make you angry or envious and realise that they're reflections of yourself. Recognise your attractions – the events which leave you feeling happy or sad.

What events do you avoid? Does fear hold you back from things you want to do? Do you envy other people and the things they achieve? Are there times when you say, "I could never do that", and is this a true statement or a belief you could discard?

> Although George visited soon after the workshop, Judy took a little longer before coming to see us. She'd thought she had everything in her life under control, and had been intent on turning over a new leaf and forging healthier relationships with her employers. As things turned out, however, these intentions hadn't lasted for long. "It was a great idea," she said, "and really in line with the owners' image for the company. They still turned me down, though. I was so angry I immediately started looking at the job boards. I think they just need to be in control."
> "So, when someone in your life is controlling you get angry?" we asked. "Have you always been this way?"
> She thought for a minute and then said, "I grew up in a house which was always in chaos. I suppose I'd forgotten just how crazy it could be. I remember making plans to do something with friends, for example, only to have my parents make other arrangements at the last minute. It got to the point where I stopped making plans altogether."

Self-Discovery: Feel & Accept

Some feelings are easy to accept and others are not – the latter are the real keys to self-discovery. Some feelings seem easy to accept but are actually challenging, too. As an example, while most people would say that accepting happiness is easy, a great number find doing so to be incredibly difficult. These people, constantly worried about good situations not lasting, are essentially saying, "I don't believe I deserve to feel happy", or "I'm waiting for the other shoe to drop." This shows a System at work.

Are you afraid of a particular emotion? That could point to an underlying belief. Does it seem that you only feel one feeling? This may reveal an underlying belief about feelings being 'appropriate' for a man or a woman. Is your life committed to feeling up and happy, down and sad, or emotional and chaotic? These are pointers to the unconscious: memories of a certain feeling, or a belief that a feeling isn't safe. Do you ever engage in behaviours to avoid feelings? Smoking, sex, alcohol, sugar and comfort foods are good avoidance strategies. If you didn't engage in them, what would you feel? What does your avoidance reveal?

> "What happens now when your employers change your ideas?" we asked.
> "I get so angry," Judy replied "I have to hold back my tears."
> "Why do you cry when you're angry?" She looked at us blankly. We continued, "Tears usually come when people are sad. When people are angry, they normally yell."
> She looked horrified. "I couldn't yell. Yelling doesn't do any good. It only makes people mad at you. I could lose my job for yelling."
> "Sounds like there are more childhood memories there."
> "Sure there are. Only my mother was allowed to be angry. Anyone else was punished for it – and I mean anyone, including my father. Are you really suggesting that I yell at the owners?"
> "Not at the owners, but it sounds like you could benefit from finding a safe place and letting loose."
> Her eyes lit up as she said, "That sounds like fun."

Self-Discovery: Discover

Paying close attention to what's going on in your life is the keystone of self-discovery. In some cases, though, you'll have to work harder to find out what's really going on in your subconscious mind. You may, for example, have to switch tools or go deeper into your thoughts. Let's say that you've done repeated projection work but a single event continues to generate feelings of anger. Perhaps what you're feeling could actually be sadness? Maybe anger is just one of your character traits (however, making this discovery doesn't give you permission to freely vent your anger!). Similarly, other people may respond to the majority of charged events with feelings of sadness. These people can cry and cry, but can never stop the flow of tears. If these people look at themselves more deeply, they may reveal that what they're feeling is anger – which may in turn show memories of being punished for getting angry or a general belief that anger is bad. In some cases, they may just be naturally sad people (the above note about being angry applies here as well!).

If using one tool doesn't bring about a shift in you, then try another. Even though you're feeling judgemental, for example, the judgements may be based in a fantasy and so the attachment tool may work better. Equally, feeling sad may not come as a result of attachment but from thoughts which you've failed to evaluate critically – and a critical thought may have its basis in fantasy or be a judgement and so need the use of the Projection Tool.

When using all of the tools, keep your eyes open for Systems. You will see them revealed every time you make a discovery that just doesn't seem to make sense – there is, after all, a System lying underneath a great number of discoveries. Also be aware of the constant possibilities for self-discovery that can lead you to deeper revelations. Keep your eyes and your mind open, accept all that you find out, and your life will become an endless journey of amazing discoveries.

We paused and then asked, "So what System is playing out with regard to what's happening at work?"

"I'm not sure. How can I tell?"

"Look for the contradictions. You left home saying that you wanted control, and yet you work in an environment that takes control away from you. What does that say about your System?"

"Other than I'm completely messed up? I guess it says I have a System around not being in control."

"That sounds right. Your System is ensuring you don't have control. That re-enacts your childhood experience. At some level ,you need to have someone else being in control – to be out of control of your own life."

"I really am a messed up person."

"Is that really true? Or are you a human being who's living with their System? Why do you accept these 'messed up' messages? Apply some critical thinking here."

She sat up straighter and said, "You're right. I'm not as messed up as my thoughts keep saying. That's just old stuff coming from my mother."

"Now, the feeling you had from the event was anger. If we apply the Projection Tool, that means that you're like the owners. You too are controlling."

Looking most indignant, she said, "I am not. You just told me I like other people to be in control. When I work with my staff I give them a lot of latitude."

"Sure, it's not identical to how the owners express their control, only similar. How about at home? Does your partner have the same liberties as you in the kitchen, for instance?"

"Not in your life, that's my domain..." She paused. "Hmm, I see what you mean."

Self-Discovery: Integrate & Accept

Radical Acceptance isn't about 'fixing' yourself; if you're trying to do this, then you've decided that your discoveries are unacceptable parts of yourself and so you're back at square one. Regardless of whether you uncover a memory, a character trait, a System or anything else, Radical Acceptance teaches you to say, "Yes".

In much self-help literature, there's a confusing message when it comes to these discoveries. The message is often, "Accept everything and get rid of the negative in you." So is there acceptance or a need to fix? You can't have it both ways at the same time.

Being aware of the times you try to fix yourself can also lead to additional discoveries, as they reveal deeper beliefs about your need to fix. You may, for example, discover underlying beliefs about inadequacies and a need to feel useful. In order to hide from feeling inadequate, you felt the need to fix. Exploring those discoveries may then expose further memories, attachments and Systems.

> "So now I need to stop being controlling?" Judy asked.
> "Just like you turned over a new leaf with the owners?"
> "I'm trying, really I am," she pleaded.
> "Why are you doing that?"
> "What do you mean?"
> "Why are you trying to turn over a new leaf?"
> "I don't want to be contrary. I want to get along with the owners – see things from their point of view and have peace and tranquillity at work."
> "But is that who you are?"
> Reluctantly, she said, "Maybe not, but it's surely who the owners want, isn't it?"
> "Is it? Then why haven't they fired you?"
> "But..but it's not nice to be angry."
> "And being nice is important?"
> "Sure: if you're not nice, then no one will like you," she replied.

"But Judy, you're not nice all the time. There are times when you're not nice to the owners, times when you aren't nice to your partner, and you certainly weren't nice to George. Does that mean that no one likes you?" She shook her head. "Then why do you believe that?"

Self-Discovery: Plan

The planning step continues with the theme of being aware. In this step, awareness means watching for your attitude toward the archetypes involved in planning. Do you try and shut down the Child and plan only 'adult' courses of action? Is your Adult truly being the Adult, or is your Child sneaking in as a pseudo-Adult?

To see what's going on, it can help to watch your body position and posture. The Child tends to slouch and sit in a curled up position, while the Adult tends to sit straighter and more upright. The Child will also be more judgemental and argumentative when compared against the Adult's calmer approach. Thinking that you're planning from the Adult while sitting as a Child is a good indicator that the pseudo-Adult is in charge.

Being aware that the incorrect archetype is in charge at any moment leads to discoveries about your beliefs and Systems around the archetypes. You may have a belief that being 'childish' is wrong, as you may remember those sorts of comments from your parents as you grew up. You may have a System that says growing up is unsafe: that if you grow up, then you may not get your desires or may not be able to make it as an adult. These are valuable discoveries, and are best acquired while planning.

"So what do I do?" Judy asked. "Do I let loose and become a screaming, out of control bitch?"
"And how likely is that?" we questioned.
"You're right. I could never do it."

"Then that wouldn't be a practical plan – but it is good input from the Child. How can you also keep the Adult happy?"

She thought for a bit and said, "You said earlier about finding a safe place to yell. I could do that, although it'd be hard. I guess I have strong beliefs around 'proper' behaviour." She paused, and then her face lit up. "I know – I could wait until the next time my partner makes me angry and then I could let him have it. He's safe. How's that for a balanced plan?"

"Your Adult likes that plan?"

"She sure does."

"Look at your posture. You're curled up almost into a ball. Sit up straight and say that the Adult agrees."

She couldn't do it. She sat up and then her face fell. "Damn, I was looking forward to that. But when I sit up, it just feels like I'm punishing him."

"Just like your mother punished your father."

She turned white and whispered, "Oh shit." The discoveries just kept coming. "So, I guess I find a place on my own and let loose..."

"Sounds like a plan."

Self-Discovery: Act & Accept

How you act in the world is vital to effective self-discovery. While what you say is important, it's what you do that reveals your innermost secrets.

If you make wonderful plans but fail to carry them though, then you're being invited to make a discovery. If you make a commitment to avoid certain behaviours and then do them anyway, the same applies. These failures often reveal fear-based character traits or Systems; while you may have the courage to act, you may also have a System which says that you don't have the right to act, and so this holds you back. Conversely, if you manage to carry out everything that you plan successfully, then your actions will help you to discover great strengths and disciplines which you never knew you possessed.

When discovery becomes a way of life, discoveries are made throughout the Radical Acceptance cycle; life itself becomes your teacher.

> Judy returned a couple of weeks later. She was barely through the door before she started telling us about her experience. "At first I couldn't do it. I kept putting it off, which only made me angry at myself. Finally I was so miserable that my partner asked me what was wrong. I burst into tears and told him everything.
>
> "He gave me a hug and said, 'If you want to yell at your boss, I can be there to support you.' I cried even louder. I couldn't believe he was willing to do that.
>
> "So, when I finished crying, he asked me when I wanted to do it. I said, 'No time like the present.' So we went into the basement and, with a little encouragement from him, I let loose. It was so liberating I can't believe I haven't done this before.
>
> "But that's not the best part. The best part came afterwards. I sat down and thought about what had happened. I'd actually made another discovery: I'm not as independent as I thought I was. I also realised that my mother wasn't, either. I remember how we rarely went out without our father. Although angry, she was actually quite dependent on him. That revelation changed how I viewed those memories.
>
> "Finally, I realised that I'm not as open with my partner as I thought I was: I'd kept most of this from him. As it turns out, I'm actually quite private about what goes on in my life."
>
> What could we say? She'd done all the work herself.

Self-Discovery

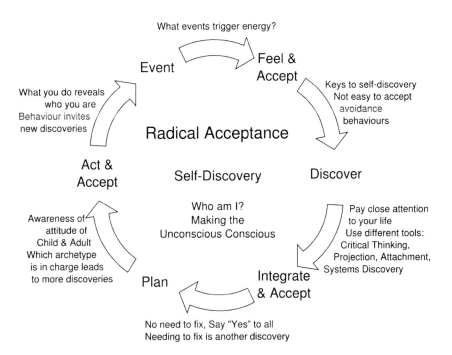

5 Self-Acceptance

Once you've put significant effort into the self-discovery process, there's still a long way to go. The next step is to accept the discoveries that you've made.

Radical Acceptance makes use of a Scoring Tool. The tool asks you to rate a discovery on a scale of 1 to 10. Each discovery is ranked twice with two separate scorings. The first scoring measures to what extent you've accepted your discovery, and the second scoring is how good you are at using your discovery.

When measuring your degree of acceptance, a score of 1 represents a discovery which has not been accepted at all. This is indicated by a desire to fix, transform, transcend or heal what you've found; all of the event's energy is directed into trying to make the discovery go away. A score of 7.5 indicates that you see your discovery as a gift, loving it as a wonderful part of you. A score of 10 is obtained when your revelation holds no energy: it's a simply a neutral fact, and is rarely even considered at all.

Despite the assumption many people make, moving from 1 to 10 is not a linear process. One moment your score may be at a 6, for instance, before falling down to a 2 only seconds later. On another occasion you may have reached a 10, and then an event happens which puts you right back at a 3. The acceptance cycle, like the six steps on the Radical Acceptance Wheel, is never-ending.

Moving from 1 to 10 is also not a balanced process, as there may be some areas of your life in which acceptance is much easier to achieve than in others. As an example, discovering that you have a character trait that gives you a tendency to be cold and distant will likely be easier to accept at work than in an intimate relationship. Similarly, you might be able to accept that being cold and distant gives you a cool head in a crisis, so that if one of your children gets hurt, you'll be able to respond quickly and effectively. The tendency may also mean a lack of closeness with those same children, however, which could be a far more difficult challenge to accept.

Furthermore, some discoveries may be so painful to accept that they'll never make it to a 10; some will just never make sense to you to accept, no matter what Radical Acceptance says. These are the ones that you deem totally unacceptable: the ones which you think will make you into a bad, unlovable person, and the ones which challenge your entire sense of self and can lead to a major identity crisis.

Don't get too disheartened, however: there are two key tools available to help you accept what you've revealed. The first of these again uses the Scoring Tool. This time it involves spending a few moments at the end of each day reflecting on how well you're using your new discoveries. For example, if you find a System which says that intimacy isn't safe, then score how well you managed to sabotage closeness over the past 24 hours. Perhaps you were busy when your partner wanted to talk? Maybe you criticised someone during an intimate moment? Did you just get into another dysfunctional relationship? Give yourself a 1 if you only managed to ruin a small amount of intimacy, and a 10 if you managed to completely stop an intimate experience. Congratulate yourself if you score a high number – take a bow and recognise that you're a highly-skilled individual. While rewarding yourself for your ability to feed your System may seem counter-intuitive, doing so is actually incredibly useful: once you recognise the skill and effort that it takes to keep a System running well, you'll become more aware of how much that System is a part of you.

Before proceeding to the second tool, it's important to understand the two forms of scoring. Although they use the same scale and are related to the same discovery, they're actually quite different. To return to the previous example of a System that feels intimacy, you might score very high in your ability to block intimacy, but very low in the degree to which you accept this attribute in your life. You may wish to stop blocking intimacy: to fix the System. That would mean a low acceptance score.

The second useful tool is the Gratitude Tool. This involves being both open to and acknowledging the many reasons you have to be grateful for what you've discovered. With the case of the avoiding intimacy System, you could use the Gratitude Tool to appreciate how safe that System leaves you feeling; most people who fear closeness (almost everyone) have a reason to do so. Learning to sabotage intimacy protects you from the kind of pain that you may have experienced earlier on in your life, and also allows you to retain a strong sense of independence and individuality. In short, the Gratitude Tool teaches you to be grateful for what the System has given you. The tool doesn't just work with Systems, though: the same principles apply to character traits, instincts, beliefs and memories. If you discover a character trait which says that you're a procrastinator, for instance, then use the gratitude tool to recognise how many times procrastination has meant that you didn't complete a task which ultimately wasn't necessary. This will help you to accept that you're a procrastinator – and acceptance is what the Gratitude Tool is all about.

The Scoring Tool helps you to realise just how prevalent and pervasive your discoveries are once you recognise them. The more aware you are, the easier it is to see your choices and end up with the outcomes you want. To stay with the previous example, if you can't see your fear of intimacy, then you can't change the choices you're making; the System will act in ways which are hidden to you. The Gratitude Tool allows you to start seeing your discoveries as gifts. This will eventually help you to let go of any judgements you might make around your findings, and will instead encourage you to use the new choices that scoring makes available.

Aside from the ability to make choices, there are several other important reasons for putting effort into accepting your discoveries. The most important of these is the act of self-acceptance itself. If you'd like to get rid of certain parts of yourself, then what does that say about your ability to love yourself? That's a very conditional love at best, and is probably better re-described as self-hatred. The new-age Self Help Movement often falls into this trap – first telling everyone how important it is to love themselves, and then in the next breath giving easy and quick ways of getting rid of their 'negative' aspects. Either you love all of who you are or you don't, without any exceptions.

Further to this is the need to keep up a front: doing things such as being nice so as to create an appearance which you think will help others to love you. It's like walking around with a cardboard cut-out in front of you saying, "Love this cardboard cut-out, because the real me is damaged and unlovable." If you do this regularly, what happens when someone tells you that they love you? Your reaction will likely be, "You don't really love me, you only love the cardboard cut-out. If you knew the dark, ugly parts of me, then you wouldn't love me." Acceptance is all about taking down the cut-out and experiencing love from both yourself and others.

Self-acceptance also helps you to see and accept others. Just as cleaning windows allows you to see out of them more clearly, when you discover unconscious material within yourself and accept it without judgement, you'll be able to see the world around you and the people within it with much more clarity and compassion. Bear in mind, however, that while you can know what someone does, you'll never be able to know why they do it. You can only ever discover the 'whys' about yourself – never those of anyone else. You can, however, notice other people's behaviour. If you're having an intimate conversation and your partner suddenly becomes critical, for instance, then this only tells you that you're in a relationship with a person who criticises. What it won't tell you is why your partner chose to be critical: no amount of Radical Acceptance can tell you that.

Seeing yourself and others clearly means seeing them without making any judgements In response to this, you may feel that accepting without judgement is the same as making every action okay – but this isn't the case. It is, however, an interesting point, and one which will be covered in detail over the next two chapters. For now, just remember that acceptance means the ability to make choices, the capability to love yourself, the ability to give and receive love from others, and the power to clean your vision and truly see the people around you for who they are. Doing these things can be a challenging process, but the results on offer are really worth working for.

Self-Acceptance: Event

Self-acceptance is measured by the degree to which aspects of your self are seen as simple, objective facts. That you have a character trait of being a procrastinator, for example, has no more charge for you than how you feel about the length of your big toe (although some people are bound to worry about the length of their big toe!).

How does this relate to events? When an event causes a feeling, there's probably an issue that's not been accepted. That isn't good or bad in itself – it's just part of being human. This also means that there's no end to Radical Acceptance: you'll never become a perfect person, totally content with who and what you are. You'll always have issues in your life, and there are always new discoveries to be made. When an event stirs anger, sadness, excitement or any of the many other feelings which colour our lives, greet those emotions as valuable mentors to guide and correct your path. Give thanks to the event which raised the feelings, knowing that all of life can be used as a grand classroom for studying the most wondrous of beings – you!

> George was having a rough time. "I wish I'd never heard of Radical Acceptance," he started out. "It seems that I'm always angry now. There's Albert, we've worked that out – but at home, with my children and with my wife, I'm constantly angry. It's the little things that throw me, too. I hate being this way."
> "So, lots of little events make you feel angry?" we asked.
> "Yes! Knowing I was coming here, I looked for a pattern. It's still any time someone is being a jerk that really sets me off, but I've dealt with that. I now know that I'm a jerk sometimes too, at least when I need to be."
> "That doesn't sound like acceptance. You're still justifying it in your mind. What about the times you're a jerk just because you're a jerk?"
> "But I really thought I'd already accepted everything.," he admitted.
> "Not according to your reaction to these events, which suggest that you're still projecting being a jerk onto others. This implies that there's more in you yet which you need to accept."

Self-Acceptance: Feel & Accept

Feelings can be particularly difficult to accept. The big feelings like rage, terror and depression are, for many people, the ones which are most problematic. It's particularly common to fear getting swamped by these big emotions if you accept them – especially if you've been dealing with the matter for a long time.

The only thing more difficult than accepting your feelings, though, is not accepting them. Feelings which you don't accept are feelings which you have to fight, and this fight can quickly turn into an exhausting and never-ending struggle. If you accept who you are, then you can work with it – something that's true for anger, love, depression, terror, courage and everything in between.

Acceptance of these feelings won't always take the same form, however. For the clinically depressed or those with anxiety disorders, acceptance includes knowing that you'll take medication for the rest of your life. For the angry, it can mean keeping a careful eye on your words and actions at all times.

It doesn't matter how much you might wish that you didn't feel what you feel – you do, and that's that. To make the best out of the situation, accept what you have and work with your emotions. Fighting them will only intensify your suffering.

"So I'm a jerk? That's why I wish I'd never heard of Radical Acceptance. I'm tired of being angry. I don't want to be angry."
We looked at him and said quietly, "But you, Sir, are an angry man."
"No", George yelled angrily, "I'm not!"
"That's not really very convincing George, is it?" we retorted.
"See what I mean? My temper is on this constant short fuse."
"What would it mean to accept that you are an angry man?" we asked.
"Angry men are violent and abusive; no one wants an angry man as a husband or father." He hung his head in sorrow. "I'm afraid that my

anger will push everyone away, so it's easier just to convince myself that it doesn't exist."

"George?" He looked up at us. "When did this anger begin?"

"With that Radical Acceptance workshop."

"No, George", we answered. "You didn't suddenly become angry then: that was just when you became aware of your anger. It's really been there a long time: it's just been hidden and passive so you haven't realised that it was there. Now it's open and active. Think back to all the times you distanced yourself from your wife or children, for instance – giving them the cold shoulder or hiding behind the paper at meals."

"What, you live in my house?" he asked with astonishment.

We laughed, "No, we just know what passive anger looks like. We've lived with it and been through it too."

"So I just say, 'Yup, I'm angry: too bad for the rest of you?'"

Self-Acceptance: Discover

Self-discovery and self-acceptance work go hand in hand: first you discover an aspect of yourself, and then you work to accept it. As you accept your discoveries, new layers emerge within yourself – ones which can lead to deeper discoveries on the same issue. When these get accepted, new levels emerge, and so on. As such, it's important to look at discovery and acceptance as a process, not a destination: just like the rest of life, you'll constantly be building on what you've done previously.

To understand this matter further, consider the example of lying. Once you've identified that you're a liar, your first discovery on the topic may reveal that you lie to protect people's feelings. When you accept this, you may see that you avoid giving complete answers when feeling attacked – which is another a form of lying. After subsequently working to accept this new discovery, you'll perhaps discover that you lie to yourself. The discover-acceptance process won't ever stop – it'll just go deeper and deeper into the infinite layers which make up your psyche, every discovery and acceptance building on the ones which have come before.

This discover-acceptance process isn't the only way in which self-discovery and self-acceptance can work together, however. Another example occurs when old acceptances get rediscovered: when an issue you'd previously scored as a 10 suddenly reappears as a 3. When this happens, it's possible to become unsettled as you realise that a situation you thought had been dealt with a long time ago still carries charge. The whole situation can cause you to question how effectively you deal with the discoveries that you make. Don't focus on such insecurities, however – just do the work, accept the discovery and move on with your life. You even may find yourself dealing with the same situation several more times: some issues, called core issues, just keep coming back no matter what you do. When they do return, though, don't let the repetition get you down: just accept what you find and move on as before.

"When you get angry, what do you do?" we asked.

George thought for a moment before saying, "I think really angry thoughts. I walk around with a stormy look on my face. Then I remember that damn Radical Acceptance, so I start trying to see how I'm like those people that angered me – but it's just not working."

"Yes, you said earlier that you only accepted that you were a jerk when necessary. Maybe it's time to discover and accept how you're a jerk at other times?"

"Oh great! Not only am I angry, but I also get to discover that I'm an inconsiderate, selfish jerk as well! You call this therapy? I call it crap. Other therapists would help me to stop being angry and to stop being a jerk. You guys just sit there and say, 'Accept it.'"

At this point, it was clear that George was exhibiting a reluctance to discover – a reluctance to really go inside and see what was there. We just smiled, though, and said, "It's wonderful to see you expressing your anger so well. When we first met you, you had your anger stuffed so far inside yourself that you were begging for a medical breakdown. It's also nice to see you openly being the jerk that you've always been. That's the point here, George – you've always been a jerk. An inconsiderate, controlling, angry jerk. The only, and we mean only, difference is your awareness of that. If your wife were here, she would be able to make a long list of just how much of a jerk you really are and always have been. They only person who doesn't know is you! So, take a breath and see just how deep this jerk goes into your life."

He sat stunned for a long time, and then finally said, "It's like the Wizard of Oz when Dorothy pulls back the curtain to reveal not some wondrous wizard but a nasty, angry, old man."

Self-Acceptance: Integrate & Accept

Once you've discovered hidden aspects of yourself from your unconscious, the next step is to accept that they're a part of you. What's more, many of the things which you discover will have been with you all of your life: the only thing which will have changed is the way in which those discoveries express themselves over time. This is another important part of the Integrate and Accept step: accepting that who you are was essentially fixed by the time you reached the age of maturity.

Having fixed patterns isn't something that sits well with most people – their natural reaction is to cry, "What do you mean fixed? I'm absolutely not the same person I was 10 or even 5 years ago!" This is true: they aren't. However, although they've changed how they express themselves over time, the person they are underneath has remained the same.

Let's return to the example of someone with a System which works toward a lack of intimacy to help clarify this point. When that person is young, the System may lead them into fierce fights and huge amounts of drama. As they get older, the System may encourage them into a safe relationship – one which doesn't foster personal growth, and is really more about dull co-existence than passion. Older still, the System may express itself as breaking free from that safety and exploring independence, maybe by having a series of more superficial relationships. Finally, in old age the System might leave the person wondering why they never found the same level of intimacy that others seemed to discover. The System keeps evolving over time.

The question often asked at this point is, "If we don't change, then what's the point of doing personal growth work? What's the point of Radical Acceptance?" The answer to this is simple: Radical Acceptance helps you to alter your awareness of and response to your underlying patterns. When you know what you're dealing with, you'll be able to work with it instead of constantly fighting against it.

If you have a character trait of being a procrastinator, for instance, then accepting this means that you work with it. This work could mean setting intermediate deadlines so you don't finish everything at the last minute. It could also mean warning people who work with you of your working style so that they don't get caught off guard. Whatever your choice, allow your procrastination to serve you rather than fighting against it. You can only do this, however, once you've fully integrated and accepted that you're a procrastinator.

> After discovering the extent of his jerk, George continued, "So I see, finally, just what a jerk I've been. I accept it. Does accepting it mean it goes away?" he asked, hopefully.
>
> We just burst out laughing. "George, you're too funny! Being a jerk has been a part of you since you were a child. It's lasted through all of your life's ups and downs, and it's persisted despite your efforts to stuff it, repress it, hide it, kill it and avoid it. It will survive acceptance as well." We then became serious and added, "We used to think that our negative attributes could be healed, cured, transformed, etc. as well. Then we kept noticing them coming back. That was when we tried another technique, and another, and another. We're very thorough people.
>
> "Next, two things happened. The first was that we began questioning why we labelled those aspects of ourselves as negative: they were just as much a part of us as the things we labelled as positives. From then on, the labels 'positive' and 'negative' began to lose their meanings.
>
> "The second thing that happened was our realization that who we are wasn't going to go away. Both of these led to Radical Acceptance."
>
> "So I can fight or accept it, but it will stay either way? So why not keep fighting it? Why let it win?"
>
> "Those are excellent questions, George. They show that you're really thinking about this. In response, let's talk about one of Radical Acceptance's clichés: 'What you fight wins. What you accept serves you.' What this means is that the jerk will have his day, and that the more you fight him, the stronger he becomes. Accepting him brings him out of the unconscious mind and into the open — where you can see him and deal with him."

Self-Acceptance: Plan

If you know that certain character traits and Systems are a part of who you are, then how does that change how you approach life? If you're a member of an addiction recovery fellowship and have accepted that you're an addict, then how does that affect your decision to go out after work to a bar? Self-acceptance doesn't mean that you shouldn't go to the bar, only that you need to make sure that you have both support and an exit plan ready. A common coping strategy involves making sure someone else knows of your addiction – so that, in the bar example, you can share your concerns with them if you're starting to crave a drink. You might even think about creating a signal to show that things are getting too tough. This way your support person can discretely make your excuses as you leave.

The same applies to your dealings with other people. If you know that your boss likes to keep a close eye on things, then don't be shocked when he or she does just that. Similarly, if you know that your partner is forgetful, then make sure that he or she knows about a special date coming up. Hoping that they will suddenly change from who they are is like wishing your cat could bark like a dog. Getting this right is especially important in relationships, as couples often live wishing for the early days of a relationship to return – the time when their partner was different. Those days are gone, however. Now it's time to accept your partner for who they really are – not who you wish they'd be.

On a related note, if you know that human nature on a wider scale isn't going to change, then how does this change your plans to stop war or save the planet? If this knowledge makes you downhearted, then you've failed to really accept the human condition. True acceptance makes character traits, Systems, other people's behaviour, wars and eco-devastation neutral. When you've mastered this, you'll be able to plan from a place of wisdom – without the emotional charge that may have hindered so many of your earlier plans. A simple example of this occurred when energy campaigners approached businesses and showed them that different manufacturing processes would not only save electricity, but would save their companies money. By discovering, accepting and appealing to a basic commercial desire for profit, the campaigners were able to successfully get companies to change their practices – a very different result from when they offered angry and emotional appeals to those same companies centred around the issue of saving the planet.

"Once you've accepted your jerk and made him a part of your conscious mind," we continued, "you can begin to make plans which include him."

"Like inviting him along on a picnic?" George asked sarcastically.

"Sort of," we replied with a smile. "It definitely includes asking him what his needs are. "Trying to bring him along and not asking him what his thoughts are is rather inconsiderate, don't you think?"

"So you're telling me that I've been a jerk to my jerk?"

"Yes, exactly. He's going to show up whether you invite him along or not. Just like the crazy uncle that upsets everyone at family gatherings."

George smiled, "Oh yes, we have one of those. Everyone pretends to be shocked, but I think we're pleased that he's shown up, really."

"How do you explain your uncle to strangers?"

"I take them aside and explain. Then, if he gets too out of hand, I take him aside until he settles down a bit."

"Wonderful. Pretend your jerk is your uncle and your family are the strangers."

He looked confused for a bit then his face brightened as he said excitedly, "You mean speak to them and explain about my jerk? Tell them that his presence doesn't mean that I love them less – it just means that he's a part of me? That might work. But my jerk is hardly the life of the party…he's more like a party spoiler."

"What does the jerk have to say about that?" George looked confused

"In your head, ask your inner jerk what he says about being a party spoiler, and then speak the first thing that comes to mind."

"He says," he began slowly, "that he is present when I feel passionately about something. He wants the best for me and my family. Wow! I never realised!"

"So, the jerk is the voice of your passion?"

Dazed, he said, "Yes."

"How does your wife feel about this emerging passion?"

He blushed and admitted that there was a new life and energy in other areas of his life. "It's a plan. I'm going to speak to my family, telling them about my jerk and that I only want the best for them. And then, when things get out of hand, I'll remove myself from the situation until I'm less angry."

Self-Acceptance: Act & Accept

To act from a place of self-acceptance is to act in accordance with who you are, not who you want to be. On some issues, this will mean that you're restricted in what you're able to do. For someone whose body doesn't fit with the current ideal of beauty, for example, then dreams of becoming a model are pointless; no amount of dieting with make a person taller. For a person who's tone-deaf, then taking up a musical instrument is best done for personal enjoyment rather than with hopes of becoming a rock star. It's crucial to act while accepting these limitations, as fighting them will only lead to disappointment in the long run.

On other matters, there are things which can be done – so long as you set out a clear plan for overcoming any discoveries which might get in your way. A self-admittedly lazy person can join a gym with a friend, for example – a friend who loves working out and who's not afraid to prod the lazy one into action. Similarly, a person with a System of failure can start a project with concrete plans in place for when their System tries to sabotage their efforts.

How well you've worked with your discoveries – and accepted them as integral parts of yourself – is indicated by the results that you achieve. Are you going to the gym? Are you completing the phases of your project? If the answers are no, then go back to the planning stage, accepting more fully who you are. Self-acceptance is only truly measured by your ability to work with what you have.

George was back two weeks later with a definite limp, a black eye and looking a little sheepish.

"What happened to you?" we asked, worried about him. "Did your family gang up on you and beat you up for being a jerk?"

He laughed, "Nothing like that. In fact, that actually didn't go too badly. I don't think the kids fully understand it yet, but we're moving in the right direction. No, these wounds weren't caused by my failure to accept that I'm a jerk – but rather my failure to accept that I'm not 19 any more.

"There I was claiming my passion when I saw my kids out throwing the football. I remembered playing football as a teen and, bursting with energy, I went running out to play with them. They first looked at me strangely, as I guess I haven't done too much of that over the years. Anyway, I played quarterback for a while and then tossed the ball to my oldest and said, 'I'm going deep. Throw me the long bomb.' My son shook his head, but agreed. I started running while looking over my shoulder for the ball." He paused and winced. "I forgot about the maple tree."

We all groaned. Ronna then started telling George about some of Chris' failures to accept his age and how some had even resulted in trips to the hospital. We shared a good laugh.

Self-Acceptance

6 Principles

In Radical Acceptance, a principle is defined as 'an intention to guide how I behave and a plan for when I miss.' An intention is like a bulls-eye in a target; a goal you aim to achieve, sometimes succeeding, sometimes missing. The plan is an attempt to correct matters when you missed in your intention. To make this clearer, here's an example. You might intend to work through the steps of Radical Acceptance whenever you come across an event which is charged with a feeling. Furthermore, when you realise that you've missed your goal, your plan will be to make appropriate amends, take yourself back to the feeling, and then try the Radical Acceptance steps again. In other words, principles are just ways of setting out how you want to behave – and then putting a process in place to catch yourself when you don't quite manage. Over the course of this chapter, you'll be encouraged to explore your principles. Before doing that, though, it's necessary to understand a little more about exactly what principles mean.

One of the biggest mistakes which people make when referring to principles is to confuse them with rules. Unlike principles, rules are fixed statements about life which, when followed or broken, result in either a reward or a punishment. In contrast, principles are flexible – and when they're followed, the consequences of any actions are the natural outcomes of those actions. It's easier to understand this difference if you compare two different attitudes to speed regulation. In most countries, rules apply: if you're caught driving over the speed limit, you'll receive a fine or imprisonment. There's no flexibility – the law is the law, and if you break it, then you get punished. On the German Autobahn, however, a principle applies: drivers choose an appropriate speed for the weather, their vehicle and their driving ability, and if they get into an accident for ignoring any of these, then they're held responsible for damages. Unlike with the rule, drivers in Germany have to face the consequences of their actions – and not just an inflexible punishment. In short, the flexibility of principles allows them to meet unique situations appropriately and also ensures that outcomes flow naturally from your actions (offering natural guides to behaviour instead of the more arbitrary nature of rules).

Once people are confident of what a principle is, many still have problems in defining their own principles – instead opting to take an extreme view of how principles should be set out. Most often, one of four different extreme views can be found. The first of these is trying to find one principle to guide all aspects of life. This view is overly simplistic. Take the 'treat others as you want to be treated' golden rule, for instance: in this case, how you want to be treated may not be clear to others unless you clarify it – and when you do this, you're back to having more than just one principle. Similarly, how you want to be treated won't always be the best approach to every situation. Imagine that one of your friends is an addict, for instance, and that they've asked you for money to buy drugs. No matter how much that person might want you to help them – and how much you can imagine yourself wanting the same help if you were in a similar position – fulfilling their wish could be hazardous to their health. In this situation, the overly-simple golden rule clearly falls down. The second, opposing extreme is having too many principles – trying to define your response to each and every possible situation which could ever occur. Doing this is pointless, as life is full of infinite variations. No matter how much you try, you'll never be able to cover them all.

There are two other extremes as well. The first is to simplify a principle so much that it becomes essentially a rule. An example might be, "I will never lie." This, like all rules, is too rigid to deal with the complexities of life. The other extreme is to make a principle so complicated that it becomes incomprehensible and thereby useless. An example of this might be, "I will only lie when to tell the truth would cause unacceptable levels of pain to another person - unless that pain is for their benefit. I also won't lie if the person really isn't open to receiving any help (though I'll still lie if I think they're actually seeking help, even though they're denying that)." The goal to strive for when creating a principle is to try for the middle ground between all of these four extremes.

When you strike this balance then your principles will become useful aids in guiding and directing life. If you miss, ending up close to one of the four extremes, don't worry, life will encourage you to move into balance.

Having covered the potential pitfalls of defining principles, it's now time to consider some principles which are common to most people. While these principles are common, however, different people will express them in different ways. They are:

1. Treating others and yourself with respect. This can vary quite a lot between people. A common variation is to respect those who respect you and not those whom you deem unworthy of your respect. For other people, a fear of being seen as disrespectful leads to their being subservient to everyone; the classic ever-changing person who always wants to please.

2. Being kind to yourself and others. Being kind is also quite varied, with some people applying kindness to a select few and others attempting to be nice to everyone. Niceness, in this latter case, is trying to prevent any kind of hurt and upset in others.

3. Seeking to improve yourself. The self-improvement principle can vary from claims of already being good enough without the need for any personal growth work through to self-flagellation in response to a perception of repeated personal failure.

Give some thought to how you apply each of these principles in your life. As well, consider what you do when you fail to live by these (and your own, more specific) principles. If you fail to respect others, for example, then avoid excusing yourself or blaming other people. In this situation, a more effective plan is to consider possible amends for your actions which, in hindsight, lacked respect. When your actions have failed to be kind when kindness was called for, an apology is often the best plan for making amends. The final principle covered above, self-improvement, typically comes with a plan for trying harder or giving up after you've missed the mark. This approach flies in the face of Radical Acceptance, which calls you to accept your misses instead of trying harder to fix them. As such, a better strategy would be to identify the area of your life that you wanted to fix and turning your attention to accepting it.

Having given some common principles, it's also important to remember that Radical Acceptance invites you to take responsibility for your life by developing your own personal code of conduct through a set of principles. These principles shouldn't be fixed and static like rules, but should instead grow and change over time as life experience invites you to revisit them over and over again.

The planning step is the most common point on the Radical Acceptance Wheel for looking at principles. There are two points to consider during this step: the first is to see how your discovery affects your principles. In most instances, this will be clear – if you have a principle which says that you consider certain people unworthy of your respect, for example, then discovering and accepting that you're actually the same as those other people can cause a major adjustment to that principle. On the other hand, if one of your principles tells you to respect everyone, then discovering that you can be disrespectful might shift the principle into a more balanced place. There are also times when new discoveries create new principles. If you discover that you're a liar, for instance, then you might develop a new principle regarding truth and lies as a result (though this new principle would still be influenced by the principles which you already have).

Once the work on creating or adjusting your principles is feeling complete, then it's time to consider point two: does your plan meet the goals of your principles? When creating your plan, it's important to check it against your principles. Two problems often come up during this process. The first occurs when a plan exposes conflicting principles – when a choice is in agreement with one principle and in disagreement with another. If you've promised your children not to tell your spouse about a surprise party, then what do you do when he or she notices unusual behaviour and asks you what's going on? To tell the truth would agree with your honesty principle, but would also disagree with your principle on keeping your word to your children. Not telling the truth would have the same problem in reverse. The problem with conflicting principles is that they take away your guide for directing your choice.

The second common problem found in planning is the desire to act in conflict with your principles – even principles which have just been created. Again returning to the example of lying, imagine that your partner lies to you. Through the discovery and integrations steps, you accept that you too are a liar. Now in planning, you decide that since lying is neither right nor wrong, you're going to respond to the event by telling a lie back. You may convince yourself that that would be an 'appropriate' level of truth. However, when checking it out against your principle of respect and kindness, you see that you were excusing an inappropriate level of truth in your first attempt to use the principle.

Principles are guides, and in many respects are more demanding guides than rules. Unlike rules, they require you to plan and act with thought and responsibility – to be aware of what you're doing and why. With principles, no action is right or wrong, and this can make living a lot more demanding. On the other hand, principles also mean that you can respond to situations with intelligence and flexibility, rather than with the inflexible approach offered by rules.

Principles: Event

When life throws difficult events your way, what stops you from reacting – from striking out in anger, for example? If you tend to strike out, what could you use to prevent yourself from striking out in the future? The solution is a strong principle: a principle such as, 'I will acknowledge that each and every event is neutral, and that no matter what feeling I have in response to an event, I accept that feeling as belonging to me. Furthermore, if I take an event personally, I will return to it after calming down so as to find out why it meant so much to me.' Such a principle constantly reminds you that events are neutral: not to be taken personally. This doesn't suggest that you won't have feelings in response to events, but instead sets out that you intend to see the feelings as belonging to you, and not to the event.

This principle is true for events where you feel excitement, fear, hate and more. No matter what feeling you experience, attributing it to an event – taking the event personally – will often get you into hot water. Even an event which generates a loving response isn't personal: if the event is your intimate partner saying, "I love you," for instance, then that speaks to their state of feeling and their reaction to your presence. Interestingly, if your partner had said, "I hate you," then that event would also be neutral, but something which you might have an easier time accepting.

Since you're human, you won't always remember the principle of neutrality, especially when you're just beginning with this work. That's okay: just come back to the event later when you have a cooler head. Then ask what it was about the event that hooked you – a question which requires the use of the tools of self-discovery.

Living by a principle of neutrality instead of taking events personally is difficult to implement when the event is heated, but it's an essential skill to develop if you want to live a life based on Radical Acceptance.

Judy was in love: his name was Robert. The only problem was that she was in a relationship with, and living with, Frank. Robert was a man whom she had regular dealings with through a volunteer group. "He's everything I want in a man; everything my current partner isn't. And he's so sexy, too, he makes my heart flutter and my knees go weak!"

"So, why haven't you left Frank and moved in with Robert? Or maybe you could just have an affair with Robert?"

Judy looked horrified. "I couldn't do that!"

"Why not?"

"It'd be wrong...wouldn't it?" she asked a little hopefully.

"No idea. Would it be wrong?"

"Of course it'd be wrong. Having affairs is immoral."

"According to whom?"

She puzzled over that one. "I guess the Church, but I don't go to church. Maybe society, but then affairs happen all the time. It's no longer a crime. Then...not according to anyone but me, I suppose. I wouldn't want Frank to have an affair, though, so it wouldn't be fair to him if I then went out and had one."

"So your sense of fairness is what prevents you from having an affair?"

"Yes."

We smiled.

Principles: Feel & Accept

In the Feel & Accept step, you're aided by a principle which says, 'I will stay in a feeling: I will not run from it, no matter how hard staying might be. Those times when I do run from it, I will go back and find out why I couldn't stay.' Following such a principle is as important for feelings of happiness as it is for feelings of the darkest depression.

Illogical as it might initially sound, even happiness can be a difficult feeling to stay in. How many people keep 'waiting for the other shoe to drop'? This worry can lift you out of your happiness and instead feed a System which says that you don't deserve that happy feeling or will be punished for being too happy. The same is true for feelings of depression: it's important to stay with the feeling and to work through it, fully learning from everything that it has to teach you. Trying to escape the feeling and force happiness won't get you anywhere.

If you combine the importance of staying with your feelings with the neutrality principle from the previous step, then you'll eventually be able to stop yourself from acting on your feelings straight away (at least on a good day). Instead, you'll have space to work through the Radical Acceptance Wheel; to use your feelings as your teacher and guide into the subconscious.

Beware, however, of a common mistake with accepting feelings: indulging them rather than just feeling them. If you're feeling depressed, for instance, then indulgence means staying in bed and losing your job. The alternative is to acknowledge the feelings and then get up and go to work anyway. Feel and accept your feelings – don't become them.

Similar to the event principle, when you miss and avoid a feeling, then the principle calls you back to review and learn. Recall the event and feeling and be aware of how you avoided your emotional response. Then go back and make use of the tools of Radical Acceptance.

"So this is love with Robert?" we asked.

"It certainly feels like it."

"It didn't feel like that with Frank?"

Judy looked confused. "It felt like it when we first met, but not any more. I guess it wasn't real love."

"Because real love never dies? Or was that a song title?"

"I'm not sure," she replied. "I just know that I want that feeling."

"Yes, and I want to be twelve feet tall. Keeping a feeling and becoming twelve feet tall are equally likely."

"No", she wailed, "I want it to last!"

"Want away," we retorted. "That won't change life. Feelings, all feelings, come and go. Look at us, we have a fabulous relationship — but we're not constantly in love. It's nice when it's here, but we've got no expectation that it will stay — so when it goes, it's no big deal."

"Then how do you stay together?"

"We have principles: personal intentions for how we choose to live our lives. Those principles don't depend on feelings. In fact, they often move counter to feelings."

Ronna then added, "Yeah, when Christopher leaves his socks on the floor again, I feel like whacking him. But I have a principle about hitting, so I accept the feeling and choose not to."

Principles: Discover

One of the goals of Radical Acceptance is to continue digging for discoveries no matter how dirty and ugly they get – no matter how much you want to stop looking for them. A useful principle for this step is, 'I will have the courage to go into my subconscious and see what's there for me – no matter how uncomfortable those things might be. If doing this becomes too uncomfortable and I end up stopping, then I will work with my fear so that the next time life calls me into the depths, I will be more likely to stay.'

One of the implications of this principle is the commitment to look within yourself to discover issues instead of blaming other people, places or things. This is particularly tricky in an intimate relationship. When your partner repeats the same annoying behaviour despite the number of times you've asked, demanded and even begged that he/she stops, it can be hard to remember that it's actually your issue and not your partner's. The principle doesn't change the fact that your partner is doing what you object to – yet your response to that behaviour is still all your own. If, for example, your partner drinks, gambles or does no work around the house, then those actions are their behaviour. That belongs to them. The only thing that belongs to you is that their behaviour upsets you. To find out why their behaviour upsets you means going within.

The other part of the principle pertains to those times when you miss – when you try to blame your feelings on external events, or those times when the discovery work seems too hard or too scary. These times mean going back later to complete the discovery work – perhaps even asking for help with this from a friend or therapist. Then, when life provides another chance to go digging, you'll be better prepared.

"So, what should I do with these feelings of love for Robert?"

"Hmm, Radical Acceptance says to use feelings to lead yourself into your unconscious."

"Yeah, but that's only for negative feelings. Not love."

"Negative feelings? What happened to feeling and accepting all feelings?"

Judy looked horrified. "You want me to process my feelings of love?"

"You said in the last meeting that you wanted to use Radical Acceptance in your life. Now, are you going to or not?"

"Wow, I guess that's where the Adult comes in, isn't it? My Child just wants to bask in these feelings. Is there a Radical Acceptance principle?"

"No, principles are personal: there isn't a one-size-fits-all Radical Acceptance Principle. In this case you might have a 'I made a commitment and I want to stick with it' principle."

"Yes, I do. Okay...as far as I remember, there was no tool for processing love. What do I do now?"

"Love is similar to anger: it's a form of projection. It shows you what you like the most about yourself — except you see it in another. When you think of Robert, what's the most appealing thing about him?"

"That's easy, he's strong. Not just physically, but as a person."

"So how are you strong?"

"It's funny that you should ask, actually. I've been feeling quite weak over this whole work stuff, and while Frank has been great, he often backs down in situations. Robert is so confident and assured — he never backs down."

We laughed, "That strength you love today will become the stubbornness you curse tomorrow. So how are you strong?"

We discussed this further until she could see in herself the strength and power that she saw in Robert. She added, "Damn, I don't feel as much in love now. You guys spoiled my wonderful feelings."

"Yes," we replied. "Love based on projection has a way of fading as the projection is seen."

Principles: Integrate & Accept

Not trying to fix a discovery takes work, self-discipline and a firm principle. The principle might go something like this: 'I intend to accept my discoveries without trying to fix them. When I find myself wanting them to go away, I will return to scoring and being grateful.' This is the core of the Integrate & Accept step: to hold on to this principle of acceptance, no matter how ugly the discovery first appears to you. You'll find that underneath all the ugliness is a gift – a gift that contributes to the unique person that you are.

If you notice yourself working to fix a discovery, then call on this principle and return to the work of acceptance. Remember to score how well you used the discovery, and then go deeper within yourself to find the reasons for gratitude – ultimately letting go of the desire to fix. Perhaps you have a character trait of lying when you feel defensive? A situation comes along which challenges you, so you lie – and before you have a chance to correct the situation, someone discovers the lie and it causes problems in your life. While it might be tempting to try and remove your character trait, that would not be acceptance (and attempting to do this would only fail, anyway). Instead, notice your desire to fix, and then step back and work the tools of self-acceptance. Begin by scoring how well you lied (although don't score too highly, because in the example, the person you lied to caught you out fairly quickly). Then think about how the character trait is a gift. Maybe it helped you to avoid punishments as a child? Maybe it gives you a sense of control when things start feeling uncontrollable? Whatever the reason you come up with, give thanks for having such a wonderful character trait.

"So, you're a strong, powerful woman, just like Robert is a strong, powerful man?" we asked.

Judy hedged, "It sounds right when we talk about it, but to come right out and say it sounds conceited."

"And being conceited is bad?"

"You guys keep asking me that question; I don't know what's right or wrong any more."

"Maybe as a strong, powerful woman you need to figure that out for yourself..."

"I wish you'd stop calling me that."

"Are we lying?"

"No", she paused, "It just doesn't feel right. It feels like claiming that will make me less of a woman and turn me into a bitch. I know you guys preach acceptance, but I'm not sure that I want to accept this."

"So which are you going to choose: acceptance or continuing to pretend that you aren't a powerful woman?"

Judy thought for a bit, and then she sat up straighter, put her shoulders back and said, "You're right. I am strong and powerful, and I said that I was going to accept that. That's why I'm choosing to say yes to this. I have principles, after all."

Principles: Plan

A strong principle is also an aid to planning, as it can help to ensure that the Child and Adult archetypes are in balance and that your plan doesn't conflict with your other principles. The principle might read as follows: 'I will ensure that my plans are formed on a consensus between my Child and Adult and that the option which I select is in agreement with my principles. When I realise that a plan does not meet this principle, I will re-plan or, if I've already acted, I will make amends.' The first part of the principle ensures that you include both the Child and the Adult's point of view in every decision that you make, which is an essential part of making the most reasoned choices possible. The second part of the principle is your plan for when balance between the Child and the Adult hasn't been achieved – or when your plan is in conflict with your other principles.

Common errors here are the tendency to ignore the Child when making a plan and for the Child to pretend to be the Adult (to become the 'pseudo-Adult'). In the first case, the Adult may have noble ideas on the best plan, but without the support of the Child, acting on the plan can be very difficult – after all, the Child knows how to dig in his or her feet and cause real problems. The pseudo-Adult comes out when the plan sounds good – all the words are right – but the motivation comes from self-interest and conflicts with other principles. Having a clearly-defined planning principle means that you have the intention of pausing and evaluating all of your plans so as to ensure that you've avoided both of these errors.

This principle is especially important when a plan is likely to raise strong feelings in someone else. There are instances, for example, where the most appropriate course of action will raise angry, defensive or sad feelings. One such instance may be a parent refusing a child's request when the request is inappropriate for the child's age or is likely to result in harm to him/her. Other examples of plans which are likely to generate strong feelings can be: ending a relationship, confronting another on inappropriate behaviour, giving praise, proposing marriage and so on. Each of these actions can be either appropriate or inappropriate depending on the specific circumstances. What's important is that the Child and Adult archetypes are in agreement on what you're doing and that the plan has been aligned with your principles.

When you realise that a plan misses either of these intentions, then your course of action depends on how far things have already gone. If you've yet to act, then no harm has been done: go back to the drawing board and re-do your planning. If you've already acted, then you'll need to plan for appropriate corrective action. This might be an apology, or it could be something else. Consider an example: you've refused a child's request to attend an event based on their age, but after thinking on it more, you've decided that you made the wrong call. Corrective action would now mean going back to the child, explaining to them about your new thoughts and giving them permission to attend.

Having a clearly-defined principle to aid in planning and using this to verify your actions will result in having fewer regrets and more often achieving your desired outcomes.

> "Speaking of principles, what are you going to do about Robert?"
> Her face fell. "Oh yes, Robert. I'm feeling caught. On one hand, having an affair would run counter to my principle of respecting Frank, but on the other, there's still a zing when I think of Robert."
> "But you're already having an affair. You may not be having physical sex with Robert, but emotionally and mentally you're with him and not Frank."
> She looked up in shock, "Oh no. That's just wrong." We waited. "Alright, it's not wrong, but that's unfair to Frank." We waited again. She began to get frustrated. "I know: the fair word is from the Child. Arrrgh! You two drive me nuts. I can't even think without hearing your voices in my head!"
> We laughed and said, "Let's step back a bit. To date you've had rules about fidelity. Now it's time to figure out your principles. To do this, it's best to start with an outcome. There are two points to consider here. Firstly, what do you want in terms of a relationship? Secondly, to feel proud about how you've behaved, what would you choose to do?"

"The second one is easier to answer: I would have trouble looking at myself in the mirror if I slept with Robert. The first one is harder. I'm not sure if I want to be with Robert or Frank."

"Back away from the specific question and ask yourself what you long for in a relationship with any man."

"I want the relationship to be based in love, caring, strength, great sex, etc."

"What about intimacy?"

"Of course."

"There's no 'of course' about it. Most people say that they want intimacy, but in reality they work hard to make sure that they never get it. It's interesting, for instance, that after Frank saw you being angry and then intimate and vulnerable, you're suddenly drawn to another man."

She turned pale. "Oh my God! You're so right! What do I do?"

"I don't know, we're working with your principle around relationships. This needs to come from you."

She thought for a bit and said, "I now see what you mean. Principles aren't black and white. Yes, it's my goal to build intimacy and when I don't – when I become aware that my actions are destroying intimacy – I will speak to my partner." Then she added, "And I'm going to tell that asshole Robert that he can get lost." She put up her hand to stop us from speaking and added, "I know that would conflict with my principle of respecting others..but I do need to end things with him."

Principles: Act & Accept

Having made a plan, it's now time to consider a principle that will guide you through the final step. Two principles are important here: the first applies to acting, and the second applies to the consequences. When you're carrying out your planned action, the principle says: 'I intend to act regardless of my fears and anxieties. I also intend to keep things simple, firm and clear. If I fail to act, then I will re-plan – being aware of the reasons for which I failed to act.' This principle reminds you that the plan has been thought through and that it's your best course of action. Carrying it out might upset others, but even this upset is for the best in the long run.

The second principle might be: 'Having acted, I accept the consequences of my actions. If I realise that I'm trying to avoid responsibility for the consequences, then I will take corrective measures to change this.' In many cases, plans which are put into action don't work out as intended: even though the plan looked good on paper, there will have been another person involved – and other people aren't always predictable. Radical Acceptance invites you to accept all consequences – whether or not they're the consequences that you'd planned on accepting.

As an example, if you decide to end a relationship, then how your partner will take this news is unpredictable. They may agree easily, leaving you tempted to ask why ending the relationship was such an easy process. Asking this question is likely to prolong the discussion and may even lead you into suggesting that you give the relationship one more try. The acting principle reminds you to be clear, direct and firm when speaking, which will help you to avoid this potential pitfall.

On the other hand, your partner may strongly oppose the break up suggestion – reacting angrily and attempting to intimidate you into giving it another try. The firmness aspect of the principle will help here too. Your partner's most likely response, however, is an attempt to persuade. He or she may use words, tears or even hints of suicide and other forms of manipulation to win you back.

If it was a long-term relationship, they will know what buttons to push: what forms of manipulation work best. By strongly standing by your principle of being clear, direct and firm, you'll avoid being manipulated and achieve your goal.

There has been much said about consequences, but to reiterate: life can throw some expected twists. Even when the consequences are unpleasant, remember the principle, take a breath and step up to the plate. You may not like having to do this, but those consequences are still yours to accept and respond to.

> It was two weeks before Judy came back to see us. She practically threw herself into a chair and said, "Wow, who ever knew that principles could be so hard?!"
>
> "Robert give you are hard time?" we assumed.
>
> "Robert? No, not Robert. Well he did, but I went in really clearly and spoke about my principles. He gave me a bit of a hard time. I saw him as stubborn and controlling rather than strong and assertive – it's funny how that shift occurred really quickly, actually. Once he saw that I wasn't going to budge, he called me a few nasty names and quit the volunteer group."
>
> She sighed, "No, that was easy, though. It's Frank that's hard. I spoke with him about Robert and he had the nerve to respect my new principle. When I told him about our discussion on intimacy, the jerk thought that you two made sense and invited me to go deeper and be more intimate in our relationship."
>
> We said, with a hint of sarcasm, "He wants to go deeper into intimacy and vulnerability with you? That sounds horrible, I'd run!"
>
> She looked at us and said, "That's just the point. The deeper we go, the more I want to run. The really hard principle to keep is the one about honouring intimacy. This intimacy thing is really hard."
>
> "Yes: conscious, intimate relationships are one of the hardest jobs in life."
>
> "Hmm...so much work! Meeting you two was a good thing, right?"
>
> We all shared a good laugh.

Principles

7 Responsibility

Responsibility is a broad theme in Radical Acceptance, bringing all of the previous themes together under a single heading. However, as a term, it is also extremely subjective: it means different things to different people. In fact, 'responsibility' can even mean different things to the same person depending on the situation they're in. To help narrow down this concept, the first objective of this section will be to give the term a more concrete definition – not necessarily the 'right' one, but nevertheless the one used by Radical Acceptance.

In light of responsibility's scope, its definition is split into two parts. The first part states that 'everything you do comes as a result of choices that you've made'. Some of those choices are made consciously and some unconsciously, but from the words you speak to the things you do and everything else in between, all of your actions come from a choice made by you, not anyone else. Regardless of how tempting it may be to move blame away from yourself, in reality no one and nothing ever forces you to decide to do anything. You're the one who chooses to act or not to act – just as you choose to smoke a cigarette or to not light up; to have junk food or a piece of fruit; to have an affair or to resist the temptation. The list is endless. In this first part of the definition, responsibility is about accepting your role in your choices.

It's important to note that while your actions are the result of your choices, the actions of others are the result of their choices, too. As an extension of this, how someone responds to something that you do is a decision which they make. No matter how much you might try, you'll never have the ability to control any other person. This idea is based on the Radical Acceptance teaching that events are neutral; since any reaction or feeling which the other person experiences in response to what you do is their own, only they can deal with it. Believing that you can control another person's feelings is nothing but a fantasy of the Child archetype.

The second part of Radical Acceptance's definition of responsibility states that 'the consequences of your actions are yours to accept'. Initially, this may sound like it contradicts what was just said about other people's responses being their own – but that isn't the case. Here, 'consequences' is the keyword: other people's reactions aren't anything to do with you – but you do have to own and accept how those reactions affect you. If the other person decides not to talk to you as a result of your actions, for instance, then you have to accept the silence which comes as a consequence, even though it was their choice to stop talking. What's at play here is a subtle distinction, but also an important one. Although you didn't cause their refusal to talk – they made that choice themselves – your actions created the environment in which they made their decision. Similarly, if you speak angry, hurtful words to your partner and they respond by offering you a hug, then this consequence is also something for you to accept.

The second part of the responsibility definition, however, doesn't extend to taking on the consequences of other people's actions (the only exception to this is if you've chosen to take on consequences for someone who is unable to take them on themselves, such as a child or someone who is mentally ill). As an example, imagine that a friend comes to you and asks for money. When they explain why they need it, it turns out that they lost money on a venture which you had brought to their attention. According to Radical Acceptance, what responsibility do you have in this situation? The answer is simple: you don't have any. You made the other person aware of the venture, but it was their decision to invest – and, critically, also their decision to invest more than they could afford to lose. While it's understandable that you feel compassion for them, taking on the consequences of their actions yourself isn't 'responsible' according to Radical Acceptance. Instead, it's just the Child talking: wanting to be liked by all, this archetype will immediately want to jump in and try to rescue the other person. A more mature response is to spend time processing your feelings around the event. Ultimately, doing this might lead you to offer them some money, either as a gift or as a loan – but since you don't have to accept the loss under the Radical Acceptance definition of responsibility, this decision would be your choice. It absolutely wouldn't be your obligation.

In summary, therefore, responsibility in Radical Acceptance is all about saying, "Yes, my actions are a result of my choices, and yes, I accept the consequences from acting on those choices". Living this definition of responsibility will require using all of the preceding themes of Radical Acceptance, as explored below:

Maturity

The Child archetype tries to avoid responsibility in two ways – firstly by actively evading it, and secondly by trying to be overly responsible. To evade, the Child blames, rationalises, excuses and denies. In being overly responsible, the Child tries to be liked by everyone and so takes ownership of consequences from other people's actions. In most situations where the Child is present, he or she will attempt to avoid responsibility in both of these ways. An example might be a person apologising to all present for a guest of honour at a party being late, but then not apologising to the same guest of honour after being rude to them over their tardiness. To help overcome these pitfalls, the more mature thinking of the Adult needs to be brought in as a balance.

Self-Discovery

When you find yourself wanting to avoid responsibility for your actions, you can use this desire to discover more about yourself. Similarly, when you feel guilty, angry or sad as a result of the consequences which you've caused, those feelings can also be put to good use for the purpose of self-discovery. To continue the earlier example of the person who lost money through a venture which you suggested: if you feel guilty for suggesting the venture, then you can use the guilt to take a trip into your subconscious. You may find a belief that needs questioning – perhaps a belief that it's your job to take care of other people's misfortune.

Self-Acceptance

When you choose your actions unconsciously – based on forgotten memories, unconscious beliefs, undiscovered character traits and instincts or under the influence of your Systems – undesirable consequences are likely to follow. Upon reading this, your first reaction may be to condemn those undiscovered parts of yourself as useless and unhelpful. This, however, is not self-acceptance. On the contrary, taking full responsibility is about overcoming the desire to condemn and instead fully accepting who you are – along with any resulting consequences.

Principles

Principles help you to remember two things: firstly that your actions are the result of choices that you've made, and secondly that the consequences from those actions are yours to accept. The second part is especially important in situations when you feel like shirking your responsibility due to a consequence's particularly unpleasant nature. In the case of the friend who lost money, it was their choice to invest an amount that they could not afford to lose. It's therefore up to them to accept the consequences of this choice. If they call on their principles, then they'll stop trying to blame anyone else for their own choices.

Now that you know what responsibility involves, how can you start to become a more responsible person? As the last item on the above list indicates, you stand firmly on the principle of being responsible. Then, when you find yourself avoiding responsibility or trying to take on another person's consequences, you'll be able to stop and take corrective action. Similarly, if you find yourself dealing with the consequences of your actions by blaming someone else or excusing them, then it's time to stop, apologise and do things differently. Responsibility in Radical Acceptance might sound quite simple, but it's unquestionably challenging in practice.

Responsibility also extends to how you act – and Radical Acceptance provides several tools and strategies to help you act responsibly. In some instances these will help you to be responsible to yourself, and in other instances will help you to be responsible to those around you. To be responsible to yourself is to work actively to release attachments to memories, especially traumatic ones; it's about clearing out the parts of your past which still hold energy. The tool to use for this process of self-nurturing is called 'Cutting Cords'. Cutting Cords is a simple, meditation-based exercise that can be used on any type of event: from major events in your distant past through to smaller events which only happened five minutes ago. To try it, you'll first need to find a quiet place where you won't be disturbed. Then make sure that you have fifteen minutes of uninterrupted time and next sit or lie down – making sure that you're comfortable and relaxed.

When you're ready to begin properly, close your eyes and start taking a few deep breaths.

With your eyes still closed, begin to imagine the event. It doesn't matter what the event is – it could be someone who cut you off when you were driving earlier in the day or a fight you had with your sister ten years ago. Your only task is to see it clearly: the sights, the sounds and the smells. When you've created a strong picture in your mind, next imagine that there are cords of energy which are attached to you and going out to the past. Sometimes these cords will be small, like strands of string or telephone cords. At other times, they'll be as big and thick as redwood trees. However they look, see them and imagine energy flowing through them – out from you and going out to the memory, keeping the past alive. This is energy you could be using in the present – energy to feed your dreams, your health and your creativity. To stop the cycle, imagine yourself cutting those energy-draining cords. You can use any imaginary tool at your disposal to do this: scissors, axes, dynamite – whatever it takes to cut them. Once the cord is cut, make sure that you pull out any remains which are still attached to you: pull out the roots from deep within your body. Finally, imagine filling the new gaps you've made with healing light – maybe even apply some 'energetic cream' to ensure that the healing process is complete. If you're not a visual person, then you can do the same exercise by just thinking: your mind will tell you how big your cords of energy are, and you can think about how to cut them and repair the holes that they leave. Whether you visualise or think it, the end result will be the same.

When all the cords are cut and the holes are filled, re-imagine the event. How does it feel? How much energy are you now spending on it? If there's still energy flowing out, then you'll need to repeat the exercise either immediately or in the future. For some people, effective cord cutting can take a long time: you're only done when you can imagine the event without feelings (or in other words, when the event is fully neutral).

The other aspect of responsible acting relates to how you act around others. This is specifically targeted at how you speak to them; the words you use and the clarity with which you talk.

There are three tools which can be used to improve your communication. The right one to choose depends on what you wish to convey. The first tool is used to communicate a feeling in response to an event. This tool is called 'I' Statements. The second tool, Boundary Setting, is used to set a boundary with another person. The third helps you to communicate a clear and concise message, especially when that message may not be well received. This tool is called The Broken Record.

The 'I' Statements tool is a responsible way of telling someone how you responded emotionally to an event. When using this tool, however, it's particularly important to remember that the event is neutral; it did not cause your feelings. Instead, the feelings are yours, with the event only acting as a trigger in activating an aspect of your subconscious. Keeping these facts in mind, how should feelings best be communicated? Blaming the feeling on the event would not only be incorrect, but it would also be irresponsible – it would fail to recognise that the feeling is yours and that it originated from within you alone. Using 'I' Statements ensures that the feelings are kept personal. To make it work, change, "You made me feel...", statements into, "I felt..."

Here's an example of this tool in action. Your good friend, one that you've known for years, forgot your birthday. In response, you felt sad. It would be tempting to think that the sadness was caused by the forgotten birthday, but doing so would be incorrect: the sadness is yours and may originate from times as a child when your parents forgot a special occasion. In other words, the forgetting incident is the trigger of your feelings, and not the cause. If you choose to speak with your friend about how you felt, then it would be unwise to simply say 'You made me feel sad'. Instead, phrase the conversation through 'I' Statements: "Last week was my birthday, and although you usually remember, this year you forgot. When I realised that you'd forgotten, I felt sad. I'm not blaming you; I know we all get busy. In fact, your forgetting helped me to do some healing around times when my parents forgot special occasions. I just wanted to let you know how I felt – and to ask you to join me for a drink to belatedly celebrate my birthday."

The second tool for responsible communication is used when it's time to communicate a boundary. Simply put, Boundary Setting means telling someone which actions you'd like them to start or stop. In all such situations, what's key to remember is that the boundary belongs to you: you're the one that finds the other person's behaviour in some way uncomfortable. Clearly they don't – if they did, they wouldn't act that way. If you link this to events being neutral, then what the other person does is just what they do. Their actions are neither right nor wrong, nor good nor bad - they're just actions. Any discomfort belongs only to you. However, just as they're entitled to do what they do, you're entitled to your discomfort. The other point to remember is that you have no control over the other person. You can ask them to respect your boundary, but expecting them to honour that is likely to lead to disappointment. When planning your speech, expect your message to be received with either shame or defensiveness – and plan possible responses to both eventualities.

An example of where the Boundary Setting tool might be appropriate would be approaching a co-worker who likes to click their pen repeatedly throughout the day. You could say: "I'd like to mention to you that when you click your pen, I find it difficult to concentrate. I was wondering if you'd please stop?" If the other person responds with shame, you might add, "I'm not saying that there's anything wrong with you or with your pen clicking. The problem lies with me and my lack of concentration." If the response is defensive, on the other hand, with the other person maybe even refusing to change, then you could add, "I know that you have every right to click your pen. I'm only asking this as a favour so I can get more work done." However it goes, you'll have tried to communicate that the problem is not their pen clicking, but your distraction. The other person may not stop, either deliberately or because their pen clicking has become a habit – but in both situations, you'll have done what you can (and will need to either grin and bear it or seek another solution such as requesting a desk further away).

In the prior example, the other person's actions were relatively innocuous. Even if the boundary involves a more serious activity, though, the same rules apply. Imagine that you're receiving unwanted sexual advances from a co-worker. You've tried to be polite and evasive, hoping that they would get the hint, but it's been to no avail. Finally you decide to make your stance clear. Here, the same principles apply: the sexual advances are not right or wrong, good or bad – the issue is that you're uncomfortable with them. To deal with the situation, plan your response thoroughly and then express it clearly. If they refuse to stop, be explicit about how you intend to enforce your request: you might say that you intend to file a grievance with Human Resources, for example, or even to make a complaint to the police. It's important to understand that these requests might not get your boundary respected – but they will mean that you've acted responsibly.

The final tool is used when you need to communicate a strong, clear message, especially when that message may not be well received. This tool is called The Broken Record. To use it, start by sitting down – either by yourself or with a friend. Then come up with a short, clear message (no longer than two sentences) which clearly communicates your position on the issue at hand. Next, memorise this message until you know it inside out and are able to repeat it even when under stress. When you've done this, meet up with the person with whom you have the issue and speak your message. If they object to your message in any way, simply repeat it. Then keep repeating the message until it's been received without further objections. Say nothing else; just keep repeating your message. Any deviation from the memorised text will only prolong the discussion. No matter how angry they get, just keep repeating the same words.

This tool works well when you need to communicate any potentially unpopular decision. It's also an extremely effective parenting tool, as it communicates clearly without the need to get angry. While the child may get angry in response to its use, you'll be able to remain calm and level-headed, which is what responsible communication is really all about. There's an extended example of this tool in Chapter 10.

Responsibility: Event

Being responsible with respect to events is largely about knowing which events happen as a result of your actions and which are totally outside of your control. When this distinction is clear in your mind, you'll be able to see what's yours to take responsibility for – and also what isn't.

In the Spirituality Movement, there's a belief that every single event which you experience was created by you. Everything from a friend giving you flowers to an international bomb scare – all are created by and for you. Another belief suggests that events are influenced by your thoughts, and still another group claims that all events are totally random and that you have no part in any of them. Each of these arguments has a group within the Spirituality Movement which backs them up – though in the end, since there's no definite evidence either way, all followers can really do is move into speculation or fall back on a belief.

In contrast, Radical Acceptance teaches that some events come about as a direct result (a consequence) of your actions, whereas others just 'come'. Speculating on this latter point is a fruitless activity which can even be destructive in certain situations. An example of this destructive potential is apparent in a parent who's wracked with grief over the death of their child – feeling guilty that the death was somehow their fault because of their 'negative' thoughts. Since no evidence can conclusively 'prove' this position either way, why give speculation a chance to ruin a life?

Responsibility isn't about carrying around the weight of every unpleasant event which happens in your life: if this is what you're experiencing, then the Child and your System of suffering are both having fun at your expense. You're only responsible for those events which are a direct consequence of your choices – so let all the rest go.

George came in complaining of the week from hell; it had come to his attention that one of his staff had stolen money from the company. We let him rant for a while and then shrugged before asking, "So what?"

I thought he might slug one of us (Radical Acceptance therapy is an exciting occupation!) "So what?!" His face was red. "I hired him!"

"And you didn't check his references?" we pressed.

He looked confused. "No, I did. I checked them."

"Oh, so when you checked them you were told that he was a repeat felon?"

"No. The references were excellent," he retorted.

"So you hired him and, without knowing him, you immediately gave him exclusive signing authority."

"No, the company always requires two signatures and he wasn't one of them. He forged signatures."

"So why are you beating yourself up for hiring him? It sounds like you did everything right – you even had the systems in place to catch him quite quickly. Well done."

"But I'm the Head of Finance and the buck stops with me..." he answered.

"That's true, and you're responsible for dealing with the issue – but pretending that you're responsible for having created the situation in the first place is silly nonsense."

"You don't pull punches, do you?" He looked astounded.

We just grinned.

Responsibility: Feel & Accept

The origins of your feelings are buried in your subconscious. This means that you're not responsible for what you feel – but as soon as you've felt a feeling, you are responsible for how you respond to it. Will you choose to feel it fully, or will you opt to stuff it down? Will you immediately react to the feeling, or will you use Radical Acceptance to grow, plan – and only then act? The choices that you make when confronted with strong feelings in particular indicates how much responsibility you've taken for your life in general.

To understand this point more clearly, imagine that you've asked someone nicely to stop doing a certain action on a number of occasions. They agree each time, but keep doing it anyway. Finally the dam bursts and you feel a huge surge of anger. You weren't responsible for the event behind this development – but what you do with the feeling is now your responsibility. If you react in anger and start yelling or saying angry words, then those actions are the result of choices that you've made. If you take a breath, sit with the anger and then start using the tools of self-discovery, then that's also your choice.

That feelings happen is a fact of life – what we do with those feelings is entirely our individual responsibility.

> Once we'd suggested to George that he wasn't responsible for the fraudulent actions of his employee, he replied with, "But I feel responsible."
> "Yes, that's the feeling – although it'd be more accurate to call it a thought. What's the underlying feeling?"
> He considered this for a while. "I guess I feel betrayed that one of my staff members did this. I keep wondering what I did to cause him to do it."
> "So, you've taken your feelings of anger and turned them on yourself."
> "Well, I've certainly accepted the feelings of anger."
> "No you haven't. You've taken feelings of betrayal and turned them into anger at yourself. That isn't acceptance of the betrayal feelings,"

we replied. "However, the more important question is, 'What are you doing with the feeling of betrayal?' What you're currently doing is beating yourself up. That isn't productive. What would a more responsible response be?"

"Deal with the problem at work?"

"No. Absolutely not. At least not yet. What step comes after the Feel & Accept step?"

Responsibility: Discover

The Discover step in Radical Acceptance is about uncovering aspects of yourself which you weren't previously aware of. Once you've done this, responsibility involves looking back and seeing all those times when you did things which you now need to accept and make amends for. You might look back and recognise all those times you hurt people, for instance. You'll now need to go back, accept that you acted incorrectly and apologise to those that you affected.

Beware, however, of overusing this step, as making a discovery can end up being a little like a child with a hammer - everything will start to look like a nail. In this instance, everything will look like something that you need to take responsibility for. Imagine, for example, that you discover that you're a liar. After an initial period of denial, a metaphorical dam will break and you'll suddenly see that you've been lying in many different aspects of your life. As a result, you'll suddenly feel the urge to make amends everywhere – calling the Tax Department and reporting the $10 error you discovered after filing, for instance, or confessing to your young child about all the times you lied about Santa Claus and the Easter Bunny being real. When this happens, it's time to slow down. Instead of acting rashly, let the new discoveries settle for a while; when you integrate your discoveries, you'll start to see that lying isn't always 'bad'. Because of this, not every lie from your past needs to be apologised for.

The ones which are left over, however, will need to be corrected – and it's your responsibility to make this happen.

"The Discover step comes after Feel & Accept," George replied. "It's my favourite step: the one where I get to find out what a jerk I am."

Ignoring his cynicism, we continued. "So, what tool goes with feelings of anger?"

"Projection. That's where I find out how I've been a betrayer myself. Well, I'm not so sure this time. I certainly haven't stolen anything from the company!"

"Remember that it's never identical. Have you ever taken office supplies home, for instance?" He looked a bit sheepish. "What about at home?" we pressed on. "There are many kinds of betrayal which are possible. A promise to your wife or children that doesn't happen, for example."

"Sure, but that only happens because I have to work. This job is very demanding."

"That's the excuse. The fact, from their point of view, is that you made a promise and didn't follow through – just like your employee made a promise not to steal and he didn't follow through. You have a good excuse, but I bet your employee does as well."

He paled. "Oh my God I have to make amends to my family – apologise for each of the times I cancelled."

"Each and every time? Don't be crazy. You won't remember them all and they won't, either."

"Then one big apology."

"You could, but I'm sure you've apologised before. What's more important to them is that you choose them over work in the future when you've made them a commitment. It's only in new actions that they'll feel less betrayed. Besides, right now the discovery is new and everything looks like a betrayal. Give it some time before taking any action."

Responsibility: Integrate & Accept

The Integrate and Accept step is where we say yes to our discoveries. However, it's important to remember that integrating and accepting these discoveries doesn't give us permission to act on them without responsibility: you're still responsible for all of your choices and their consequences. Just because you integrate and accept an aspect of yourself doesn't mean that you can express that aspect whenever and wherever you wish. In other words, acceptance is not permission.

Integrating that lying is sometimes an appropriate action, for example, might result in a gleeful splurge of lying. After all, lying isn't right or wrong, but is rather appropriate or inappropriate to specific situations. If you forget about responsibility, then lots of situations might begin to look appropriate. There's the potential to become like a child let loose in a candy store, happily lying whenever you feel like it.

To avoid this danger, always remember that responsibility means that you have to live with the consequences of your choices. Give this some thought before acting. While it's true, for instance, that many people lie on their tax returns, do you want to live with the worry of being audited? You'll be responsible for the consequences of the lie if you are – so are you prepared to pay the potential fines? That most people don't get caught doesn't mean that no one gets caught, after all. Choosing to lie to your children will similarly mean that you're responsible for remembering your lies; you can rest assured that your children won't forget what you've said. Integration and acceptance is not permission to disregard the consequences of your actions. Instead, it's an acceptance of the choices you've already been making and taking up the responsibility for those choices.

> After George realised how he betrayed his family, he wanted to fix all of his past betrayals. Instead, we suggested that he give it some time first. This would let him respond with changed actions rather than big apologies. "Yes, I see what you mean," he replied. "I just hope it'll be

different from the anger experience. When I discovered my anger, I was suddenly angry all of the time. Now I've discovered that I've got a tendency to betray my family, what if I betray them more often? My wife had to take me aside before I realised what was happening with the anger...and I don't want to hurt my family any more."

"Yes, seeing and expressing the discovery more often is a danger. It will take awareness not to repeat that." We paused and then continued, "You've seen that you're a betrayer. Now, how are you going to integrate that?"

"It really hurts to admit it to myself." George held his head. "It completely blows my illusions of my personal integrity. I'll do the usual, I suppose: look for the gift and score my ability to betray others."

"Don't forget to be aware of your ability to betray yourself. Think of the commitments you've made to yourself – perhaps in getting fit. Remember how you've betrayed those aims as well. Take responsibility for them all. Then accept that you're a betrayer."

Responsibility: Plan

Planning and responsibility go hand in hand, as good planning can help in preparing you to accept responsibility for your actions. Spend time asking yourself several questions before you do anything in response to a feeling: which actions would most likely lead to regret? Which ones would leave you feeling unhappy with yourself? Which ones have better alternatives? By spending time thinking about these issues, you can choose the best course of action for each specific situation.

What of those times when you don't like any of the consequences, however? As an example, imagine that your relationship just isn't working: the feelings of love have gone and you've run out of things to say to each other. Leaving means having to start all over again with a new partner – a partner who will likely have many of the same characteristics since that's what you're drawn to. The other option is to stay in your current relationship with mounting feelings of anger and frustration. The decision to stay in the relationship or leave will be a difficult one, requiring you to use each of the themes covered in this book to form a final decision.

Regardless of which choice you make, responsibility will play an important role. You could avoid choosing at all, for instance, which is really making a choice not to choose. Alternatively, you could take out your frustration on your partner – which is a choice to end the relationship while hoping that your partner will get fed up and be the one to actually call it quits. These are both choices which you make, and both have consequences. In the first option, the consequence will be living in a state of limbo. In the second option, you'll live with anger and resentment – and your partner may not decide to leave in any case. A firm, responsible choice to either stay or go will make things clear and avoid such consequences.

Planning is to make a choice: a responsible choice as to how you'll respond to an event. Not choosing is to make a passive choice with its own consequences – consequences over which you'll have very little control.

George thought for a bit. "Okay, so I'm a betrayer and my employee is a betrayer. Do I forgive him, give him a pat on the back and offer him his job back?"

"Would that be a responsible course of action?"

"Of course not. I just don't get how acceptance and kicking his ass fit together."

"Kicking his ass is about punishing him. That's your pattern."

"So I just let him get away with it?"

"That's up to you. You could do that or you could act from your principles and plan a course of action."

"I have a principle of being nice, so I guess I let him get away with it."

"Is that the responsible thing to do?" we challenged.

"No, I guess I need a principle about allowing people to be responsible for their own actions," he concluded.

"Yes, that will serve you well in this situation, as well as in the wider context of being a parent."

"Then I'll press charges. That's an appropriate consequence of theft. I did feel guilty about doing that, but as I work this through, I don't any longer."

"Pressing charges will mean dealing with the police, going to court, producing documents, being questioned by the defence and so on."

He squared his shoulders and said, "I can live with that."

Responsibility: Act & Accept

Once you've planned, it's time to act. If things don't quite go according to plan when you act, though, what are you responsible for then? After all, life is often difficult to predict. You might well end up being faced with a consequence which you hadn't considered – and it might be one which you really don't want to take on. Is that consequence still yours to accept?

One option is to try and wriggle out of the situation. Avoiding the consequences like this isn't the responsible thing to do, however. Since your actions created the environment for the outcome, the consequences are now yours to accept and handle.

To continue the example from above, imagine that you decided to leave the relationship. You expected your partner to be hurt, sad and maybe a little angry, and you prepared for the arguments which he or she might have raised to get you to reconsider. Instead, when you broke the news, your partner got instantly furious, picked up a valuable, treasured possession of yours and smashed it. When you were planning, this didn't seem like even a remote possibility – if it had, you would've planned to do the break-up on neutral ground such as in a coffee shop. Now what do you do?

As much as it might be hard to accept, your possession was destroyed as a consequence of your actions. This means that it's now your situation to handle. The first step to take is a trip around the Radical Acceptance Wheel – ending up with a new plan and a new set of actions. In doing this, keep in mind that even though the consequences were your responsibility, responsibility isn't about becoming a doormat. As such, you might consider pressing charges or filing a lawsuit. If you do so, however, remember that these actions have consequences, too.

George called us back a couple of days later asking for an emergency session. We booked him in, and when he arrived, he looked completely dazed.

"What happened to you?"

"Nothing happened to me and nothing happened to my former employee. I was ready for the hassles of a court case: I'd even psyched myself up and was looking forward to the challenges. I went into the owners to let them know that I would be calling the police to press charges, and then." He stopped and ran his hand through his hair. "I still can't believe it. They told me not to. I was told to use the threat of charges to settle with him and then to let the whole thing drop."

"That's their right, of course," we told him.

"It may be their right, but it's not the right thing to do. To make matters worse, he and I belong to the same social club. I'm going to see him and know that he's gloating."

"Yes, you'll see him. You don't know if he'll be gloating, though."

"Yeah, I know. He was quite apologetic when I discovered his crime, but when I approached him with an offer to settle, I could see the self-satisfied look in his eyes knowing that he'd got away with it. I'm not looking forward to seeing him at the social club meetings – but there's no way I'm leaving those groups.

"To be totally honest, though, I just don't know if I can keep on working at the company any more. I need to know that my bosses will back me up. Judy may be able to live with their constant mishandlings, but that's not something which I can accept."

"Then I guess you start polishing up your resume," we said.

"I guess I do," he replied.

8 Observer

The final theme is that of the Observer. This is another archetype, just like the Child and the Adult. Specifically, the Observer is the archetype which observes all life. It notices all thoughts, feelings, behaviour and events, but it doesn't engage in the emoting or reacting. Living from the Observer doesn't mean that you'll become a robot or that you'll stop feeling your emotions. In fact, feelings are actually more intense with the Observer – you're just not engaged in them. On the Radical Acceptance Wheel, the Observer is most closely-associated with the Event step, which is normally the first step of the Radical Acceptance process. As a theme, however, the Observer comes as the final one: it's the theme which covers all of the other themes.

To better understand what the Observer is like, imagine that you're sitting in an office with beige-coloured walls. How excited do you get about those walls being beige? How sad are you with the walls being beige? How angry do the beige walls make you? In all likelihood, the colour of the walls would register in your mind without any emotional reaction at all. It's simply a fact that the walls are beige: a fact which you accept. The Observer is just about looking at all of life with that same detachment. When people consider how they'd live in this state themselves, they often imagine extreme forms of disengagement – such as spending their days sitting in an ashram, meditating. In reality, however, the Observer can be achieved without doing anything like that. Your life will largely continue as before – events happening, feelings arising, discoveries taking place and being integrated, plans being made and actions being taken. The only difference will be that the Observer sees all of these experiences with the same detachment as looking at beige walls. Without the Child or Adult archetypes interfering and without re-labelling or rationalizing your emotions, you'll be able to observe pure feelings.

Why would you want to do any of this, though? From the perspective of the Child, the Observer can be a problem. The Observer gives a sense of disengagement with life, while the Child prefers being caught up in life's dramas. Finding the Observer may also cost you friends and family. In these relationships, you will have played roles – and many relationships are sustained by the roles you play. What happens when you stop playing? What happens when the people in your life can no longer count on you to get angry when you used to, to get sad at what makes them sad, or to judge others in the way you did before? These changes will create conflict, and you may end up getting accused of being uncaring, insensitive and unfeeling – even when your own experience is one of being more caring, more sensitive and more feeling than before.

Despite all of these disadvantages, however, there are also advantages of finding the Observer. You'll know inner peace even in the midst of turmoil, conflict and strife, and you'll also reach a state of 'equanimity', which is a point where all feelings and events are seen as the same. From then on, happiness and sadness, love and hate, peace and conflict, wealth and poverty, justice and injustice are all seen as equal states. This reduces the dramas of life, allowing you to go within and do the work of Radical Acceptance. Finally, you'll know freedom. This isn't a freedom which allows you to act as you please, but one which is much more powerful. It's the freedom to choose: to choose how to respond to thoughts, feelings and events without being caught up in them. It's the freedom to set the direction of your behaviour in response to, but not in reaction to, external circumstances.

Once you've balanced up the pros and cons of the archetype, if you do decide to develop the Observer, then you'll need to know what tools to use. The most basic tool is called 'Moment to Moment Awareness', and involves being aware of what's going on within and around you. This tool is very closely linked to the overall work of Radical Acceptance, with awareness inviting Radical Acceptance work and then the Radical Acceptance work opening up new awareness. Moment to Moment Awareness can simply be a part of your day – or you can develop a more formal meditation practice (if you're interested in meditation, there are many good books available on the market). Whether you go for simple awareness or meditation, keep on observing – no matter what you experience. For example, a feeling may arise. When this happens, just watch the feeling. Initially, you may find yourself caught in the feeling – but later you'll just notice it: notice it come and watch as it leaves. Over time, this practice will give you a new perspective on life. You may notice your language changing from, "I am angry" to "I feel anger," for instance; from "I am thinking" to "I had a thought". In general, you'll become less identified with individual thoughts, emotions and physical sensations and more able to experience them as the Observer. From this place, you are not your physical sensations, you are not your feelings and you are not your thoughts. Instead, you are the Observer: the archetype of pure observation.

But what of those times when you just can't reach the Observer, when the issue which you're trying to observe seems just too much to be able to step back and assess objectively? In these cases, treat the inability to step back as an event. Then take it for a trip around the Radical Acceptance Wheel.

Over time you'll find that you're not as reactive as you were before, and that you're generally less attached to the dramas of life. Using the tools will also make it easier for you to call upon the Observer when it's needed. Most importantly, you'll begin to appreciate that no matter what you think or feel, everything will pass. This is really the key to the Observer: knowing that whether you experience pleasure or pain, happiness or sadness, heaven or hell, silly thoughts or monumental thoughts – everything shall pass. The passing will be watched by the Observer with a gentle bemusement: it knows that nothing lasts forever, so why get caught up in something as fleeting as a thought or a feeling? The Observer calls for a detached attitude to life, watching as you get caught up in drama and emotions and, at the same time, having a gentle smile at the foolishness of it all.

The Observer is an integral part of your journey – providing peace, equanimity and freedom. Be sure to remember, however, that life is about balance: you don't develop an Observer instead of the Child and Adult, but alongside and in balance with them.

Observer: Event

From the Observer, not only are events neutral, but all of life is neutral. What does this mean? It means that on one hand you are engaged in life, while on the other you have an ability to watch what's going on – to observe without taking things personally. This means that you see events, thoughts and feelings as simply occurring. They won't be happening to you, they'll just be happening.

The idea of not taking things personally is an important one. Any time you think that an event has occurred for your personal benefit or suffering, you've taken the event personally. While it's true that you can use any event for your benefit (taking a ride on the Radical Acceptance Wheel) or suffering (through Feel-Act-Regret), that's different from thinking that the event occurred for those reasons.

There are several statements from the Spirituality Movement that reflect taking events personally, including: "All things happen for my benefit", an event was "meant to be", and that "Everything happens for a reason." The Radical Acceptance response to all of these is 'maybe...or maybe not: there's just no way to prove either position'. Regardless of how an event came to be, Radical Acceptance says that the event was neutral, not personal. By using the Radical Acceptance Wheel, you can also use that event for your personal benefit. Only then does the event become personal.

Judy had barely sat down when she started talking. Her life was a series of crisis: there were crises going on at work, her friends were having crises, and her partner was in crisis. After letting her spew for a while, we said, "Judy, we're exhausted just listening to you."

"Yes, it's exhausting for me, too..." she wearily replied.

"That's not what we said. We said you're exhausting us. All the drama."

"But what about work and my friends and Frank?"

"They're all doing their own things. Why are you so caught up in all this drama?"

"It's important. These are the people I care about."

"Sure, but you're totally useless to anyone in this state. At the moment, with you so caught up in their dramas, all the caring in the world won't help them."

She looked at us suspiciously, not certain where this was going – but knowing from experience that she probably wasn't going to like it. Not knowing else to say, she tried again, "I care about these people."

"We hear that, but we're wondering how you're going to help them. You're like the person who, on seeing a person drowning, wants to show their caring nature by jumping into the water and drowning alongside them. To help the person who's drowning, it's best to stand back and observe the situation. From there you can see the life buoy and toss it in."

Observer: Feel & Accept

One of the things you notice as you watch your feelings is that they come and they go. No matter how high the highs or how low the lows, they all pass. The Observer watches the feelings come and go much like you might watch waves washing onto the shore: they're sometimes fierce, sometimes gentle, and sometimes still. The fierce times and gentle times are just accepted – one state is not better than another. The still times are when you're not feeling anything at all: when you're in a 'neutral place'. The neutral place is neither happy nor sad, neither excited nor fearful. It contains no feelings at all. The more you use the tools to engage the Observer and the more you do the work of Radical Acceptance, the more time you'll spend in the neutral place. The more time you spend watching your thoughts and feelings with total acceptance, the more the neutral place emerges.

Watching your feelings also has other effects. When you get really good at it, you'll begin to notice energy within yourself which hasn't yet formed into feelings. It's amazing to watch this energy grow, become an emotion, return to energy and then fade. Over time you'll notice energy rising and fading without ever becoming a feeling.

Here's an example of how this might progress. When you first discovery Radical Acceptance, you may discover you've been suppressing your anger, maybe by relabelling it as tears. Then you come to really feel and accept your anger. At first this will be uncomfortable, but over time and with work, you'll come to accept it. Then, spending time in the Observer, you'll watch anger come and go and learn of its passing nature. Then, one day while meditating, you'll see energy rise – just energy. As you watch it, it'll become anger. Then it'll return to energy and pass. Later, the energy will arise again, but this time you'll see that you can choose to call it anger or just leave it as energy. As you leave it as energy, it'll pass. You'll realise that emotion is just energy, coloured by your memories and your beliefs.

However, even knowing all about energy rising and falling, there will be times when you leave the Observer and jump straight into a feeling before catching it. Such is the ebb and flow of life.

> Judy was looking at us with even more suspicion when we suggested stepping back from the crises in her life. "I once had a partner like that," she said. "He used to tell me that I was too caught up in the drama, but he wasn't touched by anything. He would just sit back and watch me spin out while he looked down his nose at me. It was like being in a relationship with a rock. I don't want to stop feeling for my friends."
> We spent some time talking to her about the Observer archetype – about how the Observer feels and feels deeply, but how it just isn't attached to the feelings. We explained that what her former partner was doing was shutting down his feelings, not observing them. She looked a little sceptical, but said, "I can try the Observer."
> "We're going to ask you some questions and you let us know how well you can stay in the Observer. Remember, the Observer sees everything as the colour of beige walls." She nodded. "So..there are possible layoffs happening at your work?" we asked.
> She was okay with that one, "Yes, but..that's like colour of the walls to me. Although I'm aware of the situation and do have some fear for it."
> "Excellent. Be aware of the feelings, but don't become them. Well done."
> "What about Frank's thoughts about changing jobs?"
> "That's definitely the colour beige."
> "Good, then I guess the friend in the potentially abusive relationship is easy too?"
> "No! That's terrible. How can I just sit back and ignore that? Just observe it while he gets her in deeper and deeper?"
> "We never said to do nothing, we said first stop jumping in to drown alongside her. You're useless to her unless you can stand back from these feelings."

Observer: Discover

The discovery step is an excellent time to see obstacles to the Observer: those parts of yourself that prevent you from being in the Observer state. The process of discovery, along with meditation, is the core of the work involved in moving toward more time in the Observer. The more that's brought from the unconscious into the conscious, the more there is for the Observer to watch and the less there is for the other archetypes to get their hooks into.

The Observer also aids in the discover step, especially with tools like Critical Thinking and Projection. In Critical Thinking, you observe your thoughts. That can be tricky without an Observer. As such, meditation can be used as a tool to assist in Critical Thinking, as it teaches you to see your thoughts and feelings instead of becoming them. Seeing a thought is to say, "I'm having a thought about being stupid." Becoming your thought is to say, "I am stupid." If you've become your thoughts and feelings, after all, then you can't watch them.

In the Projection Tool, you're asked to find how you're similar to the one you're feeling angry or envious toward. If what you discover is highly charged, then it's difficult to see ways that you're similar, as the Observer is now in the background and the Child is in the foreground. In this state, you're caught in the emotion of the moment instead of standing back to objectively have a look. In other words, if someone ignores you and that generates a lot of anger, and the idea that you might be inconsiderate to another also fills you with a sense of self-disgust, then it'll be difficult to see how you can be inconsiderate. The Observer helps you to step back from the intensity of the situation and allows you to be more open to the idea of being similar to the one who ignored you.

Having a developed Observer lets you see your discoveries in the same way as the colour of the office walls.

When asked to stand back from her feelings around her friend being in an abusive relationship, Judy said, "But I can't." We waited. "I don't know why I can't, I just know what he's like..", she paused, then started sobbing. Through her tears, she said, "Oh my God! When I was younger, one of the older boys tricked me into going a closet with him. He started touching me. I tried to get away, but he was bigger. Finally, he told me that if I told anyone he would really hurt me." She looked at us through the eyes of the little girl – so afraid of being hurt. "I've never told anyone until this moment." She cried anew as we waited. Finally, she said, "When I see my friend with him, deep inside all I can feel is the helplessness of being trapped in the closet." She shook her head, "No wonder I despise the man. So what do I do?"

We said, "It sounds like the little girl inside is needing to feel safe. How can you do that for her?" Ronna reached behind her into a trunk of extras and pulled out a teddy bear. She handed it to Judy and said, "Hold her and tell her that she's safe with you." We watched as all her love and fierce she-bear came out as she spoke with her inner child and reassured her. Only when she was done did we speak again, saying, "How does that feel?"

"Much better. Can I take teddy home with me..? But seriously, I can see how my feelings had me all caught up in my friend's problems. I really was useless to her in her abusive situation. I can see that now. Imagine how my inability to be of help all stemmed from not being able to step back and observe my feelings!"

Observer: Integrate & Accept

The Observer is a great aid in the Integrate & Accept step. The goal of the step is to be become neutral about discoveries made. The Observer gives you a sense of distance from the immediacy of situations – especially those situations in which a character trait or System is acting out. The distance allows you to do the work of

Scoring and Gratitude – which in turn helps to bring you out of the drama and into the Observer.

When struggling with a discovery that you really don't want to integrate, remember that being a liar, a victim, a bitch or an asshole are facts of being human, and that they have no more excitement than the beige colour of office walls. Having a System that says you're unlovable, that intimacy isn't safe, that you're a failure or that life is suffering are facts that have no more excitement than beige walls. When you feel angry, happy, in love, sad or afraid, similarly remember that these are just facts – facts which also have no more excitement than beige walls. Any additional charge belongs to you: step into the Observer, see the facts, see the charge and use Radical Acceptance to discover why the charge is present.

> After Judy had composed herself, we continued, "You've shared a deep, shameful memory of being powerless. These kinds of discoveries often arise when you investigate why you can't step back into the Observer. I'd suggest that the discovery is part of the System that you play out at work: being powerless to bring about change in the office."
> "Shit, you're right! You know, I really haven't done much with getting my resume together. I'm so messed up."
> "Well done", we exclaimed. She looked confused. "You just used your System. You just took a powerful situation – making things safe for you inner Child – and turned it into a state of powerlessness with your self-criticism. Now score that. Give a rating to how well you used the System of powerlessness."
> She looked at us strangely and said, "Yeah, that was pretty good. I'd say I scored a 7 at turning a powerful situation into feeling powerless again."
> "And how do you feel now?"
> "That's funny, when you asked me to score, it brought me out of the powerlessness into...into the..Observer. I started looking at it instead and suddenly it seemed rather silly. Of course I have Systems. And I'm damn good at them!" She laughed, really laughed, for the first time in that session.

Observer: Plan

The Observer helps during planning, as it's the archetype that keeps an eye on things; like a referee watching a contest between players, the Observer watches the tug and pull between the Child and Adult as they work to develop a plan, identifying which one is running things at any point in time. It also helps to catch the Child when it's play-acting as a pseudo-Adult, trying to trick you into thinking that it's really the Adult archetype. The Child may say Adult-sounding words, but it's still the Child, and the Observer can help you to recognise this. As an example, imagine that you're planning how to respond after your partner has lied to you. Your Child immediately suggests lying to your partner as a punishment. The 'Adult' may respond that, "Although revenge isn't a noble idea, demonstrating the pain caused by lying will be an excellent teaching tool for my partner." In this situation, the Observer will immediately blow its whistle and identify the pseudo-Adult trying to rationalise punishing behaviour: the real Adult wouldn't try to excuse actions which violate your principles.

More importantly, the Observer sees original events and the response to those events impartially. For example, if there's a need to reprimand an employee or a child or to set an unpopular boundary with a partner, then this can feel overwhelming. Having the Observer available can help you to remember that both event and actions are neutral: that to be attached to an outcome is pointless because we can't control another person. Remembering this opens more options for planning. Here's an example. You need to tell your partner you've been laid off at work – but how do you tell them? What do you reveal, and what do you hide for their peace of mind? You stop and realise that you're trying bring about a certain outcome – your partner not being worried – and you pause knowing you can't control their response. This opens the option of just speaking the whole truth, an option closed to you when trying to control the consequences.

Now that Judy had returned to the Observer, we were ready to bring things back to her friend in the abusive relationship. "So what are you going to do about your friend?"

"Yes. I can observe the situation, but it's not a state that I want to continue. She's my friend: I need to at least try."

"Yes, we agree. But do so without attachment to her agreeing. She has her Systems playing out too."

"So how do I plan for that?"

"What are your ideas?"

"The only thing I can think of is to kidnap her and force her to see what's happening."

"Yes, as long as you are attached to an outcome, your choices will be limited."

She cried for a bit, had a long sigh, and then she sat up, moved out of the Child and into the Observer. Then she spoke, "I'll use Radical Acceptance. I'll point out that she may have a System that needs to feel misery. I'll show her how well and how often she's chosen misery, and then each time she comes back to me with more tales of what's happening, I'll congratulate her on how well she's chosen more misery and ask her to score her skills." Her whole body slumped and she added sadly, "What if this fails?"

"Remember," Chris said, "you're no longer a little girl forced into a closet. And neither is your friend."

Observer: Act & Accept

Observing while acting reduces attachment to outcomes and helps you to accept consequences more easily. Imagine backing your car out of a driveway, for instance, and not seeing the car parked behind you across the street. That feeling of dread comes when you hear the bang. Now what? Your principles are suggesting that you should let the car owner know who's hit their car, while your Child's panicking, knowing that you really can't afford to pay for the car repairs and that if you drive off, no one will be the wiser. Besides, their insurance will pay.

What to do? Your Child and Adult archetypes are locked in conflict; you're vacillating between the two choices. Instead, take a breath and call on the Observer: step out from the midst of the conflict and view it from above. From the Observer, you can see what the Child wants and what the Adult wants. From that viewpoint you can make a choice without the emotional attachments to the outcome and consequences.

Beyond a conflict between archetypes, the Observer can help with other inner conflicts: those between thinking and feeling, between conflicting principles, between two strong feelings and so on. An example might be when you promise to keep a secret and then need to tell a lie in order to keep that secret. Here, the choice you have to make rests between two conflicting principles: one principle speaks of an intention to honour your word, and another principle speaks of an intention to be honest. Both principles have some flexibility to them, but which principle should be the one to bend? Being caught in the midst of the conflict makes it difficult to see which way to go.

Stepping back and into the Observer gives you the time and space to take another look. If lying is likely to cause problems, then breaking your word would be the better solution. If the secret is an important one, then choose either to lie or to say, "I can't answer that - I've promised to keep it secret". The best choice for your situation will obviously vary in every instance, but this is where the Observer comes in, allowing you to evaluate your priorities and select your course of action with emotional distance.

Once again, the advantages of developing this archetype are clear: by giving you time and space to step back and consider the situation objectively, the Observer can help you to act on your plan and accept whatever consequences those actions might bring.

> We saw Judy a few times over the next weeks, and each time she was hurting because her friend was still in the abusive relationship. For the

most part, she was holding strong on her decision to congratulate her friend on her ability to choose misery. Once she'd broken down and begged her to leave, but neither course had worked so far. The last time Judy visited us, her friend had stopped seeing her; she'd become angry at Judy for not caring.

We encouraged her, "Judy, we know that this is hard, but your friend needs the anger to break the pattern. Yes, the anger is initially directed at you instead of her partner, but it may be the beginning of the shift. Remember that she has her own Systems and that she may decide to stay with this guy. There's nothing you can do about that except the ongoing work of accepting your friend, her partner and your powerlessness."

Judy chose the hopeful path, "It's the first time since this began that she's been angry at anybody or anything." She paused, "This Observer place is both hard to be in and all that's saving me from going crazy. Without it I'd be over at her house with a gun – or at least constantly nagging her to leave, which I know does no good." Looking reflective, she added, "It's helping at work, too. When the owners change my ideas, I notice and go with them." She smiled for the first time in a while and added, "They're not sure what's going on. I think they were also wrapped up in this drama that I used to provide."

It was a buoyant Judy who came in two weeks later. "I'd have come last week, but I was too busy with my friend. She moved in with me and things around my place have been a bit crazy." She shook her head. "Thank God for the Observer. It's been quite the drama. We had a late night visit from a drunken ex-boyfriend who put a rock through my front window when we wouldn't let him in. I called the police and he now has a peace bond out against him. When he came by, I was so scared – but I also noticed that the Observer provided a place of peace in which I could make my plans and stand strong. My friend was all caught up in the drama. I know what you mean now when you told me that it's exhausting." She gave us a hug and added simply, "Thanks."

The book now shifts from explaining the themes into a time of storytelling. We've drawn on the experiences of seven of our long-term clients, changed their names and fictionalised some events from their lives so as to protect their identities and the identities of other people talked about in their stories. Despite some fictionalizing, though, we've worked hard to maintain their central issues and some of their personality quirks. Each of these people has read the chapters and agreed that they capture their life. A couple of them have also made direct contributions to their chapters.

Before each story, we've repeated the Cheat Sheet from the end of each theme to act as a reminder of the theme being discussed. The idea of the Cheat Sheets was made by 'Kathy' from the Observer story, and for this we offer her our thanks.

> "If history were taught in the form of stories, it would never be forgotten."
>
> Rudyard Kipling

9 Linda: The Wheel

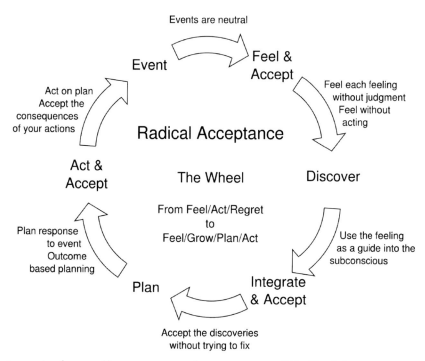

As part of our efforts to expand awareness of Radical Acceptance, we speak to groups of all sizes in a variety of forums and countries around the world. A number of years ago, we were speaking at a Lunch and Learn session at a local college. There were about 20 people gathered in the room from a variety of programs offered by the college. We introduced ourselves, gave a brief history of who we were and why we were there, and then asked each of the students to stand up and give their names.

Once the introductions were over, Chris began taking the group through the six steps of Radical Acceptance. "We begin with Event. What's important to understand is that every event in your life is neutral. As such, if you ever feel an emotional charge – whether it's a feeling you like or dislike – then you know that you have work to do. When…."

A young man sitting in the front row jumped in and asked, "So if I punch you in the face, that event is neutral?"

Ronna responded, "Yes, even if someone punches you in the face."

"So if I walk up there and punch you, you won't have any feelings? You'll just be neutral?"

Chris answered, "Not at all. I'd be quite upset if you were to punch me."

"So if you have feelings, then how is that neutral?"

"It's neutral because the feeling of being upset belongs to me, and not the event. Instead of speaking of a hypothetical situation – at least I hope it's hypothetical! – is there someone here who would like to give us an example of a real event that doesn't feel neutral?"

Linda, a young woman sitting at the back, snorted and mumbled under her breath. Chris invited her to speak louder, "I heard a definite snort. Would you care to share your charged event?"

"Hmm, well right now I'm pretty pissed. I handed in a paper, but my teacher lost it without any record of me handing it in – so I received a big fat zero on my assignment."

Ronna responded, "Good start, thank you for sharing that event." She then turned to the blackboard behind her and wrote:

> Step: Event
> Paper Lost = Getting a Zero

Linda said, "This is hardly a neutral event. They lost my paper so they're responsible, not me. It's not fair that I'm being punished for their disorganization."

There were a few nods from the audience. Ronna turned to the group and asked four other students, "What would your response be to Linda's event?"

Beth replied, "That's a no brainer, I'd start crying."

Tom responded, "I'd quietly ask the teacher to look for my assignment. I might even suggest places for her to look in."

Amy answered, "I'd blow my stack and probably swear at the teacher – something that's gotten me in trouble more than once already."

"I'd print off the email with the document attached, proving that I'd handed it in on time," answered Andre.

Chris turned to the class in general and said, "We asked four different people to respond to the same event and received four very different responses. If the same event generates different responses in different people, then it's not the event which generates the emotional charge, but the perceiver of that event. Each of the four people we asked heard the same event, and each ran it through their own internal filters. As the event moved through these filters, it became charged based on each person's individual programming. Part of what Radical Acceptance is about is discovering your own 'individual programming': becoming aware of what you're doing and why you're doing it.

"I know all of you are probably now keen to ask, 'How do I make these discoveries?'" He paused and looked at several of the students. "You do this by following the charge generated by the event – turning your emotions into a guide that can lead you through your subconscious mind."

The group was now fully engaged. Ronna returned to Linda and asked, "Since it's your event that we've been talking about, what have you learned so far?"

Linda took a breath and replied, "This is interesting. I assumed that everyone would feel and respond to that situation in the same way as me."

"Right, good noticing. Let's now take it one step further and look at the Radical Acceptance Wheel. We have a charged Event – an event which, for Linda, is not neutral. The next step of Radical Acceptance is Feel & Accept." Ronna added with a touch of sarcasm, "I know Linda's feeling was very subtle; I'm sure none of you noticed what she was feeling about this event."

The room laughed. Ronna returned to the blackboard and wrote:

> Step: Feel & Accept
> Anger

Chris continued by asking Linda, "You responded with anger to this event. How do you feel about the emotion of anger?"

Linda suddenly started fighting back tears and said, "I hate it. I feel so embarrassed about getting angry, and that means that I get embarrassed a lot because many things make me angry."

Ronna stepped in, "Linda, you're an angry person who gets angry a lot."

"Well I'm more than that," Linda came back. "I'm loving and compassionate too!"

Ronna repeated, "Linda, you're an angry person who gets angry a lot."

"Yes, but I really do nice things for people and help them out when they need my help and…" she continued defiantly.

"Linda, you're an angry person who gets angry a lot."

Now glaring, Linda said, "Okay, I get angry a lot…but I don't like it!"

Chris then spoke, "Linda, I listened carefully to what Ronna was saying, and she didn't ask if you liked being angry. She stated two facts – that you're an angry person and that you get angry a lot."

"Yeah, but I'd rather feel happy."

"Is being happy better than being angry?"

Sarcastically, Linda replied, "Duh yeah. Doesn't everyone think that way?"

Ronna responded, "Let's have a closer look at feelings." Grabbing the chalk, she moved to a new section of the board, divided it in half and asked the class, "Yell out feelings which you think are good."

The class shouted out words for the 'Good' column, and then Ronna continued, "Okay, let's hear your list of bad feelings." These were added until the board finally looked like this:

Good Feelings	Bad Feelings
Happiness	Sadness
Joy	Pain
Contentment	Anger
Peace	Jealously
Power	Greed
Empathy	Powerlessness
Passion	Judgemental
Harmony	Resent
Confidence	Aggression
Love	Hate

Chris looked at the list and then at the class, and said, "That's quite the pair of lists." Then he looked at Linda and said, "Anger is bad and we must get rid of it, right?"

"Yes, it's destructive. It's much better to put your energy into being happy or loving."

"So, MADD (Mothers against Drunk Driving) needs to quit their cause because it was started by an angry mother? Maybe you're suggesting that the Feminist Movement needs to stop fighting for women's rights because they're angry at how women have been treated? Certainly the environmentalists need to let go their anger and stop fighting for a healthy planet?"

Linda, "Hmm, well no, they're all good causes."

Chris asked, "So anger can be good sometimes, too?"

"Okay, I see your point. I guess anger can be good as well as bad..."

Chris said with a smile, "Actually, I lied. Anger isn't good." Several students nodded in agreement. "Anger isn't bad either, though." Those that had nodded a moment ago suddenly looked confused. "Anger is just a feeling," Chris continued. "Who here thinks that red is good? Who here thinks that yellow is bad?

They're just colours. Red beside orange can be jarring and uncomfortable, just as yellow beside orange can be soothing. It's not the colour itself which is jarring or soothing, but how that colour is used.

"The founders of MADD, feminists and environmentalists are all using anger in constructive ways – they're using it to make important changes to our laws and attitudes. In contrast, there are other people who use their anger to justify violence or revenge. The feeling of anger is actually neutral, just like events. What you do with the feeling can be either constructive or destructive.

"Trying to pretend that you don't feel anger is to tell a lie to yourself. Such lies are ultimately self-defeating, as your anger will always find an outlet – either aggressively or passively. The other problem with rejecting anger is that the feeling has flip sides: power and passion. If you can't access your anger, then you'll have difficulty moving powerfully or passionately in life. You also may have problems setting boundaries, achieving your goals and saying, 'No'."

Linda interjected, "Chris, you said that if you have anger, then you also have power, passion and the ability to set boundaries – but I get angry a lot and I don't have power or passion and I really struggle with setting boundaries."

Ronna responded, "To have the power, passion and the rest, you need to accept the feeling of anger into your life – seeing it as a valuable, important part of who you are. You don't like your anger and that's rejection, not acceptance. Rejecting it often leads to 'getting angry', when your anger bursts forth without you being in control. This is a reactive response, originating from a build-up of the anger that you've rejected. Acting on this basis is what we call 'Feel-Act-Regret'. This is where you have no ability to separate the feeling from your actions. For example, when you're angry, you yell. There's no room for feeling the anger that arose from an event and then stepping back to make a decision about what the best response to the event is. Stepping back, using the anger for growth and then planning before acting is what we call 'Feel-Grow-Plan-Act'. Notice this alternative does not include the regret piece."

Linda put her head down and said, "I think I do Feel-Act very well, and I certainly know all about Regret." The group nodded in agreement.

Chris came in with, "Let's look at another example of good and bad feelings. On the list is says that happy is good and sad is bad."

Beth said, "Please don't tell me that there are benefits to feeling sad or problems which come from being happy. That seems like a pretty big stretch."

Ronna asked, "Who here goes out to buy things when they're happy, only to then find it hard to meet their monthly budget? Who eats when they're happy and then has difficulty managing their weight? And who's taken time away from their studies because they feel like doing something fun, knowing that they'll have to cram later?"

All hands were in the air by the end of Ronna's questions.

Chris continued, "As for sadness, being aware of and accepting our grief gives us compassion and empathy for others. If we cut off the pain, we live in an emotional flatland – never feeling too happy or too sad. In fact, those who fear sadness often fear happiness as well. They find themselves always waiting for the other shoe to drop and then end up missing the moment of happiness. Sadness is just as important as happiness, and only when this is recognised can both feelings be experienced fully."

Linda pondered what had been said for a moment, and then asked, "Okay, fair enough – but what about hate and love? There's no value in hate, and love is only good."

Chris looked around the room and asked, "Everyone agree?" Everyone nodded. "So it's not okay to hate child abuse? Similar to anger, many beneficial changes have come about through the effective use of hate. And what about love – is it always good? What about the loving friend or family member who enables the addict? What about the co-dependant, staying in a dysfunctional relationship because they love their partner? Can anyone here relate to these situations?"

No one spoke, but there were several people looking very uncomfortable. "Are there any other feelings someone would like to ask about?" A loud silence followed.

Ronna picked up the discussion up from there. "So, the lost homework event was neutral, and Linda's charge on the event was anger. This second step calls Linda to accept her anger and not judge it or try and get rid of it – and instead to just feel it."

Linda said, "Okay, I'm feeling it. Now what?"

"Now you can use it."

"Use it for what, starting a 'Teachers Shouldn't Lose Papers' group?"

"That would be one option. However, we'd suggest a more internal approach. Radical Acceptance invites you to use the charge as a guide into your subconscious – enabling you to bring unconscious material into your consciousness mind."

Ben spoke up, "I've tried to do some of that personal growth stuff, but I never know where to begin. I'm told to find things in my unconscious, but if it's unconscious, then how can I find it?"

Chris entered the discussion, "Excellent question, Ben - there's no way directly to see what's unconscious. We have to rely on clues and pointers to guide us instead. Fortunately, our psyche wants to help – and one way it offers this help is by charging events with feelings. Those feelings then become pointers back into the subconscious."

"How does that work?" asked Ben eagerly.

"There are several tools we can use to lead from a feeling into the subconscious. If Linda is willing, we can demonstrate one of them for you." Linda nodded. "Good, we'll show the Attachment Tool."

Ronna spoke, "Linda, when you described the event, you said that it wasn't fair that your mark was zero when it was the teacher who lost your paper. Is that correct?"

"Yes, but there are many things in this program that aren't fair. That's just one of them."

"So fairness is important to you?"

Linda replied sarcastically, "No, I much prefer getting the shaft!"

"It sounds like you're attached to fairness."

"Isn't everyone?"

"No, and in any case, we're only talking about you. What I'd like you to do is come up here and sit in this chair." Linda complied, and Ronna continued, "Now close your eyes and allow this attachment to fairness to be present in your mind." Linda did as she was asked. "Now I'm going to ask a question to your 'Fairness', and I want you to speak the first words that come into your mind."

Linda opened one eye and asked, "Am I going to regret this?"

"Probably – do you want to stop?"

With a shrug she replied, "No. I'm a sucker for punishment."

Ronna asked, "'Fairness', tell me about yourself."

Answering in character, Linda replied, "I'm important in Linda's life. I help her get what she's owed."

"Why is that?"

"She works hard and deserves to be rewarded."

"Hard work deserves to be rewarded?"

"Yes, and I make sure that she gets what she's entitled to."

"Why is that?"

"Well, she never received it as a child, no matter how hard…" Linda turned pale and stopped talking. "Oh my God," she said. "I'd forgotten that." She returned to silence.

Chris, giving Linda time to collect herself, turned to the group and said, "Ben, that's how someone discovers their unconscious. You let the feeling lead you." Ben also looked a little stunned.

Turning to Linda, Chris then said, "The feeling led to a belief." Linda looked up a little puzzled, "The belief that working hard is always rewarded." Linda nodded. "The belief then led to the memory of what you didn't get as a child. If we go further, we'll find the System that supports that belief."

Linda, looking shell-shocked, said, "Why stop here? Go for it."

"A System is a rule which makes sense out of the chaos of your childhood. You can't see a System directly, so instead have to look for them in the discrepancies between your words and actions."

"What do you mean?"

"You say that you expect rewards for your hard work - and yet you still hand in a paper without a backup copy to a school which you know to be disorganised."

"Now you're saying that I wanted them to lose it?"

"Consciously you want to do well and you work hard so that you can do well. Unconsciously, however, you're contributing to situations which belie your words. That's the sure sign of a System at work."

"I can't wait to find out my System," she replied with her usual sarcasm.

Without flinching, Ronna responded, "We can't know your System for sure, because as Chris said, you can't see a System directly. In your case, though, there may be a rule about not deserving."

"Deserving of what?"

"In your case, deserving of the rewards you work so hard to get."

"But my attachment to fairness says that I do deserve those rewards."

"Yes, an attachment often pushes you in the opposite direction to your System. This then leads to inner conflict."

"So my System is, 'I do not deserve '- while my attachment is, 'I do deserve'?"

"Fairness didn't say that you deserved. She said that hard work deserved to be rewarded – and that's what made life fair. However, your reward is often sabotaged by your System, so you end up with hard work and no reward."

Amy spoke from the group, "Cool, I get that. What you're saying is that we're all really messed up. That makes sense, in a sick kind of way."

Andre jumped up and said angrily, "That doesn't make sense at all to me. I think it's the stupidest thing I've ever heard, actually. There's no way I do that." Amy stood up and whispered into his ear. He blushed, sat down, and didn't say another word. We never found out what she'd said to him in that moment, but she clearly made an observation which helped to change his mind. It sometimes takes someone else's insight to make us realise just how dominant (and well-hidden) our Systems can be.

Ronna turned back to Linda and asked, "How are you doing?"

Linda replied, "I'm a bit shaky, but it all makes so much sense. I can see the System, the belief, the memories…oh my God the memories…and then the attachment to fairness. How do I fix this?"

Chris stood and wrote on the board.

> Step: Discover
> Attachment to fairness
> Belief that hard work is rewarded
> System of 'I do not deserve'
> Step: Integrate and Accept

Linda looked at the board in horror, stood up and shouted, "You want me to accept this? You guys are nuts!"

Ronna asked, "What would it mean to accept that System?"

"Insanity?" Linda replied.

"Or maybe sanity at last?" suggested Chris.

"How can that be? The idea of accepting that I work hard to get nothing seems like craziness!"

Ronna suggested, "Linda, you've spent a long time rejecting the idea that you work hard to get nothing. How is that working for you? Are you getting rewards for your hard work?" Linda shook her head. "So rejecting isn't working. Besides, it's really important that we deal with the realities of life and not the fantasies. Life happens and will not 'give' us things simply because we work hard. Sometimes hard work produces the results we desire and sometimes, no matter how hard we work, it doesn't. Sometimes we get the most amazing gifts when we haven't done any work at all."

Linda lifted an eyebrow. Ronna continued, "How much work did you do to create a beautiful sunset? How hard did you work to fall in love? Instead of looking at life as a series of rewards and punishments, Radical Acceptance suggests an alternative approach. In this approach, when life gives us a happy gift, we celebrate. When we get a painful gift, we celebrate as well. If we try to hold on only to the gifts which we like, then we're setting ourselves up for a lot misery and suffering. Those doing a spiritual or personal growth journey are particularly susceptible to this trap: they expect their dreams to come true as a reward for the hard work of their journey.

"Letting go of 'fairness' is even more important for people who have a System of deserving, as those people are naturally set up for misery – always expecting to get what they feel they're owed, and then becoming miserable whenever reality doesn't turn out to be 'fair'. Begin to see both happy and painful gifts as neutral. If a gift is charged, then you still have work to do."

Ronna asked the class, "Does anyone here know how the twelve step addiction recovery programs definite insanity?"

Beth piped up, "Yeah, I had a boyfriend who attended a twelve step program. The definition of insanity is doing the same thing over and over and expecting a different result each time."

Linda said, "Shit, you're right: I'm using the same approach over and over again, thinking that I'm either doing it wrong or hoping my luck will change and that I'll finally get what I want. I've been thinking that I deserve things in life because I'm working hard on a personal growth journey. Is this my only System?"

Chris responded, "We usually have three to four primary Systems, but let's focus on your not deserving System for now."

She took a breath and said, "Okay, how do I integrate 'I do not deserve'?"

Chris began to talk about the Scoring Tool. "Scoring is an important tool to assist with the integration process. It has three benefits. Firstly, it helps you to distance yourself from the drama of the event – especially when your Systems are acting out in response to what's happened. Secondly, it helps you to look at the situation clearly and begin to plan how you want to respond. Thirdly, it gives you an opportunity to find out what very interesting and talented skills you have."

"Skills?" asked Linda.

"Yes, if you're honest and aware, then you'll discover that you're very talented at finding ways to avoid getting rewards from hard work – very talented indeed."

"Wow! I'll be sure to add that to my resume," Linda responded dryly.

Ronna asked, "Linda, on a scale of 1 to 10, with 1 being the smallest and 10 being the largest, where would you rate your ability to make sure you don't get rewarded for your hard work?"

She chuckled, "Oh, it's right up there between 7 and 8. Chris is right, I'm highly skilled at making sure I don't get the reward."

Chris replied, "Good awareness. This begins the process of integrating and accepting – but it's only the start. Scoring is one tool to aid with integration, and gratitude is the other."

"Gratitude? Let me guess: now you want me to be grateful for my System of not deserving? You want me to give thanks for all the times I worked hard and ended up with nothing? Maybe you'd like it if I went to my teacher and give her a big kiss? I could write a letter of commendation for her amazing talent at losing term papers."

"You have a remarkably smart and sarcastic tongue; I quite like it." Chris paused as Linda smiled, before continuing with, "Tell me what you did after you discovered what happened to your term paper."

"I'm not sure what you mean."

"Is this the first time, here today, that you've spoken about the incident to other people?"

"No, I've told several people."

"And did telling people generate your desired response?"

Suspiciously Linda asked, "What do you mean?"

"Did telling others give you the opportunity to relive your anger? Did you get sympathy from the people you told? Did you become the centre of attention?"

Linda glared at Chris and reluctantly nodded in agreement, but it was Ronna who spoke next, "Linda, the System has given you three gifts so far, but most importantly has enabled you to re-create your childhood experience of not getting what you wanted. This returns you to familiar experiences from your youth."

Looking a little teary, Linda said, "But I didn't like it then, either."

"Was there dysfunctional parenting in your family?" Linda nodded, "While you as an adult can see it as dysfunctional parenting, to a child, what your parents did was love. That's how Systems are formed; since what your parents are doing is love and also right, then you must be the problem. In your case, one of your parents gave the impression that if you could just work hard enough, then you would get their love and attention – but no matter how hard you worked, the parent was just too busy. To the young Linda, the fault couldn't be the parent, so it must have been with you. Coming up with a System that says 'I do not deserve' fitted the bill perfectly. Now your world made sense."

"That makes sense, in a sort of twisted way. But why does my adult keep reproducing the situation?"

"The little child hasn't gone away, at least not on the inside. Under stress, that Child will seek the same relief she felt when she first made the rule. One way your inner Child feels reassured is to work hard and not get. That's another way your System serves you – it gives your inner Child a sense of reassurance and familiarity."

"Yippee," Linda returned to her sarcasm.

"We're not done yet. Your System gives you permission to get angry. Remember, you're uncomfortable with anger. Being angry is uncomfortable, so you need a reason to get angry. There's a lot of anger wrapped up in this System. For example, if you're mad at your boyfriend, then you're unlikely to express that to him directly. What do you do instead? Simple: you work hard at something you know won't produce a reward and then hey presto, you can now get angry at that."

"Wow! I can see that so clearly! I often call my sister and try to help her with her relationship issues. It's like banging my head against a wall, as my sister won't change. It gives me a chance to work hard, though – and not only do I not get rewarded, she gets angry at me for trying to help. Then I rant to my boyfriend about my sister instead of what's bugging me about him!"

Chris excitedly responded, "That's fabulous! You have an amazing skill in not deserving. You should pat yourself on the back and take a bow: you're being really creative and effective."

Linda stood up and took her bow. Then she started to walk away. Ronna stopped her by saying, "Umm, where are you going?"

"We're done, right? I've accepted this…"

Ronna looked at her with a raised eyebrow and said, "You've started the integration process, but what are you going to do about the missing paper?"

"Shit, there's my System kicking in! I did the work and was ready to leave without doing anything to change the situation – work without reward."

Chris said, "Once again, good noticing. Now it's time for the next stop on the Wheel."

Linda sat back down on the chair and asked, "What's the next step?"

Ronna grabbed the chalk and wrote:

> Integrate and Accept:
> Scoring - 7-8
> Gratitude - the many ways it serves you

Then she added:

> Step: Plan

"Oh, this isn't good - I'm a horrible planner," Linda proclaimed.

Ronna chuckled, "That doesn't surprise me."

Chris then continued with the explanation, saying, "Planning is a vital step to Radical Acceptance. If we don't plan, then we end up making decisions unconsciously and those decisions often feed our Systems. Planning gives you the opportunity to analyse the situation and then choose the appropriate action in response to an event. Before we talk about Linda's event specifically, though, let's describe the process of planning."

Beth asked, "The old pro and con list?"

"You could use that, but we have other tools which work better. Firstly, we shift the focus of your planning from 'What will I do?' to 'What do I want'? This is called Outcome-Based Planning. We'll start with a hypothetical situation that everyone can participate in."

Chris moved to the board, and while he cleared off the good and bad feelings list, Ronna gave out the situation. "Imagine you have your own place and a friend's causing a problem: he keeps coming to your apartment with a group a people and partying. While you don't mind the occasional party, it's becoming disruptive to your studies. You've gone around the Wheel for the event, and have now come to the Plan step."

Ronna paused and Chris wrote:

> What's my desired outcome?

Then he responded to this question with, "Setting a boundary with the friend without ending the friendship seems ideal, doesn't it? What's wrong with this outcome, though?"

Amy raised her hand and said, "If you set a boundary with the friend, then they may choose to end the friendship."

"Right. So outcomes which depend on another person will often lead to disappointment. What else is wrong with it?" The group was silent. "It talks about what you might do rather than the outcome that you wish to achieve. What is the outcome you wish to get from your actions?"

Beth suggested, "Peace and quiet!"

"Is it? There are lots of times you enjoy noise, aren't there?"

"But not when I'm trying to study."

"And why are you studying?"

"To get good marks so I can get out of this dump and get a job." The group laughed.

"Let's stick with your key point. The outcome is to get good marks. Are there other outcomes?"

There was silence, so Ronna asked, "How important is it to keep the friendship?"

"I thought we shouldn't base our plans on another person?" said Linda.

"But nor should you ignore them. So, in this hypothetical situation, let's also make keeping your friend important. Now think carefully about the outcomes and consciously decide what your real priorities are. If it's to keep your friend happy, then there's no shame in that. Just be clear and plan accordingly: if you think that you 'should' put marks ahead of friends when you really prefer friends over marks, then you'll create a plan which is doomed for failure."

Chris drew a line across the board. At one end he wrote, 'Marks' and at the other he wrote 'Friend'. Then he said, "Alright folks, I want some suggestions for what to do with this partying friend. Remember that this is a brainstorming session and that any idea is accepted. As you come up with ideas, we'll add them to the line."

One person called out, "Party on!" The group laughed. Chris asked, "Okay, where on the line does it go?" Most people agreed that this idea belonged closest to the 'Friend' end of the line. Someone else called out, "Tell the friend to get lost. Who needs a friend like that?" That one ended up closest to the 'Marks' end. Several others followed, and the final result can be seen here:

"Okay," Ronna said, "let's review these. Remember that this activity is about deciding on the outcomes and their priorities. 'Get Lost': how does that fit with the desired outcomes?"

A discussion on this and the other suggestions ensued, with some in the group preferring one option over another for each of the five points. Ronna listed the people under each of the options. Then, for interest's sake, she asked each person to give their average from their last report card and how they would rank themselves as social people. The people with the highest social ranking tended toward the two extremes. If they had a lot of social confidence, then they didn't worry about telling a friend to get lost as they knew that they had other friends. The ones with lower social confidence but high social needs tended toward the party on option. The students with the highest marks tended toward the middle options.

Chris commented on this spread, "Notice how people's priorities reflect across their lives. Even this hypothetical situation shows patterns in how each of you live." The grouped looked reflectively at the board and each other. Chris continued, "Now let's take a look at Linda's situation." Turning to Linda, he asked, "What are the outcomes you seek?"

"Well, getting a mark higher than zero is one." She thought for a bit and then added, "But I don't want to antagonise my teachers either. After all, there are still several months of school left."

"So the two ends of the line are 'Mark' and 'Teachers'." Ronna wrote these on the board and then asked the group to offer suggested responses. Again, any idea was welcomed. At the end there were seven options:

1. Go straight to the Dean to complain about the teacher
2. Write an article in the school paper slamming the school and the teacher
3. Accept a zero mark without complaint
4. Keep backup copies in the future
5. Ask the teacher about resubmitting – if no, then accept the zero
6. Ask the teacher about resubmitting – if no, then go to the Dean

After listing these options, the group placed five on the line so it looked as follows:

"Let's have a look at the other two options," said Ronna. "The option to keep backups in the future can apply no matter which option is chosen. It's also a good general strategy to follow whenever submitting documents to the school, the government or even an insurance company. Linda can keep that in mind for the future. The final item is to write the article in the school paper.

Let's have a closer look at this one. How well does it meet the goal of getting a better grade?"

Linda, who had championed this idea, agreed that it wouldn't get her a better mark. "Then how will it work to keep you on good terms with the teachers?"

"Not well, but it would make me feel better."

"True, and this is why planning is such a good idea. If you'd gone off, acted on your feelings and published the article, then you'd have hurt your chances of getting either of the outcomes that you wanted. Thinking about your goal is crucial to effective planning."

Ronna turned to Linda, "Which of these options works best for you? Which one makes the most sense, based on your priorities?"

Linda thought for a moment. "My marks are more important than being friends with the teachers, so I will first ask my teacher and then go to the Dean if that doesn't work." She looked at Ronna, "Am I done yet?"

Ronna laughed, "No, not yet. There's another aspect to planning, too: you need to consider the possible consequences of your actions."

"Those are easy – I either get the mark or I don't."

Ronna looked at the class and asked, "Those are the only possible consequences?"

Andre said, "No, I don't think so. She'd also have to plan for the unexpected, as people are often unpredictable."

"That's a good awareness, Andre," Ronna replied. "Unpredictability is important to plan for, although we can never think of every possible action that another person might take."

Chris inserted, "So if Linda's teacher hears about her going to the Dean and starts yelling at her, would this be Linda's fault?"

Ben said, "Before today I would have said yes, but now that I know this information, I'm going to say no. The teacher's reaction would be their event, so they'd need to go around the Wheel themselves."

Ronna smiled as she watched people in the room discover and integrate the work being presented, "Wonderful discovery there, Ben. You're 100% responsible for what you do, what you say and how you say it. Similarly, the other person is also 100% responsible for how they receive and respond to those actions."

Chris stood up at the board and said, "Okay Linda, let's begin with your list of possible consequences." She gave as many as she could think of, and the group also added their ideas.

At the end, the list looked like this:

- Get a zero anyway
- Antagonise the teacher
- Annoy the Dean
- Get the chance to resubmit your paper

Chris asked Linda, "Are there any of these consequences that you can't accept?"

She looked at the list, "There are some that I don't like. I really want a mark other than zero, and I also don't want to antagonise my teacher. In the worst case I could end up with a zero and piss off my teacher." She fiddled with her hair. "I'm not sure I want to do this."

"Excellent," declared Ronna. Linda looked at her with bewilderment. Ronna continued, "You've just shown the other important aspect to planning: a plan that you can't carry out is a waste of time and effort. Just because an option looks good on paper doesn't mean that you can actually do it. This is why looking at consequences is so important."

Turning to the class, she added, "Some of you are more comfortable with conflict than others. That's neither good nor bad, but simply a fact. To push at your comfort zone can be liberating, but to try and be someone that you're not is damaging."

"Damaging," asked Amy? "Isn't that a bit of an exaggeration?"

"Not at all. If you're set on facing a conflict and have promised yourself that this time you're going to do it, then what happens to your self-esteem when you back down – or start the conflict only to pull back once it gets too much?"

"Oh, I see what you mean…"

Ronna turned back to Linda, "Is this option a gentle push at your boundaries – or way beyond what you can handle?"

Linda squared her shoulders, "I can do this."

Chris asked, "How does that decision feel?"

Linda responded, "It's a radical plan." She smiled and added, "It feels solid. I'll be disappointed if I get stuck with the zero, but I see that I have some responsibility in the matter as well. I'll do all that I can and accept the outcome, whatever it is."

Chris wrote on the board under the plan step:

> Ask teacher then go to the Dean
> Step: Act & Accept
> ???????

Ronna then asked, "Linda, why are you still sitting here?"

The group burst out laughing. It was a wrap for the day.

* * *

Three weeks later, Linda called requesting a visit. She began by sharing some of her history. At that time she was 21 years old and attending college in Hotel and Restaurant Management. She was also a middle child, having an older brother and a younger sister. When she was younger, her parents had both been factory workers, although her father had also been in and out of jail numerous times on a variety of different charges. Her mother ran the family, but Linda described her as being emotionally withdrawn and 'over the top' when it came to being critical and wanting things done a certain way. Linda's father was more emotionally available, so when he was around, he was the preferred parent. After Linda left home, her Mom divorced her father and met a wealthy man. She and her new husband then moved to a big house in a small town.

As a teenager Linda was a good student, although she worked harder at staying out of her mother's way than she did on her school work. At seventeen, she dropped out of school and worked a number of short-lived, minimum wage jobs. She managed to enter the college program as a mature student. She was now living with a male room-mate in a platonic relationship, but it wasn't working out very well. Linda had become sexually active at a very young age and her inter-personal relationships were fraught with drama with shades of abuse.

Linda went on to share how her paper incident had been resolved. "I was really nervous. I knew I had to be firm but not combative. I spoke with the teacher, and she'd been surprised when I hadn't handed in my paper as I'd always done so before. She understood my concerns and agreed to consider possible options. Then she went back and looked for my paper. It turned up filed with some papers from another class." She smiled, "It was an A."

* * *

Linda continued coming to us for sessions. She completed her college course, albeit with a few more bumps and bruises along the way. Then she began her search for work. It didn't take long. She arrived at one session very elated, "I'm so happy. I have this great job offer. I'll be starting in a big hotel chain working in Reservations. I'll have to start out at the desk, but they have a great advancement program with a clear path to work my way up to being a manager. I worked there as part of my work co-op and they really liked what I did then. I applied as soon as I graduated and they hired me straight away."

Chris said, "Okay, let me grab the chart and write down the event."

Linda looked puzzled and said with a nervous laugh, "But I haven't talked about the event that I came here to discuss: it's about…"

Chris cut her off, smiled and said, "But Linda, we do have the event." As he spoke, he wrote down:

> I have this great new job

Linda was still puzzled, "Yeah, but this is good news. There's no charge here: everything is going great."

Ronna went on, "Happiness is a feeling – and just as much of a charge as anger, sadness or whatever else you might feel."

"Yes, but I really wanted to talk about…"

Chris laughed, "Your great job…we know, we're very intuitive folks."

"Well, I hate to burst your intuitive bubble, but I was only sharing my happiness with you… But I'm so happy that I'm willing to let you have your chance to take my job around the Wheel."

Ronna said seriously, "Linda, this is important. We'll give you lots of time to discuss your other issue later on."

"Okay. That's cool, because now my curiosity is peaked as to why you'd want to put my job down as an event."

Chris wrote down:

> Step: Event
> Great Job
> Step: Feel & Accept
> Happiness
> Step: Discover

Linda flared, "Oh my God. You want to make my job neutral? You want to take away my happiness? Why would you want to do such a thing? I worked hard to get…" She suddenly stopped talking. After a few seconds, she continued, "Shit and God damn it to hell, there's my System again."

Ronna said, "I repeat, your happiness is not neutral. What happens when events are not neutral?"

Linda sulkily responded, "The feeling is part of a System and the System will come up to bite me."

We nodded, knowing that Linda would begin to go around the Wheel on her own with only some minor assistance.

"So, happiness is charged – and it fits into my deserving System. I could just cry right now. I want to rant and stomp, saying that I worked damn hard to get the job and that I deserve to be happy... I know that when I've gone into a job only looking at how it can make me happy, though, I've done something to sabotage my job and put myself in some kind of financial crisis."

Chris asked, "So what can you discover through the work we're doing around happiness?"

Linda sat and pondered, before eventually saying, "I'm discovering that happiness can be just as destructive as anger, depression, jealousy or any other feeling."

"Yes, but what of the unconscious?"

"I'm not sure."

"Tell me, what will be the result of you getting this job?"

Linda smiled and said, "I'll be done with all those menial jobs I hated. Instead, I'll have a job which I look forward to each day. On top of that, I'll quickly move my way up to be a manager so I'll finally have enough money to live comfortably."

"Wow, you haven't even started yet and you're a manager already?"

Becoming defensive she replied, "They said there's training and lots of room for advancement."

Ronna asked, "How old is the current manager?"

"He's in his forties."

"You've been at some of the other hotels. How old are those managers?"

Looking down, she mumbled, "Also in their late thirties or early forties. I see what you're saying. I'm not going to get there any time soon: I'll have to work my way up and that'll take time. I guess I discovered that I'm in a hurry."

"Why are you in such a hurry?"

"Things will be better in the future; I'm tired of being poor and hating what I do."

"Is there a belief in there somewhere?"

"No belief, I just know that things are better when I have the money that I need to take control of my life."

"Money gives you control?"

"Poverty certainly doesn't."

"Your Mom went from being poor to being rich. Is she now in control?"

"If she wants to go somewhere, she just goes. If she wants something, she just buys it."

"And that makes her in control?"

Getting angry, Linda said, "No, damn it. Her relationships are out of control. She was with a lot of men between my father and her current husband, and they're always fighting."

Ronna responded by writing:

> I need to be in control
> Step: Integrate & Accept

"Now you're calling me a control freak." Silence followed. "Okay, I like to know how things are going to turn out." More silence. "Alright! I'm a control freak. When your life has been as crazy as mine, it's important to have some control."

"You're a control freak," said Chris. "I wanted to start a group for control freaks, but everyone wanted to be in charge and I couldn't allow that!"

Linda smiled. Ronna didn't, as she'd heard the joke before. Linda then said, "So I get to accept that I'm a control freak?" She straightened up and added, "Why the hell not, actually? I'm damn good at what I do. When I'm in charge, things just go better."

Ronna said, "But nice women are biddable."

"Not this one!"

"You should be more like me; I don't have a need to control," Ronna replied. Chris started coughing. "Something go down the wrong way dear?" she asked.

"You could say that!" Chris answered. We all laughed.

Linda then continued, "A few months ago, I was only angry when I could justify the feeling and call it righteous anger: I was nice and loving and never needed to be in control. Now I'm messed up, angry and controlling. Gee, I'm so glad I have you two in my life. I feel so much better than before I met you!"

We smiled. Ronna leaned over to Chris and whispered loudly, "Do you think she's being sarcastic?"

"Arrrgh, this really hurts though," Linda carried on. "What else am I going to have to give up? Tell me now so I can do it all in one swoop."

"Linda, do you really think that we have the answer to that?

"No, I just wish that you did. Okay, so now the Plan step."

Chris asked, "What's your score on accepting that you're controlling?"

"It's about a 6."

Chris wrote on the board under the integrate step:

> Controlling – Score of 6
> Step: Plan

"This is the step where I find the plan that best suits my desired outcome. I want to have money, because being poor does suck. I want to be happy and enjoy my job. None of those are the point, though: the point is about letting go of the fantasies and just being with life as it unfolds. I'm not sure I see how to do this as an outcome."

"Who do you want to be as a person?"

"I'm not sure that I want it, but I seem to be driven to do personal growth work. Before I met you, I was trying to be a 'good' person – a happy and loving person. Now I'm working to accept all of me. The happy and loving work was more fun, but it forced me to try and stuff down even more thoughts and feelings. The Radical Acceptance work is certainly not fun, but it addresses the goal of becoming aware. Who do I want to be as a person? I now see that I really want to be fully and authentically me."

"Then what's your plan?"

"To be aware of and to accept all of myself: my beliefs, my attachments, my fantasies, my character traits and whatever else I discover."

"What's your plan heading into the job?"

"To see the reality of the job instead of the fantasies, and to work my ass off to become the youngest manager they've ever had."

"Sounds like a plan."

Having covered the happy event, we then returned to the event Linda had originally come to discuss.

*   *   *

Over the next few months, Linda continued occasional visits and emails. On one visit, she remarked, "I've been practising Radical Acceptance for a while now and it's made a huge difference in my life. The Attachment and Projection Tools have been especially invaluable. I find the Scoring very useful too, and have come to appreciate aspects of myself that I used to hate. I'm also watching my outcomes when it's time to make a decision. I know I'm babbling here, but I don't know where to start." She paused, "Here's an example of a problem: I was at an office party the other day, and I could barely function."

Ronna said, "Tell us more."

"I just went through the motions of enjoying myself. I was there, interacted and did the social niceties thing, but I wasn't engaged. I couldn't get up any energy for the event, and just couldn't wait for the appropriate time to leave. I'm normally such a social butterfly, too! I just don't know what's going on."

Ronna responded, "So when you were at the party and didn't feel engaged, what was that like for you?"

"It was like I didn't belong there."

Chris grabbed the markers and wrote:

```
Step: Event
Party
Step: Feel & Accept
Not belonging/Not fitting in
```

Linda turned white, "Not belonging… It can't be… Oh God, I try so hard to belong…to fit in!"

Chris asked, "Where have you fit in, in the past?

"I'm not sure. I was the black sheep in my family – always getting into some kind of trouble. At school, the teachers would get fed up with me for being opinionated or challenging them in some way. They liked me okay, but I didn't really fit in. The kids in the school yard would also get tired of me trying to control them and boss them around. They wouldn't choose me to be on their teams. I did my own thing in high school as well – found the wrong group to hang out with and skipped more and more school until I dropped out. I fitted in only by doing drugs and alcohol, but that doesn't count. In college I had a few more social skills, but I still irritated the teachers and other students by speaking out – saying things that people didn't want hear.

"When found this job, I thought that I'd finally found a place where I would belong. While I get along with a few co-workers and we go out together once in a while, they have so much drama in their lives and I don't have the energy for it any more Since I won't support their drama, people don't bother to include me at lunch or on breaks. Man," tears started to flow, "I don't think I've ever fit in or belonged anywhere."

Chris spoke with great seriousness, "The people we work with are often the ones who have never fit in. They're the seekers – the ones unwilling to accept the norms of family, society or even the norms of the modern Psychotherapy Movement. They're the ones called to seek, the ones drawn to a therapy as radical as Radical Acceptance. They never have fitted in, and they never will fit in."

Linda said, "That makes sense. I'll score the integration at a 4 for now. It'll take some time before I can let go of the longing to belong."

Chris then wrote down:

> Step: Integrate & Accept
> Score – 4
> Step: Plan

"My plan is to work to accept that I'm never going to fit in," Linda continued.

"Yes, but I would imagine there are more office parties coming up. What about those?"

"I'm tempted just to skip them all."

Ronna said, "That's Chris' strategy. He avoids as many social gatherings as possible. I, on the other hand, choose to go to some of them. It feels like part of my job to connect socially with my co-workers. The same is true for family events. I choose to engage more in family than Chris does. You'll need to think about how you want to handle things in your life."

"Yes, a plan would help. I like the idea of going to the social events as part of my job. I've always heard that important work goes on at social events."

Chris wandered back to the board and added:

> See office events as part of the job

"What are the consequences of this plan?" he then asked.

"I know that others see me as cold and isolated. I'm not interested in working to change that. Treating it as part of the job will mean that I won't be the life of the party, but I can live with that too."

"What about your bosses?"

"The biggest consequence may be a slightly poorer evaluation – a low score under the category, 'Is a Team Player'. I prefer that to the alternative of pasting a fake smile on my face and pretending that I have something in common with people I can't relate to."

* * *

Linda is still working in the hotel business – no longer in Reservations, but in a niche where she's content. She's still working toward being a manager, and we're quite sure that she'll make it one day. She's also using her many years of trying to fit in as training for being a friendly, helpful person who both her guests and the management will appreciate.

Her journey is no longer something that she does, but has become who she is.

10 Yvonne: Maturity

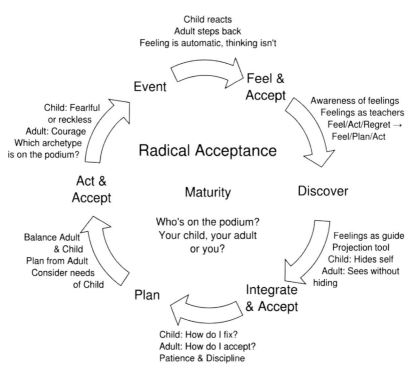

Yvonne came to Canada from Poland when she was 13 years old. A few years later, she married a man from Sudan, Hassan, and had 6 children with him – all while running her own business importing material and clothing from the Middle East. Even though Yvonne had been in Canada for many years, the influence of her Polish upbringing, her marriage to Hassan and her career choice all did little to bestow her with a true understanding of Western culture.

Our initial contact with Yvonne took place over the phone. She'd left her marriage six months previously, and came to us for therapy because she was feeling depressed and needed nurturing. We tried to explain that Radical Acceptance is an intense and rather confrontational form of therapy, and so perhaps not exactly the nurturing she wanted – but she was adamant: acceptance was what she needed most. After a few more failed attempts to convince her otherwise, we set up her first appointment.

When Yvonne arrived, she began talking about her failed marriage and her business – a business which she didn't just dislike, but which wasn't making enough money to pay her bills. "The business belonged to my mother, and I started out working with her. She died about 12 years ago and I took it over because I couldn't do anything else. I really don't like it, but it's all I have. My husband, Hassan, won't pay anything to help me raise the kids. It's all leaving me feeling depressed and overwhelmed."

Chris spoke softly, "Wow, you've a lot on your plate."

"Yes, and I'm also in mediation with Hassan. It was suggested by our lawyers, but it's just an exercise in frustration because he lies and never follows through with the things that he says he'll do."

Ronna said, "Separation and divorce proceedings are never easy, so let's have a look at how you're contributing to the difficulty."

"No, you don't understand – I'm trying everything I know to make this go as smoothly as possible. I don't want to fight him, but he provokes me until I lose it. Then he sits back and says to his lawyer, 'See what I have to put up with?'"

Ronna nodded, "Hmm, hmm."

"I put up with his shit in the marriage, and when I left, I said I wouldn't do it ever again. That's why I fight back during the mediation sessions."

Ronna said, "You sound like one angry woman."

"I tried being nice. For years I did everything his way, and where did that get me? I'm tired of being nice."

"So you've tried both sides – being subservient and now getting angry," Ronna summarised.

Chris then asked, "How's that working for you"?

"I'm not sure I understand."

"Is fighting him and getting angry with him helping you to achieve your goals?"

Yvonne looked perplexed, and said, "Goals? I only have one goal: to get rid of him."

"Who set that as your goal?"

"I know English isn't my first language, but I've been in Canada for most of my life and I thought I understood the language well. But...to tell you the truth, I don't have the slightest idea what you're talking about."

"What I'm asking is, 'Who's running your life?' Is it your inner Child or your inner Adult?"

"I don't know much about the inner Child or the inner Adult."

"Then we'll explain, because it's important to know who's in charge." Chris starting the explanation by asking Yvonne, "Have you ever been to see an orchestra?" She immediately looked confused again, but said that yes, she had. "There are all these instruments spread out across the stage. Then there's the man standing on the podium and waving his baton. What's the purpose of the conductor?"

Yvonne replied seriously, "The conductor guides and directs the various instruments."

"But he doesn't play an instrument. So why does he get so much credit?"

After thinking for a moment, Yvonne replied, "It's because he's the one who calls on the various instruments to play at the right time. He also directs them to play louder or softer, faster or slower. He's the one in charge. If he wasn't there, then the instruments wouldn't be making beautiful music: they'd all be in conflict and making a horrible sound."

Ronna continued, appearing to change the subject. "Yvonne, have you ever had the experience where it seems like there are different voices in your head, all urging you to do different things?"

"That happens all the time."

"Are those voices in harmony, or are they in conflict with each other?"

Yvonne laughed, "They're definitely in conflict."

"If those voices each represent an instrument in an orchestra, then where's the conductor?"

Yvonne thought for a bit, "I don't think there is a conductor. That's why I live with such chaos."

"We would agree."

"So what do I do? Can you jump into my head and start waving your baton?"

"No I can't, but you can. You can take charge of the discordant voices to bring them into harmony."

"How? Whenever I try, they just yell louder."

"It's done through choice – you choose which voice to listen to. That will give your life a sense of harmony, even if the inner voices are less in harmony."

"Earlier, we spoke of the Child and the Adult. These are two of those voices. The Child's voice tends to be very loud and demanding, while the Adult's voice is quieter and less insistent. Most people hear the Child and never stop to listen for – or call on – the Adult voice. Maturity is hearing both voices and making a choice as to which one is the best for the situation at hand. To make things clearer, we'll begin by showing you the differences between the Child and the Adult."

Ronna set up the flip chart then divided the page in half. She then labelled one half of the page 'The Child' and began to write under that heading:

> **Child**
> Needy and seeks to get what it wants
> Wants life to be fair
> Wants conclusions and endings
> Sees things as black or white, right or wrong
> Likes to be right, hates being wrong

Yvonne interrupted Ronna, saying, "The Child wants to be right? That so describes Hassan. He hated to admit that he was ever wrong."

Chris raised an eyebrow, "Hassan hated to be wrong?"

She chuckled, "Yeah – and not only that, he wanted me to agree that he was always right, too. But I wouldn't."

"Not even when he was right?"

"Especially not then!"

"Let me make sure that I have this correctly: he hated to admit when he was wrong, and you wouldn't acknowledge when he was right?" Smiling, Yvonne agreed. "If he was right, then wouldn't you have been wrong?"

Still not seeing the point, she said, "I still wouldn't have said anything. Doing that used to make Hassan so angry."

"Did you enjoy frustrating him?"

"Now that you mention it, yes I did. I know it seems petty, but it was one of the few times in which I had a sense of power."

Chris continued, "You say that Hassan was in the Child when he wouldn't admit being wrong. You just said that if you were wrong, then you wouldn't admit being wrong either. When you wouldn't admit being wrong, what archetype was in charge for you?"

Yvonne was speechless for a few moments. "I thought Radical Acceptance helped me to feel better about myself..."

Ronna grinned and said, "I warned you before you came: our work isn't gentle or nice. Acceptance isn't easy or fun." Without pausing, Ronna continued writing on the board under the 'Child' heading.

> Sees simplistic solutions to complex problems
> Reacts to life – operates from Feel-Act-Regret

Yvonne stopped us to ask, "Feel-Act-Regret, what's that?"

Chris responded, "When you're in mediation you get angry – that's the feel part – and start yelling – there's the act - and then feel like a fool for losing it again – giving you the regret."

Yvonne replied, "Okay, well I'm an expert at that, then."

We continued listing aspects of the Child.

> Wants things NOW

"Have you guys been living in my house? That point about the Child wanting it now fits me exactly. I'm often out buying things for myself and then worrying about how to pay for them. My credit cards are usually maxed out, and I have several pieces of furniture on a pay-later plan. I just keep hoping that later will never arrive."

Chris said, "Yes, our world is based on the Child, so that's not unusual. It's why we have fast food, drive-thru banking, massive credit card debt, pay-day loans and get now, pay later arrangements. The idea of saving until you can afford it is foreign to the Child."

Ronna added, "This is unless your Child comes from a place of financial fear, of course – for example someone who grew up where there was never enough money to provide adequate food, clothes and shelter. In that case, the Child will be afraid of spending any money, and no amount of savings will ever be enough."

Yvonne said, "I try to save, but something always comes along that's even more important than what I'm saving for. Sometimes it's a new pair of shoes, and other times it's clothes for my children. They want those things now, too."

"You could say no – both to yourself and to your children."

"If I say that to my kids, then they get sad or angry. It's easier just to buy things for them."

"Ah yes, parenting via the Child; wanting to be liked by your children."

Yvonne looked shocked, "Isn't what you're supposed to do? I thought parents were supposed to be a friend to their children. My mother came from the old country and she ruled firmly. I promised myself that my children wouldn't have to go without the things that they wanted."

Chris said, "The job of a parent is to parent – being friends with your children will come later when they're older. For now your role is to set limits and teach them that life doesn't come served on a golden platter. Teach them the tools to develop maturity in their lives."

"But my mother was firm, and I didn't learn from that."

"Yes, but what about your father? When you couldn't get what you wanted from your Mom, did you go to your father and ask again for the same thing?"

"Yes, I did. He was such a softy. I really loved my dad. Funny, Hassan used to get angry with me when he'd say no to our kids and then I'd give in. Like my dad, I'm a softy when it comes to my little ones."

We looked at each other, silently agreeing to catalogue this information for a future session. For the moment, however, we resumed our explanation – adding more items to the 'Child' list.

> Wants life to be easy, fun and happy
> Loves drama
> Will express anger with temper tantrums, sulking, punishing behaviours or by becoming cold and withdrawn
> Is controlling and wants everything to happen in a certain way
> Feels guilt when errors are made

Yvonne sat stunned, her eyes glued to the flip chart. Within moments, her eyes had begun to water, "So you are telling me that I'm a child?"

Ronna asked, "Did we say that?"

"Well not verbally, but that's me what you have written up there – almost all of it. I'm a forty year old child with six kids!" Yvonne started to get agitated, "I feel bad enough about my situation at the moment without you guys making it worse."

Chris responded, "Yvonne, the Child likes to …"

Her anger started to boil, and cutting Chris off, she said, "No I don't believe this. I'm no different from a lot of other people, so why are you labelling me like this? This is so negative and bad. You don't know me. How can you just step in and say all these things?"

Ronna turned and wrote, 'The Child loves to have temper tantrums to manipulate others into doing what they want."

Suddenly, it was as if someone stuck a pin in a balloon; all her indignation quickly disappeared. After a pause, she said, "Now I see why I'm here. No one has ever called me on my shit before. I used the tears and anger on my father, and he always gave in. I've usually been given what I want."

She started crying again, and Ronna handed Yvonne a box of tissues, saying, "You know, the first box of tissues is free – after that, we start charging."

Yvonne smiled at Ronna's joke, blew her nose, and said, "So what you're telling me is that I'm a child?"

Chris replied, "No, what we're saying is that the Child archetype is on the podium, making your decisions."

Yvonne could do nothing but nod while she continued to look at the flip chart. Ronna said, "I'd now like to introduce you to the Adult archetype. Let's go through the list again and discuss how the Adult would react to each of the items on it."

Child	Adult
Focused on neediness - it acts to get - self centred	Also self-centred, but acts on principles
Wants life to be fair - as defined by the child	Sees life as it is and does not expect fairness or even justice

"Doesn't expect fairness?" interjected Yvonne on the last point, looking totally confused. "Life should be fair."

Chris responded, "Who was it that declared life should be fair? When I look around, it doesn't seem fair at all."

"But it... It should be fair," she repeated.

"Just because you'd like it to be fair, the world should co-operate?"

Yvonne opened her mouth to speak, and then shut it several times. Finally she said, "Damn it all. Do you two like spoiling my illusions?"

"We challenge the Child and her fantasies; that's part of what we do."

Child	Adult
Wants conclusions and endings	Lives for life's journey, not its imagined final destination
Sees things as black or white, right or wrong	Sees the world as endless shades of grey - knows right and wrong are subjective and situational
Likes to be right, hates being wrong	Can accept being wrong, and has no need to be right
Sees simplistic solutions to complex problems	Sees the complexity of life
Reacts to life - operates from Feel-Act-Regret	Responds to life - operates from Feel-Grow-Plan-Act

Ronna paused the list to say, "Feel-Grow-Plan-Act is when you feel your emotion, but do not act on it – that's the Feel. Next you use the feeling as a teacher to Grow, and you think about an appropriate response – Plan – and only then do you respond – Act.

Child	Adult
Wants things NOW	Can wait until an appropriate time before acting on what it wants
Wants life to be easy, fun and happy	Takes life on life's terms
Loves drama	Doesn't need to create drama – keeps a level head and sees drama as a distraction
Will express anger with temper tantrums, punishing behaviours or will be cold and withdrawn	Uses anger as a tool for self-discovery and empowerment
Is controlling and wants everything a certain way	Knows that controlling everything is a futile exercise and so accepts things as they are
Feels guilt when errors are made	Understands that mistakes occur, and so accepts the errors along the path and learns from them
Criticises, blames and rationalises their behaviour	Accepts responsibility for their own actions

They reviewed the chart until Yvonne was able to distinguish the difference between the Child and the Adult archetypes. By then, she was able to agree that her Child has been the primary figure on her podium.

Chris explained, "The chart makes it look like the Child is bad and the Adult is good. However, a rich life includes both the Child and the Adult. Life lived only through the child is dysfunctional, and life lived only through the adult is dry. Together, they combine the fantasy and dreams of the child with the well-grounded nature and practicality of the adult."

Ronna said, "Earlier we were talking about your goals, and you said that your only goal was to get rid of Hassan. That's when Chris took us off onto the tangent about the Child. Going back, is your only goal is to get rid of Hassan? There's nothing else you want?"

"Well of course I want him to make his child support payments."

Ronna repeated, "So you want to get rid of him and you want child support payments. Is that all?"

"I would like things to be friendly and amicable between us and for him to take the kids when he's supposed to."

Chris stated, "Sounds like you have a few goals here, so let's review what you have so far: 1, You want to get rid of Hassan; 2, You want him to make his child support payments; 3, You want things to be friendly and amicable between the two of you; and 4, You want him to take kids when he's supposed to."

"Yes, that's what I'd like. Why do I need to define them?"

Ronna said, "Yvonne, it's important to know what it is you want so that you can know if your behaviour is helping or hindering those objectives. You said you were getting angry in mediation, for example, so let's see how that helps or hinders you in attaining your goals."

Chris continued, "Let's have a look at goal one – that you want to get rid of your ex-husband. Is losing it in mediation the way to meet this goal?"

Yvonne began squirming in her seat, and her voice began to raise a notch, "Well, getting angry shows him that I'm not going to put up with his shit any more!"

"We hear that, but does it meet your goal?"

"It may help with that goal, but if I get rid of him totally, then I don't get the child support."

Ronna asked, "So what do you want to do with the goal of losing him?"

"I guess I scrap it."

Chris said, "Or maybe we just need to revise it. Let's continue and see where this takes us. Goal number two is that you want him to pay his support payments. Is losing it in mediation the way to meet this goal?"

Yvonne raised her voice, "God damn it, you're taking away my one and only weapon here! If I don't get angry, then I have nothing!!"

Ronna said, "It feels like anger is your only weapon for protection."

Yvonne's eyes swelled with tears as she said, "Yes: otherwise I just break down and can't cope."

Ronna restated, "Anger is your friend and helper." Yvonne nodded, unable to speak. "This is important: anger can be your friend, but anger erupting all over the place is hurting the goals that you'd like to achieve."

Yvonne responded, "I don't understand what you mean by anger being my friend. Everyone tells me to get rid of it – that it's negative – and I know that they're right, but if I get rid of it," she paused reflectively for a moment, "then I have nothing. I don't know what to do."

"There's an important difference between the Child's handling of anger and the Adult's. As we said while building the list, the Child operates from Feel-Act-Regret, while the Adult uses Feel-Grow-Plan-Act. Feel-Act-Regret is where you feel anger, act in anger and then regret what you did."

Yvonne smiled a little, "Like when I lose it in mediation and Hassan turns to his lawyer and says, 'See what I have to put up with?' At those times I feel like such a moron. I know all about regret when acting in anger."

Chris added, "But Feel-Act-Regret doesn't just happen when you're angry. When the Child is feeling happy, it can still engage in Feel-Act-Regret. Let's say you feel really great and decide to reward yourself with an expensive new pair of shoes, for example. Later, you realise that the money you spent on them was supposed to be savings for your daughter's college fund. The same can be true for love; there's even an English saying that goes, 'Marry in haste, regret in leisure.'"

Yvonne said with gusto, "I'm a living example of that one. I can see that my Child makes most of my decisions. No wonder my marriage was such a mess."

We smiled and nodded, and then Ronna said, "Yvonne, you're similar to many other people. We hear how difficult your Child has made your life. By using the tools you learn here over time, you'll build some useful skills that will assist you and make things a little easier. However, let's get back to your anger. You need your anger to stay strong, but you also don't want to act in anger and so cause feelings of regret later."

Yvonne nodded saying, "Yeah that's it." Her face fell, "But I thought anger was negative – that you had to get rid of anger?"

"Anger is just a feeling; an integral part of being human. It's not better or worse than any other feeling. It's what you do with it that matters. Do you use it to move toward your goals or away from them? In the Hassan situation, you can use your anger to be powerful or you can let loose during mediation and then feel regret for what you've done."

"That's what I'm trying to do – to be powerful and not let him get away with things. When I actually do this, though, I either end up sounding like an angry idiot or I start crying."

"So you sometimes cry about these situations? Why's that?"

"I don't know. I just do."

"I can understand yelling, but crying is what you do when you're sad."

"But I don't like anger. Tears are much safer. You don't look like a screaming idiot when you cry."

"Nor do you get access to your power." Ronna paused. "Yvonne, you've re-labelled anger as sadness. You now see anger as being 'bad' and sadness as acceptable. Since sadness is more acceptable, it gives you permission to express yourself through tears. The problem with re-labelling the anger as sadness is that it's not an effective strategy for dealing with the true feeling – which is anger. In fact, the more you cry, the more you suppress your anger and the less powerful you become. To find the power you need to deal constructively with Hassan, you'll need your anger. You'll need to feel it fully, but without becoming it – without becoming the screaming idiot. Other relabelling can happen: for some people it's not okay to feel pain and so this gets re-labelled as anger, for instance. Those people are unable to access their tears and instead get angry. Of course, no matter how angry they get, getting angry will never deal with the grief that they carry."

Yvonne, sitting reflectively, then said, "I get it: my job is to identify my true feelings and deal with them appropriately."

Chris followed up with, "That's right. This issue of anger is an important one, so let's return to the goals and see how they relate to your sense of power."

Reluctantly, Yvonne agreed – not sure what other landmine she was walking into. Ronna took up the next goal, "Firstly, you want things to be friendly and amicable".

Yvonne smirked, "Okay I get it! Losing it doesn't make for friendly relationships."

Chris nodded and continued, "You want him to take the kids when he's supposed to."

Yvonne spoke with more assurance, "No, losing it won't get him to see the kids when he's supposed to." As she thought more about this, her panic began to return, "So how the hell am I going to get him to take the kids?"

Ronna said, "Yvonne, we're noticing that your goals have everything to do with Hassan and nothing to do with yourself. What will happen to these goals if Hassan doesn't change? What if, no matter what you do, he won't make his support payments, he isn't interested in a friendly or amicable relationship, and he doesn't want to take the children? What then?"

She looked at us with a sense of powerless frustration, "I was hoping that now we're apart, things would be different – that he'd start to take up his financial and parental responsibilities."

Chris responded, "I know we must sound repetitive, but it's the Child that hopes for a 'better' future. In contrast, the Adult accepts what is. The Adult might say, for example, 'Hassan is unlikely to become the man that I want him to be given that he hasn't been that man for the past 17 years.' Then the Adult might start making his plans around that realisation."

"But Hassan might change!" Yvonne protested.

"If he does, then it's a bonus. In the meantime, your hoping is only leading to disappointment and frustration."

Ronna continued, "Let's have another look at those goals. We'll begin by seeing what you really want and then reshaping the goal as expressed by your Adult. Adult goals do not depend on another person changing – they're directed at how you conduct your own behaviour. Let's start with goal one: you just want to get rid of him. Now talk about what you want – but just you, not Hassan."

Yvonne looked lost. "I want… I want… Damn, I don't know what I want – other than for him to stop looking at me with that self-satisfied smirk whenever I lose it in mediation."

Ronna asked, "What do you feel when he looks at you like that?"

"Like an idiot."

"So are you really saying 'I want to stop feeling like an idiot'? Maybe the goal has nothing to do with getting rid of him, since you also want him to make support payments and take the children…"

"Yeah, that's true. So my goal is to stop being an idiot?"

"How would you phrase that in positive language? Instead of what you don't want to be, what do you want to be?"

"I want to be strong and to stop losing it."

"Good, so you could restate the goal as 'I want to speak with firmness and clarity without expressing my anger whenever I deal with Hassan.'"

She looked at Ronna and said clearly, "Yes, that's what I want. That's exactly what I want. Why couldn't I think of that?" Ronna waited, "I know, the Child."

"Yes, it was the Child who set the original goal – a goal that leaves you dependent on Hassan changing. This new goal is a more mature goal – one that includes input from the Adult. It depends on you as well as honouring the desires of the Child to not look like an idiot. How about the rest of your goals? What are the Adult equivalents?"

Yvonne still wasn't sure, "I haven't clue. How can I have goals about the separation which don't include him?"

Chris looked at the time and said, "Think on it. Remember, the first goal started out as wanting to get rid of him but ended with you wanting to be firm, powerful and in control of your actions. We'd like this to be your homework – to come back with mature versions of the other three goals: versions which have a firm basis in your Adult."

* * *

Yvonne returned in a week with a piece of paper in her hand. "This was hard – I almost bought the entire stock of paper from the store! I'd get started and then notice what I'd written was actually about Hassan, so I'd have to rip the paper up and start again. Here they are, though: instead of, 'I want Hassan to make his support payments', the Adult says, 'I expect the full support payments on time.' The second goal was, 'I want him to treat me amicably'. I realised that this one was from the Child because, as you guys said, people don't change who they are. So I figured, 'Once a jerk, always a jerk'. The new goal is, 'I will return respect when respect is given.' The third one, that he'll take the children when he's supposed to, took me the longest. I finally decided on, 'I'll be fully honest with my children as to just why there was no visitation whenever the situation arises.'" She looked up at Ronna and Chris proudly and said, "See, three goals without ever mentioning 'he who won't be named'".

Chris replied, "We can see these must have taken you some time to pull together. It's clear that you've worked very hard. Now let's talk about the Pseudo-Adult."

"The what?"

"The Child pretending to be the Adult."

Yvonne's face fell, "You mean these are still from the Child?"

"Let's have a look at them. The first goal is for the support payments to magically arrive on time."

"Yes, I read that if you expect something to happen, then it will happen."

"That's what's called 'magic thinking' – or the belief that you're so powerful that you can alter another person's behaviour just by expecting it to change. It's one of those fantasies of the Child which we spoke about. We often use magical thinking when we're feeling powerless and want things to be different from what they are."

Reluctantly she agreed, "Damn."

Ronna picked up on the second goal, "Your second goal was that you would respect those who respected you."

"Sure, what's fair is f..." Before she finished, she started to cry. Chris handed her a new box of tissues, and after a few moments, she continued, "That's the Child wanting things to be fair. I guess that the Adult just lets everyone walk all over her. The Adult's goal would be, 'No matter how badly he treats me, I'll just grin like a moron and take his shit.'"

"So who's on the podium now?"

"My Child – and she's having another temper tantrum. I get so frustrated with myself." Yvonne took a deep breath and shifted out of the Child so that she could listen more attentively.

"The Pseudo-Adult talks about appropriate actions, but only on the condition that she gets treated in the way that she wants. The Adult acts based on principles first, and how others act second. As an example, she might choose to be polite – no matter how rudely someone else is behaving."

"So how does the Adult avoid becoming a doormat, always giving in to others?"

Ronna handed the question back to Yvonne, saying, "What do you think? How does your Adult avoid becoming a door mat?"

Yvonne thought for a moment and then added reflectively, "I guess I can say 'No' – either politely or rudely. It doesn't really help being rude, though, as all it ends up doing is antagonizing the other person and escalating the rudeness."

"That's an excellent response, and clearly from the Adult. Remember, it's not that the rudeness is ignored – just that it's a secondary consideration when you're choosing how to behave." Ronna continued. "Your next goal was an attempt to punish Hassan through the children."

Suddenly the Child reappeared, saying, "So he shows up when he wants and the kids think he's wonderful – and I'm left with six children and no break! I can't do it any more," she added as the number of tissues in the box continued fall.

Chris spoke, "Remember your first goal? It started with you wanting to be rid of Hassan and then ended up being about you wanting to be clear and firm at mediation." She gave a teary nod. "Let's do the same thing with these other goals." Again she nodded. "The second goal was that Hassan would pay the support on time. What is it that you really need?"

"For him to be something other than a dead-beat dad," Yvonne said with resentment.

"What is it that you need?"

"I need the money."

"Why do you need the money?"

"Raising six children is expensive."

"Yes, but you've put no limits on your spending – whether spending on yourself or on the children."

"So the children and I have to suffer while he's well off and not paying a cent? It's not right."

"Right or wrong have nothing to do with this. Whether he should pay or not is a distraction from the issue at hand. And no, it's not fair, but that too is a distraction. Notice how the Child gets caught up in distractions to avoid the real issue."

Frustrated, Yvonne asked, "Then what's the real issue?"

Ronna answered, "The issue is you living within your financial reality. It's about accepting that he isn't going to pay – or at least that he isn't going to pay very often – and planning for those circumstances."

Yvonne wailed, "But that's so unfair!" With a pout, she added, "I don't care if that's the Child. So my Child is in charge: is that so horrible? I don't think that I'm a horrible person. Do I make promises to my children that I keep breaking? No! Hassan does that. Do I promise to pay in front of the mediator and then break that promise? No! Hassan does that. I'm not the guilty one here. Why are you making me feel like the evil one? When do you say all this shit to Hassan?"

After a few moments of silence, she calmed down. Ronna broke the tension with, "It's a good thing we buy tissue boxes in bulk!" Yvonne gave a sheepish grin as she took another tissue. Ronna followed up with, "Are you feeling better?"

Returning to the Adult, Yvonne replied, "Yes, I am. I needed that. I know that you're not really making me the evil one. It just seems so unfair that Hassan is free, rich and happy while I'm bound to the children, poor and so unhappy. Why is it wrong to see the situation as unfair?"

"I notice you've shifted back into the Adult. Nice work, you're showing an increasing level of maturity. I also want to point out that the Child is right: it's unfair and there's nothing wrong with seeing the unfairness of the situation. The problem comes when the Child expects life to be fair. Those expectations lead to disappointment and frustration. Life isn't fair. There are wars, famines and torturing. There are guilty people walking the streets and innocent people in jails. The list goes on and on. The Adult sees this – yes, the Adult sees it – and doesn't expect it to be different.

"In your case, the Adult sees that Hassan is getting the better deal financially. She sees it quite clearly. Then she plans based on this being unfair. Instead of expecting Hassan to pay and then getting into financial trouble when he doesn't, the Adult expects him not to pay and then any money that does arrive is a bonus."

Yvonne reluctantly said, "That makes sense – I just don't like it."

"So how is your liking related to any of this?"

"What do you mean?"

"Remember how we said that when you let anger direct your actions, you're operating from Feel-Act-Regret?" She nodded. "Well, the same is true for liking situations or not liking them. Instead of letting the feeling of like or dislike direct your actions, notice the feeling and then do what makes sense. Can you see how that would work better?"

Yvonne agreed. Then Chris said, "So the goal from the Child was, 'I want Hassan to pay all of the support.' The goal from the Pseudo-Adult was, 'I expect the money to arrive.' What would the Adult say?"

"She would say, 'Be sensible in my spending and budgeting – as if Hassan will not pay.' But that mentions Hassan…"

"That's okay, because it isn't counting on him to change. How does that goal feel?"

"It makes sense," she said reluctantly. Then she started crying again, reaching for another tissue, "But I don't want to say 'No' to myself or my children! I hate saying 'No', I hate seeing the disappointment in their faces, and I hate feeling the disappointment in myself."

"That's the feeling, and if you keep the Child on your podium, then the outcome will be financial disaster. If you want to avoid bankruptcy, then you'll need to take back the podium and call in the Adult when it comes to managing your finances."

"I know."

Chris continued with the next goal, saying, "What does the Adult have to say about the goal of, 'I will respect those who respect me'?"

"The Adult? She says that my behaviour is up to me, and not dependent on how others behave. This one I can see clearly. I don't know if I can do it in the heat of the moment, but I can see that this is what makes sense."

Ronna gently smiled and said, "You won't do it perfectly. There will be times when you lose it: you're an emotional person, after all. When this happens, just apologise and return to the Adult."

"Apologise? To Hassan? Not on your life!"

"Now who's in charge? Who just stepped onto the podium?"

"The Child," answered Yvonne. She paused, and then said, "The Child took over really quickly."

"Yes, when a trigger fires, the Child can jump in before you realise it. That's okay. When you notice that the Child has taken over, just take the podium back."

The session continued with a discussion of the final goal. When the time was over, Yvonne again left with homework: to become aware of when the Child was on the podium and to score how well the child sabotaged any efforts to attain her goals.

* * *

Yvonne returned a week later in tears, "This can't be happening – my week has been terrible. A real week from hell! No matter what I did, the Child was there. I went out and spent a load of money that I don't really have. I didn't do very well at the mediation session, either: I really lost it at Hassan when he told me that he didn't have money to give me for the kid's school stuff. He has the money – he always has money."

Chris and Ronna sat quietly and passed her the box of tissues.

After a few moments, Chris then said, "Nice drama of the Child by the way. What's the score?"

Glaring daggers across the room, Yvonne snapped, "Oh go to hell! I mean…. Oh God, I can't do or say anything… Compared to my week it was only a 6.5."

Ronna responded, "Good awareness. Given the need for drama, the Child often puts everything at a 10 – making it difficult to get an accurate gauge."

"What I'm really worried about is that later this week, Hassan and I meet again for another mediation meeting. I really want this session to go better."

Chris asked, "Define 'better'".

"I want to be able to talk without losing it or crying, and I also want him to agree to pay child support."

Chris smiled and said, "Yep, and I don't want to be bald. I liked the first part of your wants, though: 'I want to be able to talk without losing it or crying.'"

Ronna inserted, "Yvonne, what's the problem with the last part? 'I want him to agree to pay child support'?"

She responded a little unsurely, "Is it the Child wanting things my own way and hoping that he'll change?"

Chris chuckled, "Good guess. Let's talk about Hassan for a moment. Tell us about him: what kind of personality does he have? What kind of behaviours does he have?"

Yvonne pondered this and then said, "Well, he was quiet and diligent at work – although he tended to be lazy around the house. He was more of a disciplinarian with the kids – I tended to let them get away with things. He doesn't frazzle easily like me. He makes promises, but often doesn't follow through with them. The kids are often disappointed: he says he'll do something with them, but then changes his mind or doesn't show up."

She paused to take a breath, and then continued, "He's hard to talk to because all he ever says is, 'That's your perspective' or 'Calm down'. Often I'm not even upset until he says that… Oh, there's the Child criticizing and blaming. I'll stop here."

Ronna said, "Excellent job on the noticing. Where was that on the drama scale?"

Yvonne smiled, "Ah, that was really small! Hardly any mileage on that one, so it's a 2.5 or 3 at most."

We nodded in agreement.

Chris said, "So Hassan is not a man of his word and tends to be lazy except at work. He tends to be the disciplinarian and also isn't an emotional man."

Yvonne agreed, "Yes, that pretty much describes him."

Chris asked quietly, "So if this is Hassan and has always been Hassan, then what makes you think he's going to change just because you're separated and in mediation?"

She started getting teary, so Ronna handed her more tissues. She eventually continued, "I need him to live up to his obligations. It's just not fair. God damn it, there's the Child again! I'm so frustrated with all of this!" She paused, collecting herself. "It's true that I want him to pay his support, but he may not and my options to force him are limited. That's from the Adult."

We congratulated her on her ever-increasing maturity. Ronna then said, "Let's set up a scene to help you in your mediation session. This tool is called The Broken Record. Yvonne, you'll play yourself, and Chris, I'd like you to play Hassan."

Chris started, "Yvonne, I can't afford to pay you the child support."

"Hassan, I know this isn't true: you always have money, and if you'd stop spending money on your new girlfriend and think of your children first, then there wouldn't be a problem."

"Business is really slow and I need to cut back – unlike you who keeps spending even when your business is struggling."

"This has nothing to do with my business. It's about what you're legally required to pay in child support."

"Come on Yvonne, you know that you can't manage your money. If I give you more money, you'll just spend it on something other than the kids."

Yvonne raised her voice, "I want the money you owe! All of it!"

"Like I said, I don't have it. Come on, please don't make a scene."

"You're a liar, and you owe me money."

Chris looked at Ronna and said, "See what I have to put up with?" Then turning back to Yvonne, he added, "Just calm down. Stop getting so excited."

"The children have events coming up and they need the money."

"Okay, I'll see what I can do. I'll come by on Friday."

"For sure this time?"

"I swear this will be a priority."

"I'm not sure this is a good idea, but I'll see you on Friday."

Ronna spoke, "Let's pause here. Yvonne, what did you notice about yourself?"

"I started out strong, but when he said that I'd spend it on myself instead of the children, I felt myself caving in. I began feeling smaller as my voice became louder. When he kept saying that he didn't have the money, I lost it. I get sucked in when I know he's lying. As for him paying on Friday, I gave in. I know he's unreliable and that I'm unlikely to see him on Friday."

Chris rubbed his hands in glee, saying, "I had you all right. I could feel you crumbling and I knew that I had you running in circles." He paused and added more seriously, "Good noticing on the role play."

Ronna said, "Okay Yvonne, Chris and I are going to roll play The Broken Record. This is a tool to use when you need to stand firm on a decision and not get caught up in other people's agenda or their attempts to manipulate you."

Chris began with, "Yvonne, I can't afford to pay you the child support."

"Hassan, the child support is due today."

"Business is really slow and I can't afford it now. I'll pay later."

Ronna stated again, "Hassan, the child support is due today."

"Business is really slow and I need to cut back – unlike you who keeps spending even when your business is struggling."

"Hassan, the child support is due today."

"Come on Yvonne, you know that you can't manage your money. If I give you more money, you'll just spend it on something other than the kids."

Ronna spoke more firmly, "Hassan, the child support is due today."

"Like I said, I don't have it. Come on, please don't make a scene."

Keeping her voice calm and firm, Ronna repeated, "Hassan, the child support is due today."

"Okay, calm down. I'll pay you on Friday. I swear this will be a priority."

"Hassan, the child support is due today."

"All right – just stop being a parrot and talk like an adult. Like I said, I don't have it. Please don't make a scene."

"Hassan, the child support is due today."

Chris sat in silence.

Ronna asked, "Okay Yvonne, what did you notice this time?"

Yvonne sat quietly then said, "You only said one thing over and over again. No matter what he said, you just kept repeating it." She then turned to Chris, "Chris, you must know my husband really well because he would say pretty much the same things as you did. At the end you were silent and didn't say anything."

"Where could I go? What could I say when Ronna kept saying the same thing and didn't respond to any of my attempts to push her buttons or manipulate her? Now in real life, Hassan is likely to get frustrated, yell, swear and end up leaving – slamming a door on the way out."

Ronna said, "Let's put you back in the role play and see what you've learnt."

Chris started again, "Yvonne, I can't afford to pay you the child support."

Yvonne began valiantly, "Hassan, the child support is due today."

"Business is really slow and I need to cut back – unlike you who keeps spending even when your business is struggling."

"Hassan, the child support is due today."

"Business is really slow. If you'd manage your business better, then you'd be better off."

Yvonne's voice started to escalate while she repeated, "Hassan, the child support is due today."

"Come on Yvonne, you know that you can't manage your money. If I give you more money, you'll just spend it on something other than the kids."

Ronna spoke into Yvonne's ear, saying, "Keep your voice calm and firm."

Taking note, Yvonne said, "Hassan, the child support is due today."

"Like I said, I don't have it. Please don't make a scene."

Keeping her voice calm, she repeated, "Hassan, the child support is due today."

"Okay, calm down. I'll pay you Friday. I swear this will be a priority."

Clearly affected, Yvonne slumped her shoulders and said meekly, "Hassan, the child support is due today."

"All right – just stop being a parrot and talk like an adult. Like I said, I don't have it. Please don't make a scene"

Ronna whispered to her again, this time about sitting tall and speaking clearly. She listened, and said, "Hassan, the child support is due today."

Chris sat in silence once more.

Ronna then turned to her and asked, "How was that role play for you?"

"Wow! That was amazing. I didn't know my posture changed when I'm about to cave in. Once I sat up straight and spoke louder, it was like I was serious and he wasn't going to move me. I felt really strong."

"Yes, this is how your anger can be powerful tool." Ronna then paused and added the homework for next visit: to notice how her body reflected who was in charge of her life.

* * *

Yvonne came for her next session two weeks later, and as soon as she walked in, it was clear that she was excited. "I did The Broken Record at the mediation and I held strong. I could feel the pull when he started to push my buttons, but I just kept repeating the phrase. My lawyer said later, 'It looked like you and sounded like you, but that's where the similarities ended. You were great.' Hassan got up and left before the mediation was over. This time he ended up looking the fool." She paused, "I saw how powerful anger can be and how The Broken Record tool really works." She began to cry again, so Chris handed her another box of tissues. She continued, "But I also saw that he isn't going to change. I'm unlikely to ever see a dime from him."

Ronna said, "That's the painful reality. It's good that you're well on your way to accepting that fact."

"You've been talking to me about maturity since I started with the two of you. I think I'm beginning to understand what it means." She paused. "Unfortunately, my maturity won't pay the bills. I really need the money from Hassan – my finances are in a mess."

We continued with the session, and when she left, she was feeling strong – although also still fearful about how to pay her bills.

* * *

Over the next few months, Yvonne came for several more sessions to look at issues regarding her Child and her finances.

At one session, she said, "I'm not sure what to do: I'm lousy at business – my mother was the business person – and I can hardly meet the payroll. Even though I've made advances in maturity, there are still days when I just take money and buy things without thinking about what that's doing to the accounting."

Ronna interjected, "So you're in a career you don't like and don't have the skills to properly manage it. Why's that?"

"I promised my mother that I'd keep running the business. My dad also wants my mom's business to keep going, so I do it for him. It's a way of...getting his...approval... SHIT!!! I'm always trying to please and get approval from someone – my dead mother, my father, Hassan, my kids. I'm so needy sometimes..." She burst into tears once more, and Chris immediately handed her the box of tissues which we kept on hand for her sessions. "I like to shop and buy things. It makes me feel good, and it's a way of rebelling against my mother who was so strict about money."

"Nice awareness."

* * *

Yvonne's contact continued with us on and off over the years. Her maturity continued to progress as she carried on working with her Child. She sold her business and her over-sized, over-mortgaged house, eventually moving to a new city to begin a new life. She never received any support payments from Hassan, but managed to keep herself and her children fed and clothed.

She now celebrates having less drama in her life. She's much more able to meet life as it presents itself – with goals, plans and a sense of inner empowerment. In dealing with her children, she uses tools from Radical Acceptance to be a more effective disciplinarian. As a result, she's able to set reasonable boundaries, make rules, and most importantly strike a balance between the Adult's limit setting and the Child's ability to have fun. She acknowledges and accepts that there will always be a struggle with finances. This has allowed her to put processes in place which limit the time she's able to indulge the Child financially.

Yvonne has effectively embraced the Child archetype while also adding the Adult archetype. This has enabled her to mature and, as a consequence, make more effective decisions that move her toward her goals. She's more at peace, more self-aware, more self-disciplined and more empowered. In other words, she's on the road to an ever-increasing maturity.

11 Mac: Self-Discovery

Mac was a single gay man with no children. He'd been raised in a small town and was the youngest of three brothers and a sister. His mother was Scottish and his father was American, and they'd both moved to Canada before any of their children were born. Mac's father was a dentist, and his mother worked part-time as a seamstress. He described his up-bringing as being very strict: while his parents appeared to the neighbours as bringing up a loving family, behind closed doors things were very different. There were strict rules, and breaking them resulted in severe punishments. Mac remembered lots of those criticisms – and hardly any praises.

When he first came to see us, Mac was in his 40s. He had a two year technical education back in the early 1990s that had opened doors into journalism. Times had gradually changed, however, and he eventually lost his job. Without a BA, he wasn't able to find another position in the field he knew so well. After a while spent on government assistance, he eventually took a course in bar tending and found job at a local sports bar where he'd been working ever since. He first contacted us after a workshop we'd conducted: he'd been particularly struck by the tools of self-discovery, and especially Systems.

"What you said about Systems really spoke to me, because my life isn't working. I'm in a job I hate, and I can't stop spending money which means that I'm always broke and in a lot of debt. It takes me forever to make a decision. I can't seem to find the guts to really enter the gay lifestyle, either. I have one foot in that lifestyle and the other foot running in the opposite direction. My life just sucks."

Ronna started, "You thought the Systems work might help you…"

Mac cut in, "Yeah, I think the Systems work will help me to get my life together so that I can move on. I feel like I'm on a short time line: I'm in my 40s and life just isn't happening. The Systems work sounds like it can unlock my life and get it going. I feel this wild man inside of me who just wants to burst free, but I can't release him."

Ronna said, "Yes, the Systems work might help you to put some pieces together and give you an understanding of why you make the choices that you do…"

Mac cut in again, "Yeah, then I can make the choices that set me free. There's this other side to me that just wants to burst out and do life very differently."

Ronna smiled, "Mac, we need to caution you here. The work that you want to embark on may not give you the results that you're anticipating. It involves making some very painful discoveries about why you're making the choices that you're making. This is very challenging work – unlike any other kind of therapy out there."

Mac took a breath, "I've been in other kinds of therapy and nothing has changed. Actually, my last therapist even fired me because I wouldn't change enough for him! He said I wasn't trying. I did try, but it just didn't last."

Chris inserted, "Yep, that must have been the good old 'Fix It' therapy – we're very familiar with it. Well, I guess from the workshop that you're a little familiar with our style."

Mac laughed, "Yeah, on break someone suggested that you use 2x4 therapy: if you want to drive a point home, then you hit them over the head with a piece of 2x4 lumber! I also noticed that not much gets by either of you. In a funny sort of way, even though I'm scared shitless, I feel very safe with you both. I know that you're going to give it to me straight, without any hidden agendas."

Ronna smiled, "Okay Mac, let's proceed."

Chris summarised, "You're in a job that you hate. You can't stop spending money, and you're in a lot of debt. It's difficult to make decisions. You're gay but can't embrace the lifestyle. In summary, your life sucks."

"Yep, that's it in a nutshell."

Ronna asked, "What's the pay-off for staying in a job that you hate?"

"No pay-off, in fact the pay is the shits. I took the job ten years ago until I could get back into journalism, but I'm still there."

Chris repeated, "The 'pay-off' Ronna was talking about is actually something different. We never do anything if there isn't an internal reward for doing it. It might not be a conscious reward, but the action feeds one of our archetypes or Systems."

"Well, there's no reward for me: I hate my life and I'm here to change it. I mean, I know I can't fix it – I remembered that from the workshop. But I do need to do something differently."

Ronna restated, "There is a pay-off happening. Shall we have a look?"

Mac jumped in, "I'm not sure about this pay-off. How can I possibly benefit from hating my job?"

"What is it about your job that you hate?"

"There's nothing new. I do the same things night after night."

"Well, one pay-off is that you never have to worry about change or failure. You also get to spend huge amounts of time complaining. Since you strike me as a quiet person – not terribly sociable – your job gives you a topic of conversation to use in place of small talk."

"I suppose you're right. There are pay-offs – just not the ones that I want."

"At some level, these are exactly the pay-offs you want. That's why you stay."

"I hear what you're saying, but I'm not sure about it. I still think that I need to get to the core of my problems and fix them. I remember something from one of the exercises we did at the workshop, actually – the one on the inner Child. Maybe this will get to the core of my problems? I discovered that my Child drags his feet and comes up with all kinds of excuses as to why I shouldn't do things. Hell, I sometimes do this for something as simple as cleaning my apartment. If I struggle with that, then I'm going to have real problems finding a new job."

Ronna said, "Good discovery. Let's explore that. How does it fit in with hating your job?"

"Well, I'd like to get back into journalism – but I haven't taken any courses toward a degree or updated my resume in years."

"So you procrastinate about making decisions and getting things done?"

"Yeah, I'm really lazy," he said with disgust.

"I hear your judgement on being lazy, but I said that you procrastinate, not that you were lazy. In fact, you probably work hard at procrastinating."

Mac looked questionably at Ronna, "Hmm, I work hard at being a procrastinator?"

Chris stepped in and asked, "When you see that your apartment needs cleaning, do you just shrug your shoulders and ignore it?"

"No, there's this battle: one side telling me to stop being lazy and that I live like a pig, and the other side just digging in its heels and refusing to start the clean-up."

"That sounds like a lot of work."

"Yeah, I guess you're right."

"From that and what I remember of your story, not only do you work hard, but you're also really good at procrastinating. You're one of the best procrastinators I've ever met, in fact – a real pro!"

Mac added some humour, "I'm glad that I'm good at something. Can I put that on my resume?"

After a chuckle, Ronna said, "What's it like to say yes to being a professional procrastinator?"

"It's right up there with wanting to pluck my nose hairs. I'm trying to focus on my strengths and move forward with those."

"Ah yes, let's put the procrastinator aside for a moment and have a look at your strengths. What are they?"

Mac cautiously searched his mind and tried to come up with the right set, "I'm a hard worker – at least at work. Sometimes I don't even take breaks. I'm honest and my till always balances. I come up with new drinks for the bar and that makes me creative. I'm also personable and know how to engage people, which is a real benefit for the bar."

Chris said, "Nice list. So what's an honest, hard-working, creative, and personable guy like you doing working in a job that he hates?"

"If I just forced myself to do the things that I want to do, then I'd be better off. If I could just take all of my good qualities and boost them, then I could achieve anything."

"Yes, 'Rah, Rah Therapy'. We know that one, too – it's where you pump yourself up to achieve your goals, but then a short while later everything falls apart because you can't sustain it." Chris stood up and jumped up and down, waving his arms as if he was holding pom-poms, pretending to be a cheerleader. He yelled, "You can do it, you can do it, rah, rah, rah. You can do it, you can do it, rah, rah, rah. You have strengths, you are special, I believe in you. You can do it, you can do it, rah, rah, rah. Goooooo Mac!" He sat back down. "Okay, all done. Are you all better now?"

"Okay," Mac said, bemused at Chris' antics. "So my choices of 'Rah, Rah Therapy' and 'Fix it Therapy' don't work. Instead you're suggesting that I stop focusing on my strengths and accept that I'm a professional procrastinator?"

Ronna stepped in, "That's what we're suggesting and, like we said, this therapy isn't for everyone."

Mac pondered, "I've nothing to lose; nothing has worked so far. I'll give this a try."

As the session ended, Chris gave him his homework, "We'd like you to notice your procrastinator and score on a scale of 1 to 10 how well you achieve procrastinator-dom."

* * *

Mac returned a couple of weeks later, "Well, I've discovered that I'm a master of procrastinator-dom. Most days over the past two weeks I've scored between 7.5 and 9 on the scale. The only area in which I seem to really function well is my work."

Ronna said, "You have a strong work ethic, so there would be a minimal amount of procrastinating done there. Tell us more about where you do procrastinate."

"Simple things, really – like cleaning my place, getting to a book I've wanted to read and going out to see friends. I have all of these boxes of stuff that I've collected over the years which need going through. I even wanted to sit down with my resume but didn't."

Chris said, "Well, I suggest that we set a scene for a role play and see what's happening."

Mac looked puzzled, "Set a scene?"

Ronna responded, "Yes, we'll choose some people in your life that may have influenced the patterns of your decisions. In particular, we'll take a look at your Systems around procrastinating by having a look at your family."

"Oh, okay. Let's give it a try."

Chris asked Mac to remember a common family scene. Mac chose to describe a typical family dinner, and as he described what went on at the dining room table, Chris placed pillows around an imaginary table on the floor to represent each of the family members as they were mentioned. The exercise didn't attempt to reproduce the actual seating arrangement, but rather the energetic and emotional seating of the family. At Mac's dinner, his mother sat at the head of the table; he even put her higher off the ground than the others. His three brothers were down on one side of the table, with the youngest of his brothers closest to his mother. His sister sat on the other side, as far away from her mother as possible. At the other end of the table sat his father, facing toward Mac's sister and not looking at his wife.

Chris asked Mac where he sat. After some thought, Mac placed his pillow in the corner, facing the wall. Chris then brought Mac away from the table to look at what he'd created. "What do you see?" asked Chris.

"I see my mother ruling the family, like a queen - like the Queen of Hearts in Alice in Wonderland, in fact, where she might yell 'Off with their heads!' at any time. Everyone was afraid of her; everyone except William, the one closest to her at the table and the one just older than me. He was her favourite. It's not that he was never in trouble, just that he was in trouble much less than the rest of us. He went to school forever and eventually became an actuary."

"What about the other brothers?"

"Charles was the next oldest bother. He was the family clown. He was often in trouble, but was so likeable that no one stayed mad at him for long. He ended up as an engineer. Then came John. He was most like my father, and eventually followed in his footsteps to become a dentist."

"Where did your sister fit in?"

"She worked hard to keep the family together. At birthdays and Christmas, Susan was the one organizing and encouraging the others. My mother made the house look perfect, but Susan gave it a heart. She's now a social worker"

"Tell us about your father."

"He was hard-working and emotionally distant. He was distant with everyone, including my mother. He was also a successful dentist who made a good living."

"Let me review: your mother, Mable, was the family ruler, your father was successful, and your brothers were the baby, the clown and the heir apparent. Finally, your sister was the heart of the family. They all sound like they had clear and defined roles."

Mac looked interested, "Yeah, I guess they did. I never saw it that way before."

"So where did you fit in?"

"I didn't." He paused, and then said reflectively, "This model of my family is very revealing; each person belonged in their set roles, except for me. I never fitted in."

"Right. So far you've listed powerful, successful, playful, nurturing, innocent and heir apparent. Where were the disowned parts of the family? Every family needs to have energetic balance. Where was the anger, the sexual energy, the failure and the disobedience?"

"They were there too. My mother carried the anger and violence, Charles was disobedient, and Susan carried the sexual energy. John could be arrogant, and William could be clingy and whiny. My father was passive."

"That leaves laziness, failure, procrastination and being poor."

Mac took a bow.

Ronna said, "It was important for the health of the family that you were these things."

Mac looked puzzled and said, "Then why did my mother give me such a hard time about being lazy and a procrastinator? Everything she did was successful; she always worked hard and certainly never procrastinated."

"So where did all of her laziness, procrastination and failure energies go?"

"As far as I can tell, she didn't have any; she wouldn't allow them."

"They had to go somewhere. We are all things, so what isn't owned goes into the unconscious and, in families, someone carries it. You were the designated carrier."

"Lucky me," Mac responded with sarcasm.

"So as a child you picked up the lazy, procrastination and failure roles and made a System from them. Any ideas what the System might be?"

"Not sure, how can I know?"

"Look for repetitive behaviours that are causing you problems."

"That's easy, I make plans and set goals, and then fail to act on them. I say that I'll do my resume and look for a new job, but I fail to do anything about either. It must have something to do with my procrastinator."

"Maybe, but did you notice how often you used the word 'fail'?"

"That's true, I used it a lot."

"That would suggest the System is about failure."

Mac thought for a minute before saying, "I'm a failure." He looked at Ronna and added, "That works. I'm the family failure. They've all succeeded and I've failed at everything I do."

Chris said, "I welcome Mr. Failure. You're always welcome here."

Mac's eyes grew a little misty. "You say that, but failure isn't welcome."

"Maybe not in your home, but here, in the centre of Radical Acceptance, failure is very much welcome. And, Mac, I know failure – it's not as core to me as it is to you, but it's a part of me. If I know and accept it in myself, how can I judge it in you?"

"I guess." He paused. "You said earlier that I can't fix this. So what do I do? My life isn't working. I need to do something."

Chris reflected, "You said that your life isn't working, but I see it working very well. For a life based on failure, it's hard to imagine it working any better."

Mac looked frustrated, "But it's not working in the way that I want it to work. I want a new job, I want to explore my gay side more, and I want to do many other things – but instead, I fail to do any of them."

"And how does your inability to do those things make you feel?"

"Frustrated and like a failure."

"And being a failure is bad?"

"Of course it is," he responded angrily.

"So you're fighting your System. That's doomed. You can't fight your System, because it'll win every time. You can, however, accept it. Then it can serve you."

Mac left with his homework – to have a look at how his System could serve him.

* * *

On Mac's next visit, he began by saying, "I'm not sure how the System of failure serves me. All it seems to do is make me miserable." He then started sharing some difficulties that he was having with his friend, Harry. Harry had invited him to a party in the gay neighbourhood and Mac, being Mac, left deciding to the last minute and then declined to go. He was a failure – even at going to an event that he might enjoy.

Harry was furious and had sent him a few nasty emails. Mac said, "Harry is always pressuring me to make decisions quickly. He calls incessantly asking what I'm going to do. I tell him that I don't know yet, and then I get another phone call or email. I might have gone with him, but he kept calling and calling. I find it very difficult to deal with people who are pressuring me."

Chris stated, "So your way of dealing with pressure or conflict is to become passive aggressive?"

"He's the one who's way too aggressive and demanding. I refuse to do things his way."

Ronna picked up on Chris' use of the passive aggressive idea, "So you refuse passively instead of being open and honest."

"Well, he never listens, so I get the message across another way."

Putting aside the issue of passive aggression for a moment, Ronna asked, "Have you told him how you feel?"

"Whenever I start talking about how I feel, he gets all defensive."

Ronna suggested, "Mac, please come and sit across from Chris. Chris, I'd like you to pretend to be Harry. Mac, I'd like you to begin by telling Harry how you're feeling. In this exercise, you'll be using a tool which we call 'I Statements' – a tool designed to help communicate feelings."

After we'd explained the tool in a little more detail, Mac took a breath, settling himself into the role, and then said, "Harry, I'm feeling like you're trying to control me and force me into making decisions that I'm not ready to make. I feel like you never listen to me that and that you often have your own agenda."

Ronna said, "Mac, I've yet to hear a feeling from you. This is all about what Harry does. Let's begin again, but this time tell Harry how you're feeling."

Mac, "I'm feeling…hmm. I'm feeling angry that you're controlling…"

Ronna cut him off, "You're feeling angry. Good. I cut you off – do you know why?"

"Because I began talking about Harry?"

"Yes, I Statements are about you, not Harry."

Looking down, Mac said, "Okay, so I'm angry."

"Just a minute, Mac. Take a breath. Is anger really what you're feeling? You don't look angry and you're not speaking angrily."

"Have I ever told you how much I hate talking about my feelings? They always get me into trouble and I never know what to say."

"This can be challenging for some folks. Let's take things step by step. Are you feeling anger – or perhaps another feeling?"

Mac sat for a while, attempting to come to grips with his feelings, "You're right, it's not anger: it's fear. I get fearful and anxious about being in public or being around a lot of people. At least, I'm like that when I'm not behind the bar!"

Ronna repeated back, "You feel anxious and afraid about being in public or when you're around a lot of people."

"Yeah, I didn't know that before. I'd just make up flimsy excuses and not go – feeling annoyed rather than afraid."

"Good work. Now talk to Harry again, this time telling him of your anxiety with the I Statements."

Mac attempted to look at 'Harry', but his eyes fell to the floor. "Harry, I'm feeling anxious about being around a lot of people. I don't know whether I want to go to the party or not."

'Harry' responded in a hearty voice, "Nothing to be anxious about, you'll know a few people there and there are always new people to meet. It's no big deal. How about we meet at nine o'clock at the bar for a couple of drinks before heading over to the party?"

Mac looked at Ronna, not sure what to do with this response, "That's exactly what he'd do. I say something and he steamrollers right over the top of me. I don't know what to say."

"Right. Now just tell him how you feel. This time look at him as you're speaking, too."

Mac shifted his weight in the chair and looked at Harry as he said, "I'm feeling…unheard. Yes, I'm feeling unheard. I said that I was feeling anxious about being around people…"

'Harry' cut him off, saying, "Yeah, I heard that and I'm telling you that you have nothing to be anxious about."

Mac was getting steamed, "Harry, whether I have anything to be anxious about or not isn't the issue. The issue is that I do feel anxious and so I'm not sure that I'll go with you."

Ronna applauded his response by saying, "Nicely done, Mac. You were firm and you re-enforced your feeling without blaming."

'Harry' pressed on, "Okay, so you're feeling anxious. I get that, but I want to know if you're going to give in to your anxiety or not. I need an answer soon so that I can make plans."

Mac sat for a minute and then said, "I'm feeling pressured into making a decision. If you need an answer now, then my answer is 'No, I won't go to the party'. If you're willing to wait until Saturday, the day of the party, then it could be a 'Yes' depending on how my anxiety is doing."

'Harry' responded, "Well I think it's a pretty silly thing, this anxiety stuff. Just do it anyway is my answer, but I'll wait until Saturday."

"Okay. I'll call you by two o'clock and let you know."

Mac turned to Ronna, saying, "Wow, that was different. I felt strong and knew that what I was saying was right for me. I didn't have to cave in and agree to anything."

"Or become passive aggressive."

Coming out of his role as Harry, Chris added, "I could feel you getting ready to cave in a couple of times and I thought that I had you." He paused and added, "Harry doesn't get it, but he had to respect your firm response."

"I know that leaving things to the last minute is rude and inconsiderate, though."

Chris gave a fake cough.

"Okay, it's passive aggressive – but my anxiety is such that giving him an answer at the very beginning would have meant finding an excuse not to go."

Chris asked, "Are those bad things – being rude, inconsiderate or passive aggressive?"

"Let's just say that they're not my finer qualities. I wouldn't ever brag about them, for instance. However, I suspect that when I move through the layers of accepting that I'm anxious, rude, inconsiderate and passive aggressive, this acceptance will open up new areas of my life."

"Today you shared your feelings openly. You didn't blame, and you stood strong in who you are.

"Hmm, yes. I befriended being anxious and felt stronger because of that. This stuff is crazy, but it works."

Chris said, "Once you discovered your anxiety, you didn't have to hide from it any more Now anxiety can be a gift instead of something shameful."

"Mac, I think that over the next little while, you're going to discover much more about your fears and anxieties. Once you're open to these, you can build a new relationship with them. It doesn't mean that they're going to go away, but when they're present in your life, you'll have the possibility of making new choices."

* * *

In a later visit, Mac spoke to us about being gay and how difficult it had been to embrace more of the gay lifestyle. Ronna asked, "Are you ashamed of being gay?"

"I've looked at that…but I don't think so. It doesn't feel like shame."

"How about fear?"

"I looked at that too, and while there's some fear, there isn't enough to hold me back."

Ronna asked, "How many people know that you're gay?"

"A few, very few. None of my family know, for instance. Only a handful of gay people know, and that's all."

"Tell us more about not wanting your family to know."

Mac sat quietly, "My family is pretty traditional and judgemental"

"How often do you see your family?"

"I don't see my siblings a lot; we're spread out all over the continent. While I'm fairly close to one of my brothers, I'm afraid of losing what we have. I try and see my parents every couple of weeks to help them out around the house and do some chores which they can no longer do."

Chris asked, "And what would their response be if you told them?"

"My mother would probably yell and tell me – yet again – how much of a disappointment I am to her. I'm the youngest, and she didn't want any more children – she's told me that often enough. My father would give me one of his looks and be uncomfortable around me from then on. My sister would be okay, but the other brothers would shake their heads and probably make some gay jokes to hide their awkwardness."

"That sounds like a pretty intimidating force to take on."

"Yes, and that's why I keep putting it off. It's part of the whole procrastinator-dom."

Chris added, "It goes even deeper than that, as 'I'm a failure' is certainly playing out here. You've failed as a son and a brother."

Mac took a breath, "I guess that's true. I try so hard to fit in and not rock any boats."

Ronna observed, "Yes, that's clear. How are your attempts to not rock boats working out for you?"

"Well, they keep the boat from sinking. They give me what little there is."

"Little of what?"

"Love and respect," Mac said quietly.

"How much do you get?"

Mac just sat and stared at Ronna for a long time. Quietly, almost mumbling, he answered, "2%."

Ronna asked, "So you hold back who you are for 2% love and respect? The wild man gets penned in for 2%?"

Mac nodded, unable to speak. We let Mac sit, breathing that in. When he seemed ready, Chris asked, "Mac, I'd like to explain something to you about energy. Are you up to taking more in right now?"

"Yes, I'd like to understand more."

Ronna started talking as Chris grabbed the flip chart, "This information is loosely taken from Carolyn Myss' book, 'Anatomy of the Spirit'."

Chris began with marker in hand, and drew what was supposed to look like a stick man. Ronna and Mac laughed, and Mac said, "Good thing you don't try to make a living as an artist!"

"Very funny you two, but let's stay focused, shall we?" Chris retorted with humoured sarcasm. He next drew lines pointing toward the figure's head. "Let's say that we start with 100 units of energy a day. How do you spend that energy? There are many ways of spending it. One of the more common ways it is to focus our thoughts on past events. In your case, Mac, thoughts about not having done the dishes last night might draw away 18 units of your energy." He drew lines (cords) of energy leaving the body. Continuing to draw lines, Chris continued, "Then you have 30 units of energy going out because you're remembering an argument with a co-worker. 22 units of energy are going out to thoughts about hating your job. 12 units are going out to the cookie you didn't get when you were three years old. Then…"

Mac laughed and inserted, "I hope you have lots of paper there for all these units of energy I use every day, because it's certainly more than 100."

Chris turned. "Right, that's my point. Right now you're spending 82 units and we've just begun the list. You're spending way more than 100 units. What do you think happens when you exceed 100?"

Now puzzled, Mac said with more humour, "I roll over and die?"

Ronna replied seriously, "Energetically, that's exactly what happens."

Mac sat up, "So I'm dead?"

Chris said, "Well, my friend, how long do you think you can live off of bankrupted energy without it having emotional, physical and energetic consequences?"

Mac said, "Part of the procrastinating is… I just don't have any energy reserves left to do the things that I want to do. The wild man can't make an entrance because there isn't any energy for him to use."

"And you keep making choices which deplete your energy reserves in order to sustain the System of 'I'm a failure.'"

"Christ…I even fail at dying. I'm the walking dead." He thought for a bit and then asked, "How is this related to my weight?"

"What do you mean?"

"'I've always struggled with my weight, but as I look back now, I see that the more dead I became, the more I weighed. Do you have any thoughts on that?"

"There are a couple of things about weight that are relevant to you. The first regards exercise – being dead takes away your energy for exercise. Secondly, people who are living on bankruptcy often try to fill up the hole left by the depleted energy. They might eat, use drugs or collect things – ideas, friends or almost anything else. Whatever they feel might fill the hole."

"Thanks, I'll ponder those ideas. I can see how both of them act out in me – not only in terms of food, but in collecting as well.

We nodded and gave Mac his homework: to notice what percentage of his energy is getting used each day on thoughts and regrets. We also asked him to be aware of the 2% love and respect that he's getting from his family.

* * *

Mac returned in a few weeks. "I'm so dead – scoring well over 100 units most days. Reflecting on the whole dead idea, I became so aware of how dead I really am. I've been dead for at least 15 years, but I'm sure it goes back even further than that." He took a breath, "I know you're going to tell me to accept this, but I'm struggling here between being depressed and being angry. I want to fight this, stop these patterns and get my energy back so that I can do the things which I want to."

Chris asked, "Mac, you've been fighting this for years. How's that going? Are you any closer to winning the battle?" Mac shook his head. "If you fight this you'll lose: it's only acceptance that will eventually open up some choices."

Mac was starting to become a bit more agitated, "I know, damn it. I thought about changing therapies again to focus on the positive, but I've done that before. While I gained some insight into myself, it didn't really change anything. I don't want to waste any more time. I've already wasted so many years."

Ronna added, "And you're dead."

"I'm flipping between being angry and wanting to burst into tears. I'm either dead or a failure. That's all I see in my life."

Ronna smiled, "This is wonderful."

Mac turned to Chris, "Is she for real? I'm dead and a failure and she says that this is wonderful!"

Chris replied, "Yeah, we're a little twisted that way. We celebrate death, anger, grief, fear and depression. Actually, there's not too much I can think of that we don't celebrate."

"Great, just great. 'Rah, Rah Therapy' is beginning to look pretty good right now."

Ronna gave him his homework: to watch death and failure and to continue scoring how well he worked to sustain them.

* * *

Mac called a few times over the next few months to check in. He reported that there wasn't much news on the death and failure themes, but that he was continuing to be aware of his choices and was scoring them accordingly. Occasionally he would break the mould and get out with his friends to do something he enjoyed. Eventually, he came in for a visit.

"No matter where I look in my life, I still see failure. If there's a way of failing at something, I'll find it. I'm a writer and I want to start a small business, but I've done nothing about it. I want to spend more time in the gay community, but I don't. I buy things and leave them in their packages for months. There are books I want to read, but I don't get around to even starting them. I have boxes of stuff that needs to be thrown out...and the list goes on and on. I fail to do most things – and if you say 'That's wonderful' again, I'll lose it!"

Instead, Chris said, "Mac, you're dead and a failure. What do you expect?"

"Expect, expect...shit, I don't know!!! Sometimes I can accept this and just watch it, and at other times I just want to scream. That doesn't count the times when I just want to pull the covers over my head, either. I found out this week that I have to move in three months because my landlord is tearing down the building. I think I need a plan."

Ronna said, "Yes, a plan. But what good is a plan since you won't follow it?"

Sitting with a most disgruntled look on his face, Mac said, "You're right, I won't follow it. It's like I'm this childish rebel, but the only person getting hurt is me! It doesn't hurt my family – they just roll their eyes and move on with their rosy lives. My friends just nod and help me where they can, but they're limited in what I let them do. It's only myself that I'm hurting."

"This is true. Failure after failure and leading a dead life only affect you."

Mac then left – saying that he already knew his homework and that he'd get in contact again when he needed some help.

* * *

He came by a few months later. "I've moved into a new apartment. On the failure scale, that process was a 3-4. I did procrastinate a little, but I was pleased that I was able to start noticing the procrastination and make some new choices. I also made some new discoveries along the way. I do this internal battle to get anything done, for example. One side of me wants me to do something, and the other side doesn't. At the beginning, the side that doesn't is bigger and more powerful, so I don't do anything. Then, as a deadline approaches, the side that wants me to act gets stronger. At some point – usually right at the last moment – that side wins and I do what needs to be done. With the apartment, I found a place at the last moment and packed at the last moment, but in the end, everything was done. You said earlier that this trait had pay-offs for me. I've discovered that it really does. If I leave finding an apartment to the last minute, for example, then I don't have to decide on an apartment – I just take whatever's left. Having discovered that means that I spend less time and energy fighting myself when there's something that needs to be done, freeing up more of my energy for other things."

Ronna asked, "That sounds like an interesting discovery. How do you feel about it?"

"It makes sense and explains why my life has gone as it has. I'm always going to struggle with doing things, as the failure System will always be around. However, being able to watch and observe this is beginning to open up some choices for me. Although...I do see that it's never going to be easy, and that the issue isn't ever going to go away."

Chris said, "Good awareness: we'd now like to welcome you into the Honourable Society of Royal Failures."

Mac smiled and said, "Can I be President?"

Chris smiled and responded, "We'll flip for it."

* * *

Mac returned again a few months later. "I've made some progress in starting my writing business. I took a trip with a writer friend to the States and we began doing some research into different writing styles. We're now off to Europe in a few weeks to meet with more writers. Having another person involved in my plans means that I get more done. Another discovery! Next I plan to... No, I'm not going to go there just yet. Right now, I've paid for my ticket to Europe. If I try to plan too far ahead, then it sets up my failure System, so I've learnt to stay with the current issues in my life. That's another discovery: I deal best with life as it happens."

Ronna said, "Those both sound like important discoveries."

"Oh, I almost forgot. I also told my family that I'm gay. We were all gathered for my niece's birthday, and later in the evening when the kids were in bed, we were sitting around the fire outside having a couple of drinks. I just took deep breath and let it out. Having discovered that I function best by focussing on the present moment, I didn't plan on telling them. I just allowed the right time to come along, and it did."

Ronna sat up with anticipation, "And...?"

Mac smiled, "Everything was cool. Charles looked at John and said, 'I told you so.' My parents just nodded and my sister and the brother who I'm closest to came over and gave me hugs. I think it's hard on my parents, but I didn't get the negative reaction I anticipated, so that was good. I discovered that my fears around my family are mostly in my head. I'm not really as much of the family outcast as I thought." He paused, "Here's a cute story. A few weeks after that family event, I was with a woman friend and took her by my parent's place as I had to pick up some writing papers that I'd forgotten. I introduced her and we left.

"Shortly after, I received a call from my brother William. He said that he'd heard from Mom that I was with a woman and that maybe I wasn't gay after all. We had a laugh – and I mean a real laugh. It felt so good not to be mired in all the past shit."

Chris nodded and smiled, "Hmm, everything has shifted for you. You aren't the same man who came to see us a few years back."

Mac laughed, "I've never worked so damned hard in all my life… who'd have thought that being dead, a procrastinator and a failure could be such hard work?! Or that discovering that I'm all of these things could be so liberating?!"

* * *

It was a while before Mac visited again. When he did, he started by saying, "I've often spoken of my financial issues – but now I'm in a real mess and just need some impartial ears."

Ronna said, "Okay, mine are getting a little old. However, Chris' are even older, so you'd better chat with me."

We all laughed, but Mac soon returned to being serious, saying, "I've discovered that I reward myself by spending money. When I realised this, I sat back to look at things financially and saw that I'm barely meeting my obligations. I need to figure out how to manage this. Failure is getting a lot of mileage from these financial difficulties, but for the most part, I'm just able to observe and notice failure's chatter. Sometimes it grabs me, but I'm doing okay. I'm coasting at between a 1 and a 4."

Chris asked, "What are your thoughts around the financial troubles?"

Mac said, "I anticipated that question and came prepared. Spending more than I have feeds the failure System nicely. The Adult tells me to be responsible, pay my debt off and start saving – after all, I'm almost 50 and have nothing to show for it."

We said in unison, "Good noticing."

"However, I'm way over my head in debt and am not going anywhere but further down into the hole. The interest payments prevent me from getting ahead. I'm actually trying to avoid claiming bankruptcy!"

Ronna asked, "What are your beliefs around claiming bankruptcy?"

"Hmm, bankruptcy is for weak, irresponsible people who are looking for a way out of being responsible."

Chris said, "Sure you don't want to line them up and have them shot at dawn?"

Mac grinned and replied, "Well, you did ask me. I notice that I don't sugar coat things any more I'm no longer looking for approval."

Again we laughed, and Ronna added, "We've created a monster!"

Mac continued, "I've already used the Attachment Tool. I know that I'm weak and irresponsible with money and a whole lot of other things. This is where I've become stuck, though. I don't know where to go from here."

Ronna said, "Keep going: you're doing a fine job of running this session so far!"

"I keep coming back to the idea that I have to be responsible for what I've created."

"And your belief is that you won't be responsible if you claim bankruptcy?'

"Yes, I see it as an easy way out."

Chris asked, "So what about the seven years you'll sit with no credit rating – not being able to purchase large ticket items and paying higher interest rates? And what about the years of having to rebuild everything and learning how to live within your means? Don't those involve responsibility?"

Mac sat and thought for a moment, "I didn't look at it from that point of view."

"You have two choices, and what you do is going to hurt either way: you can come up with a budget that works and pay your debt off, or you can claim bankruptcy and re-build everything from there. Either decision is going to involve consequences and responsibility. What's important is that you truly look at your beliefs and discard the ones which aren't working. Let's get together next week and see how you're getting on."

* * *

Mac arrived and said, "I discovered a number of beliefs and saw that they belonged to various people – my parents mostly, and also one from an uncle. They were all garbage. Bankruptcy seems to be a viable option, but I'm not ready to make the decision yet."

Ronna asked, "Are you okay with putting off the decision?"

"Yes, I am. It takes time for me to make decisions, and that's just part of who I am. I'm not going to change, right?" he asked with a gleam in his eyes.

* * *

Mac emailed us a few months later to say that he had his first appointment with the bankruptcy lawyers coming up – and had only scored a three on his failure scale over the whole issue. He'd finally decided that it was time to shed the weight of his debt. In the process, he'd discovered that he could make choices: choices which weren't forced by circumstances. On a parallel note, he also lost a significant amount of weight and gave up many of the items that he used to collect. All in all, it had been a huge process of letting go.

Over the course of his journey of Radical Acceptance, Mac discovered a lot of very painful patterns and traits about himself. His journey of discovery had led him on a wild and rocky road. These days he's taking a few more risks – letting his wild man out on occasion and generally feeling much more content with his life. There's also equanimity in his world; he has the ability to feel all of his emotions deeply and without judgement Does he regret the journey? "Hell no," he recently told us, "I can't wait to see what I'll discover next."

12 Anthony: Self-Acceptance

We first met Anthony a few years back. He'd led an interesting life: he was now a responsible single dad who had his own construction business, but he'd previously been a violent, drug dealing, law breaking individual. He was also a recovering addict, and had been clean of all drugs and alcohol for the past eight years. As part of his recovery, he'd become deeply committed to a twelve step fellowship program. By following those twelve steps diligently, he'd forged a new life for himself – and was now a well-known sponsor and speaker for the program. His life had hit a hit a road block, though, which is why he came to see us.

When he arrived, we asked him to give us a little more background on his situation. He began by saying, "I'm an addict. I've done all kinds of drugs, but mainly crack and cocaine. I also dealt, making – and spending – over six figures a year. I've done many things that I'm not proud of and spent more than one night in jail. When this was my life, I wasn't a nice person. Not many people would willingly get onto my bad side.

"Now I've been straight and clean for eight years, making $30-40K in my construction business and supporting my several children who are aged between five and thirty. I work 10-12 hours a day, follow the laws of the land, and go to my twelve step fellowship program several times a week. I've done a lot of personal growth work with that program; I've accepted that I'm an addict, and I'm working on my recovery. My new life is on track, and I've totally left my old life behind. I should be on top of the world, but I'm feeling … I'm not sure what I'm feeling … It's like I just…exist."

Chris responded, "That was quite the opening speech."

"Yes, in the twelve step fellowship we're encouraged not to hide behind our histories. Sometimes I just get on a roll."

Chris chuckled and said, "No problem. I hear that you've worked very hard and are feeling stuck… Feeling as if you're just existing."

"That's it, yes. I just go through life without ever feeling much excitement or zing."

Ronna asked, "Could you be depressed?"

"No, I'm not depressed: I know depression, and this is different. I just don't have any oomph."

Chris took up the questions, "You say you accept that you're an addict?"

"Yes. That's the first step of the twelve steps."

"I'd suggest that you haven't really accepted this at all."

Initially looking as if he might walk out, Anthony replied, "How else could I have stopped using? I first had to accept that I was an addict. If I hadn't done that, then I'd still be hustling on the streets and beating the crap out of anyone who annoyed me. You're a nice guy, but if you'd said something like that to me before I'd accepted my addiction and cleaned up my life, I don't want to think about what might have happened…"

Chris continued, "Let's have a look at Acceptance. How has being an addict served you?"

"Served me? It ruined everything in my life and almost killed me. It didn't serve me at all."

Chris mused, "I see. Well you must, at least, be grateful for being an addict?"

"Grateful? Man, are you crazy? You try living the life of an addict and see how grateful you are."

"Oh, so being an addict is bad?"

"I heard good things about the two of you, but I'm not impressed so far. Of course being an addict is bad!"

"So, being an addict yourself means that you're bad?"

Getting frustrated, Anthony said, "I told you when I arrived: I'm in recovery and I've been clean for eight years." Proudly, he added, "I've fought the addiction and won."

"Once an addict, always an addict. That's what I've heard," Chris replied.

"Yes," Anthony paused, "But there's a big difference between being an active user and being in recovery."

"So when you actively use, you're an addict. When you're in recovery, you're an addict – but not really an addict. Is anyone else confused here?"

Anthony ground his teeth. "You have to live it to understand it."

"Apparently," Chris replied dryly. "But I approach life differently from you: I'm not interested in cute evasions of the truth. You, Anthony, are an addict. You're just as much of an addict now as you were eight years ago."

Anthony grew still more defensive, "You're full of shit. You don't know what I was like back then, and you hardly even know me today."

Ronna entered the fray, "I'm going to guess that you're still using three different drugs." Anthony glared and looked ready to prove Ronna wrong. She continued, "They're caffeine, nicotine and adrenaline – the three drugs of choice for 'recovering' addicts." She then looked Anthony in the eye and asked, "Do you smoke?" Anthony's posture slumped a bit and he nodded. "Do you drink more than two regular coffees a day – and are those coffees heavy in sugar?" Anthony slumped a little further and nodded again.

"And finally, adrenaline. You're here because the drama of being clean is wearing off and you're hoping that we can give you your next adrenaline high."

Anthony looked a little shell-shocked. "What are you two? Some kind of therapy tag team?" He paused for a few moments before saying, "You're right, of course. I was really proud of the work that I'd done, but I was so focused on the illegal drugs and alcohol that I'd completely missed the other addictions. This drops me into a new layer of being an addict. I feel like a defensive fool."

Ronna continued, "Does this awareness change the work that you've done?" Anthony shook his head. "Then remain proud of everything that you've accomplished. We can see how hard you've worked and what a good job you've done of accepting the addict – at least as far as you went."

"But pride is one of the great pitfalls of recovery – especially pride in recovery itself."

"Does pride stop you from being cautious with your addiction?"

He pondered that one for a few seconds, and then said, "I guess not, but pride can lead to forgetfulness…"

Chris picked up on his words, "We'd say, 'When pride replaces self-acceptance, then old problems re-emerge." He paused and then continued, "Anthony, accepting your addiction is a life-long, ever-deepening process."

Anthony nodded and said, "Yes, it's a huge evil sitting inside me – waiting to jump out and take over my life if I let down my guard."

"So you're a huge evil being?"

"What? Where did that come from?"

"Anthony, you're the addict. It isn't some thing inside you. You've split yourself into 'good' Anthony and 'bad' addiction; this evil beast living within you."

"Yes, that's what it is, 'The Beast'."

"No, it's you – it can't be The Beast, because it's not separate from you. You are Anthony, and Anthony's The Beast."

He looked shattered and tried to deny this revelation, "No! If it's me, then how do I fight it?"

"Why do you fight it?" Anthony looked confused. "Fighting is the opposite of accepting."

"I'm struggling here. In the twelve step fellowship, we're really discouraged from going outside of the collective and getting involved with other therapies. Now I see why: you two just don't understand. After all, you aren't addicts."

Ronna said, "So you feel that you have to choose one type of therapy over another?"

"Yes, the twelve step fellowship gave me my life back – and now I'm learning new things here which question the very foundations of that recovery."

"So, it's either the twelve step fellowship or Radical Acceptance? There's no room for both?"

"Yes. How else can it be?"

Chris said, "You have a choice to make, then: find a way to have both; return to the twelve step fellowship and forget this discussion; or leave your twelve step fellowship and come over here to the dark side." He paused. "And by the way, the third option's out. We won't accept you as a client if you're choosing Radical Acceptance over twelve step."

Anthony looked to Ronna who nodded in agreement. "Then I guess this is it. I won't say that I understand all of this because I don't, but I will say that it's been a conversation which I'm not likely to forget."

* * *

We didn't hear from Anthony for three months. When he came back, he started talking the moment he sat down, "I've come to eat humble pie. You guys were right, but you already knew that, didn't you?" We shrugged and nodded. "I went back to the twelve step fellowship and I could hear your voices in my head. At first I was angry at the fellowship and thought that the whole twelve step thing was wrong. Then I remembered how you wouldn't accept me as a client if I chose Radical Acceptance over the twelve step ideas. I've got to tell you: you not accepting me because of that choice floored me more than anything else you said. That's why I kept going to meetings – and finally came to see that the steps weren't the problem, but how our groups have twisted them."

Ronna asked, "Please tell us more about that."

"It's like you said: we talk about acceptance and then make addiction this evil thing which we have to fight."

Chris said, "We have a saying, 'What you fight, wins. What you accept, serves you.'"

Anthony looked amazed, "Of course. I've been fighting this addiction, but all it did was find other ways of expressing itself."

"You fell into a common trap: you sought to fix instead of accept. Those two things are exact opposites. Whenever you seek to fix, change, heal, transform, transcend or make any other attempt to have an aspect of yourself go away, you've stopped accepting and started fighting your discovery. Radical Acceptance invites you to stop fighting."

"Yeah, I hear that and it makes a lot of sense. To be totally honest, though, I also have this other voice saying, 'If you stop fighting, you'll be back using'. That's why I still resist accepting."

Ronna stepped in, "In our experience, fighting it is far more likely to result in relapse."

Anthony looked truly interested, "How so?"

"When you accept, you plan for relapses: you tell yourself things like, 'I'm an addict, so this trip to the bar may be a mistake.' More importantly, if you think that you've successfully fought your addiction, then you're far more likely to ignore the signs of a pending relapse. To see the signs would mean that you'd failed in your fight."

"Yeah, I see that all the time – guys saying, 'Hey, I'm no longer an addict, I can stop going to meetings and doing the program.' Sure enough, they're all back later after a major relapse." He reflected, "So accepting doesn't mean growing complacent – it means becoming aware?"

Chris spoke, "Yes, but that's only the first part of acceptance." Anthony groaned. "The next part is to see how being an addict serves you and to be grateful for being an addict."

"That's right, you mentioned this the last time – but I still don't get it. My addiction has been the biggest problem in my life, so how can I be grateful for it?"

"But Anthony, it isn't the biggest problem; nowhere close. It's just a symptom."

"I'm sceptical. In fact, I'd call you full of shit – except that the last time you made outrageous statements, you were right."

Ronna took up the dialogue. "Here's a generalization. It's not always true, but in your case, it probably is: 'Big, bad men are little, hurting boys at heart. The bigger and badder the man, the more the little boy is hurting inside'."

Anthony looked stunned – and then, without warning, big, bad Anthony broke down in tears. As he sobbed, Chris moved beside him and began quietly speaking as if he was Anthony's parent, "Such a beautiful little boy. I love this boy of mine." His sobs increased. "I even love him when he's sad." Chris kept speaking and comforting.

The sobbing finally ended, and Anthony said, "My father never told me that he loved me or that he was proud of me when I was little. He told me that men were tough; that crying made a man weak. I believed him and wouldn't even let my Mom comfort me because of that belief. It feels like these tears today were all the years of hurt and betrayal revealing themselves at last."

Ronna said, "When it's not safe for a little boy to be sensitive, he puts up a tough front to hide from the shame of his emotions."

Anthony dried his face and blew his nose, "So this is what my addiction protected me from?"

"Yes."

Hopefully, he asked, "Does this mean that if I focus on my little boy, my addictions will go away?" We waited. "I know: once an addict, always an addict."

Chris moved back to his chair and said, "I'd prefer to say that the patterns of your personality are now integral parts of who you are. They're all part of the wonder that is Anthony."

"The wonder of me; I like the sound of that. I think I'm beginning to see what you mean. This addiction has been a real gift. I wasn't ready to handle the little boy and his feelings, and being a violent drug dealer and drug user was much safer than being with the hurt and grieving little boy. After joining a twelve step fellowship, being caught up in recovery kept me busy – so I still didn't have to feel the grief of the little boy. I guess the little boy wanted to be heard, though. That's why I had those feelings of discontent." He reflected and added, "I see now my other addictions to coffee, sugar, cigarettes, work, adrenaline and the twelve step fellowship. Should I do work to stop these, too?"

"Is acting addictively a bad thing?"

"Of course… Well…I'm not sure. I've never considered that. Certainly being a violent drug dealer and user is a bad thing."

Ronna asked quietly, "What if there are no good or bad things? What if being all of those things was just Anthony being Anthony?"

"But I hurt people – people I was supposed to care about."

"So you didn't like the outcomes?"

"No. But even more than that, what I was doing was wrong."

"It was your attempt to cope."

A few tears rolled down Anthony's face. "Since getting clean, I've hated that time of my life. Now I can see that I've hated myself – that I hate myself even now." He reflected, "So now I get to stop hating myself. That feels really nice."

Chris smiled and said, "Anthony, my guess would be that hating yourself is part of a System – one which says, 'I'm bad.' This System is part of the wonder of Anthony, too. Jumping from trying to fix the addict to trying to fix the self-hater is still fixing, not acceptance."

"My head's spinning."

Ronna said, "Yes, I'm sure it is. Let's end the session here – but before you go, I want you to begin scoring your self-hater. If you do something that expresses the hate a small amount, then score a 1. Equally, returning to the streets on crack would be a 10. At the end of the day, review your choices and score how well you've managed to hate yourself. The higher the score, the prouder you can feel. Pat yourself on the back and congratulate yourself for a job well done – the job of self-hating."

Anthony looked at us with amazement and said, "You guys are twisted." We just smiled.

* * *

Anthony came back three weeks later. Ronna asked, "How successful have you been at hating yourself?"

Anthony laughed, "That's the damnedest thing. As soon as hating myself was okay, I was able to make some different choices: I'm only using one teaspoon of sugar in my coffee now, and on good days, I'm only drinking two cups. I'm also watching the self-hater smoke, and can sometimes decrease how much I'm smoking while at other times watching myself increase it. I'm really making different choices around doing self-hating things. They didn't go away entirely, but the best I was able to score was a 4."

"So where are you on the acceptance scale with regard to self-hatred?"

"Hmm, overall I'm about an 8. Although I didn't score that high in self-hating, I could see all the ways I do little things. Similarly, I'd want to do something and could then choose not to – whereas in the past, I'd have just done it. Being aware made that choice so much easier to see."

"Yes, it's called Acceptance. When you don't accept then it's 'bad', and so you work to hide it from yourself."

"That's really powerful. Maybe you guys aren't as twisted as I thought." Chris smiled and Anthony said, "I'm learning to hate that grin." Sensing that something else was coming, he asked, "What?"

Chris replied, "I was just going to ask you how self-hatred serves you."

"Before our last visit I'd have thought you were joking. Now I know that you're not." He reflected on the question. "When I was an addict, I believed that I was bad and that gave me permission to be really bad. In recovery, I'm driven me to prove this wrong – making me work harder to be good."

"Sounds like something to be grateful for."

Anthony sighed. "You're asking me to throw out every idea and belief that I've ever had."

Ronna asked, "How does the idea of discarding those beliefs feel, Anthony?"

His eyes started brimming with tears as he said, "It's fucking scary is what it is. I don't know which way is up any more – nothing is right or wrong, good or bad. I'm being grateful for hating myself and no longer trying to fix myself. It's like I don't have any familiar places inside of myself any more."

* * *

Anthony continued seeing us on and off over the next several months. His acceptance of his addiction and self-hater grew over this time. On one particular visit, he talked about having difficulty with people taking advantage of him – in particular taking advantage of his time and his home.

"My sister, Emma, has a problem with drugs. She's not as bad as I was, but she has trouble holding down a job and my parents don't want her living with them any more so I took her in. Half the time she doesn't pay her rent or take care of her responsibilities."

Chris asked, "This surprises you?"

"No, I can see all of the addictive behaviours. I just don't know what to do about it. I'm concerned that my son is watching it all."

"Seems like a reasonable concern."

"But she's my sister."

"Yes, she's your sister. And?"

"God damn it, I don't want to kick her out. I just don't like playing the heavy any more."

"Who said anything about wanting or liking?"

"So know I get the tough love speech?"

Ronna said, "Nope, no speeches – you can give that speech to yourself later as you know it much better than I do. Instead, we'd like you to do a Child/Adult exercise on gathering information for a decision about your sister." First we gave him an explanation of the Child and Adult archetypes and then, giving him a piece of blank paper, Ronna said, "At the top of the page, put the event, "Emma Living at my House," and then divide the page in half. On the left hand side is what the Child has to say about Emma, and on the right hand side are the responses of the Adult to the Child's issues. Complete the sheet over the next week, and then we'll discuss it when you come back."

* * *

When Anthony returned a week later, his sheet looked like this:

Emma Living at my House

Child	Adult
You can't kick her out – then she won't like you	Being liked is nice, but it's not always the best basis for a decision
Think about what the family will say	The family will have plenty to say, but this is my son and my house
Her addiction will get worse and it'll be your fault	Sorry, I know too much about the addiction world to buy that one: she's responsible for her own recovery, not me
She's a help with my young son, and that saves on babysitting costs	That may be so, but I also have real concerns over what my son's being exposed to
The older kids did okay, and they saw you doing all kinds of things	They might be doing okay, but they saw things which they never should have seen.

Anthony then explained, "I hated doing that damn worksheet: it made my decision too clear. Before doing it, I could pretend to be confused – but now I know what I have to do and my Child doesn't like it. I think he's still trying to get the love from his family that he never received as a boy. I could see the hooks in wanting to be liked, having my family proud of me and not wanting to deal with the next family drama. Besides, when she pays her rent it reduces my living costs.

"Last night I went to my parents and told them that I'll be asking her to leave at the end of the month. They weren't pleased, but it didn't turn into a major drama because I remembered The Broken Record technique which you guys spoke about a few weeks back. When I kept on repeating one, simple message, it didn't take long before they understood my perspective. Tonight I plan on talking to Emma about the situation. It won't be easy, but I know that it has to be done; she has to live her own life. If that life involves recovery, then I can help her to find a good program and introduce her to some eligible sponsors. If it doesn't, then I can meet her somewhere other than at my house."

Chris responded, "It's impressive how you've worked this around the Wheel and accepted what you need to do. You've even looked at the possible consequences of your plan. I also notice that you're less black and white in your thinking; there's more grey in your decisions. A few months ago, you would have written her off completely or continued to put up with the dysfunction. Now you're willing to see her, even if she's using, outside of your house."

"Thanks for pointing that out." He paused, "Having to accept that she's responsible for her own life is another big step for me. It's helped me to realise that I can't save everybody."

"That sounds like a painful acceptance."

"I expected it to be more painful than it was – but I found out that the more I accept that I can't be fixed, the easier it is to allow others their brokenness. Actually, I've been wondering about that: on one hand you speak about the wonder of Anthony, and on the other hand about accepting that I can't be fixed. In construction, things that need fixing are things that are broken. How can I be broken and the wonder of Anthony as well?"

Chris replied, "All human beings are broken – and being broken is one of the marvels of being human. Some of us are more broken than others, but we find our humanity and compassion not in perfection, but in this brokenness."

* * *

Anthony came back a few months later. Emma had left after their conversation, refusing his help and ending up living on the streets. As he explained, "She was furious and tried every kind of manipulation to get me to change my mind. She threatened to tell my secrets, to report me to child protective services – the whole gamut. I just kept repeating the line, 'As long as you're using drugs, you're not welcome in my house.' She denied that she had any problems with drugs – and also said that recovery was my scene: if I wanted to follow some stupid agenda then I was welcome to it, but it had nothing to do with her."

Ronna observed, "It must have been difficult to stand strong."

"Damn straight. I could feel myself wanting to argue and defend myself, especially when she threatened to call child protective services. The Broken Record really is a really amazing tool of communication, though." He paused and then added, "I want to change the subject.

"I first came to see you because it felt like I was just existing. After months of work, I'm now back in this place. I've been doing my work and I've grown a lot from what you two have taught me, but I can't shake this feeling of just existing – just going through the motions of life without being fully engaged in it. I work so hard at being a different guy, a nice guy and a compassionate guy, but it doesn't change this feeling of just existing."

Chris asked, "Hmm, where's your dark and violent side, Mr. Nice?"

"Dead and gone, thank God."

Ronna countered with, "Right, just what we thought."

"Oh no, don't even think of going there. There's no way I'm going there." We could see that Anthony was beginning to panic.

In spite of his distress, Chris kept the tag team going, "What happens to the aspects of ourselves which we push down and don't accept?"

"I accept him, really I do. Now can we change the subject?" He tried to smile, but failed, "That version of me was an asshole – angry, vengeful and sometimes violent. I was an insensitive son of a bitch."

"Yep, I see that you have a good awareness of him," Chris continued, "But where's his energy?"

"I DO NOT want his energy around!" Anthony retorted.

"I hear your anger and see your fear."

"You don't understand. You met me after; you didn't KNOW me as Tony. That's what everyone called me then."

"We don't have to know him to understand that you've suppressed his energy so that he doesn't have a voice."

Anthony glared at Chris and said, "When you said my life was going to fall apart and change, I never thought that you'd be asking to bring him out again. I don't want to hurt those that I love."

Chris responded, "Hold on, hold on: I'm not saying that I want you to become violent or break laws again. It's his energy that we're interested in."

Ronna continued Chris' thought, "Anthony, when you push down vital pieces of who you are, you cut off your life source. You've judged Tony as bad, wrong and dark and Anthony as right, good and light. Think of the energy that you're using to keep Tony at bay."

Anthony asked, "And the problem with that is?"

Chris said, "The problem is the price you're paying. He holds the key to your zest for life."

Anthony sighed. "If I let him in, my life will fall apart again. Everything will change, and I won't be sure of who I am any more. I'm worried about people not liking me, causing family problems and all the old shit that started my journey many years ago. I'm so confused right now. I don't even know where to start. I want my family to be proud of me…"

"So how do you try and get them to be proud of you?"

"I'm helpful and nice. I do all kinds of chores around my parent's house. In fact, I often put aside other priorities when my mother asks me to do things. It's funny – when I come by the house to visit, she always has chores for me to do. I'm often there longer than I meant to be, and often the chores aren't that important. Sometimes they're even ones that my father could have done."

"A couple of times I've said 'No', but then my mother gets this look of disappointment – and I cave in and do it anyway."

Chris took another track, "Anthony, how does a boy become a man?"

"I used to think that it meant being tough and strong. Now I see that all I did was push the boy down; I remained a boy with this big, tough outer shell. Then I thought that being a man was about being compassionate and helpful, so I helped everyone except myself. That didn't make me a man, either. The truth is, I have no idea how a boy becomes a man."

"In his book 'Iron John', Robert Blye tells a fairy tale in which a wild man was captured and put in a cage. One day, a young Prince was playing with a golden ball when the ball accidentally fell into the cage. The Prince approached the cage and asked for his ball back. The wild man would only give the ball back if the Prince would first set him free. 'Where's the key?' asked the boy, 'Under your mother's pillow. You must steal it from there,' answered the wild man." Chris paused. "Anthony, you've put Tony into a cage. You must steal the key from under your mother's pillow to become a man. Stealing the key means setting the wild man free, and that can only happen once the wild man has been accepted. In your case, the wild man is Tony: not the Tony who's violent and tough, but the Tony who's fierce, strong and powerful. Accept Tony and set him free. That includes stealing the key from your mother."

"How about I just ask her for it?"

"No, it must be stolen; she'll never just give you the key if you only ask. A boy asking for the key will always remain a boy. The man must steal the key. Many cultures have rituals assisting the transition from boy to man. In many of these traditions, the boy is stolen away from the tribe's women by the tribe's men. Here in the West, we often talk about 'cutting the apron strings' – not untying them, but cutting them. In other words, a boy must break with his mother in order to become a man."

"I'm not sure what any of this means. I cut all ties with my family back in my drug using days, so how can I separate myself from my mother again?"

"You've never cut the apron strings, though. In the first instance, you took the strings and tied them to drugs. The second time, you tied them to the twelve step fellowship. You've never actually cut them." Chris paused, and Ronna remained silent – knowing this was best done man to man. "In Radical Acceptance, maturity means taking up your life. We use the analogy of the orchestra to explain this: growing up is taking back the podium from the Child. So, I invite you to steal the key, cut the apron strings or take back the podium. Use whatever metaphor works best for you. In the end, this will mean embracing Tony and bringing his energy back into your life."

"Then what? How does a man behave? What does he do?"

"Those are all questions asked by the pseudo-Adult – the Child pretending to be the Adult. The man doesn't look to anyone else for answers; he forges his life based on who he is, not on images of who the Child thinks he's supposed to be."

"Who am I?"

"Finding that out comes from Acceptance. So far, you know that you're a self-hating addict. You're also much more than that, of course. What else would you list?"

"I care about people – or is that the Child trying to be nice?"

"Let your actions speak. You care about people."

"I avoid conflict. This isn't an attribute of a man. For that matter, neither is addiction."

"The Child seeks to be 'right'. A man just accepts who he is: you avoid conflict and you're an addict." Chris paused then asked, "What else?"

"I'm hard working, and I do good work. Sometimes my crew call me controlling and I guess I am – but I'm also proud to deliver high-quality work. Pride also seems to be part of me." He thought again for a few moments, "And I work hard to be nice."

"Working hard to be nice and accepting what you actually are – they're two different things. The Child needs to act nice and be liked. The man doesn't. It isn't that the man seeks to be nasty, as that would be just as much from the Child (as you've already seen). Instead, the man acts based on what he knows to be the appropriate thing to do. Whether that is nice or likeable is secondary."

"Like when I asked Emma to leave."

"Exactly."

Ronna spoke into the silence. "Anthony, niceness is another aspect of you: it's a side of you that opens the door to relationships. Tony holds your zest and your power, though."

"I'm not able to say yes to this yet, but I'll consider it."

* * *

It was few a months before Anthony came back for another session. "Since I took the 'key' back from my mother, I can see both sides of myself beginning to merge together."

Ronna asked, "Please tell us more about that."

"I could see where I was really caught up in trying to live my life to please others – and how this was a way of compensating for all the havoc I'd created in my family. In trying to please people, I was being a little boy by constantly wanting their approval – and especially my mother's approval. I now see that I'm on my own journey, and that I need to accept all of myself to make this journey work. I can't deny that I'm a little concerned about letting my dark side out, but I think that I've done enough work to know that I'll never revert to being the person I was back then. I need him, however – because he's able to do the tough stuff. With Emma, he had the hard heart when he needed to… That's it, isn't it? I can use him – use his energy – to get the difficult jobs done, and then complement this with Mr. Nice so that I'm doing these actions with compassion and sensitivity."

"Yes, this is what we've been suggesting to you."

Anthony said with a laugh, "Well, you could've just come out and said so!"

Chris responded, "I think we did – a few times in fact – but it means nothing until you get the discovery and then accept it. " He paused and asked, "How did you take back the key?"

"It didn't happen all at once. It started with me asking a good friend to describe me. He described Tony. I told him that that's how I used to be, but since getting clean I'd suppressed that side. He burst out laughing, saying 'It may have been hidden from you, but it was pretty clear to those of us who know you well.'" Shaking his head, Anthony added, "So much for that fantasy."

Chris said while chuckling, "Yep, any time you want to know something about yourself, just ask a close friend, partner, a family member or your kids. It just has to be someone who's willing to be honest and not give you any platitudes. They'll be more than happy to supply the list that you think you're carefully keeping hidden. But tell me, if Tony makes you unlovable and your friends see Tony and they love you…"

Anthony reflected before saying, "The belief that Tony makes me unlovable is false – like all the other lies that I've been telling myself."

"But we digress: please continue with your story of how you stole back the key," Ronna interrupted.

"So, I opened my eyes and realised that Tony is alive and well. When I knew this, I decided to stop trying to be nice." He chuckled and added, "I didn't turn into an evil bastard. In fact, not much changed at all. I began by deciding to stop trying so hard to please my family, and especially my mother. The stealing of the key happened during an innocent visit to my parent's house. My mother asked me to do something: something that I'd have done without question in the past. This time I refused, though. I was legitimately busy, and I wasn't willing to change my plans and disappoint others just because my mother asked me to do something. Then I watched what happened next."

He broke from his story-telling to say, "I used the Observer that you guys talk about." Then he continued, "I watched as my mother looked disappointed, and then suddenly saw that 'look' as her trying to manipulate me into doing what she wanted. It didn't matter to her that I had other plans – all she cared about was getting me to do what she wanted. It was like she was asking me to prove my devotion to her. I looked back over our relationship and saw how that was our pattern. In that moment, I knew that

I'd stolen the key." He paused and said reflectively, "It wasn't a big production, and there was certainly no drama. It was just a quiet realization that I was no longer tied to my mother. At that moment, Tony and Anthony became one."

We were all quiet for a while, reflecting on Anthony's story. Ronna spoke first, "Anthony, this is what it's like to have and live with real inner power. Once we can accept the many aspects of ourselves, we no longer give our power to others and we no longer need to have power over others. We realise that real power comes in accepting everything in both ourselves and other people. A big piece of that acceptance is the merging of our violent and our compassionate sides."

Anthony nodded, "These days I find that I have a lot more energy. I'm feeling much more in touch with life, and far less like I just exist. I observe and interact with everything very differently. I'm still integrating this 'dark' side of myself – although I don't see it as being dark any more. I can feel Tony's energy, and I sometimes even enter dialogue with him about certain decisions. He has a lot of wisdom; I just have to be watchful about how he wants to protect me or how he wants to get his message across. My crew have been getting a bit more anger from me over the past few months, but I apologise and we move on. Some of them are watching my changes with amusement as I talk about my archetypes and make fun of myself. It helps to lighten the situation."

Chris said, "Wow! We celebrate the work that you're doing, Anthony. Your drive to know and accept yourself is boundless."

13 Amanda: Principles

We met Amanda about ten years ago. She was a social worker at the time, and had married, bought the house and the two cars and given birth to her two children. She and her husband, Joe, both had careers, and everything was as it should be.

Then, one day, Joe announced that he was leaving Amanda for Pam – a woman she thought was her best friend – and her life fell apart. She felt hurt, angry and afraid of being alone. She also felt deeply betrayed – not only by Joe and Pam, but by life in general. She had followed the rules: the rules she believed would keep her life safe and stable. Now she was angry that life had let her down: angry and scared of having to do everything on her own.

Here were some of the rules that she tried to live by:

1. You work hard day in and day out – because this is what you do
2. You deal with any conflict that arises either superficially or by pushing it aside – because conflict is too unsettling
3. Sex is something to be given to your husband – because that is what wives do
4. You don't ask for intimacy in a marriage – because that will rock the boat

She came to see us in the hope that we could make her fear and anger go away. After she'd finished telling her story and we'd helped her to define her rules, Ronna said, "I don't know about making them go away, but we can help you to learn from them. We can use the fear and anger to help you grow. Are you interested in personal growth?"

"I have a sister who's been into personal growth for a long time. She keeps asking if I'm interested. I say yes, but then I keep putting her off when she suggests something specific. Maybe this is my wake-up call. Maybe the bitch that Joe's with now actually did me a favour."

Amanda was on a roll, and we could see her heating up. Before she went too far, Chris said, "Before you verbally thrash Pam, let's have a look at how Radical Acceptance works. Is that okay, or do you need more thrashing time?"

Amanda looked a little stunned. No one had given her permission to be angry before. After thinking for a bit, she replied, "I guess I was getting angry, and anger is bad."

"Is that another rule that you've tried to live by? Maybe we could look at some principles instead. Principles are more flexible than rules."

Amanda looked sceptical. "I'm really not an angry person. In fact, other than some frustration with my children, this is the first time that I've been angry in a long time. I really don't like it. Will these principles turn me into an angry bitch?"

"Principles are guidelines on how you want to live your life. They're an intention for how to act and a plan for when you miss your goals."

"I don't understand."

"Here's an example. 'I'll feel each feeling fully and I'll use those feelings to guide me in my journey of personal discovery. When I miss – when I realise that I've stuffed a feeling down – I'll revisit the feeling to use it for growth.' This principle changes the focus from rejecting a feeling into using it for growth."

"That sounds good, but as I said, I'm not really an angry person so I'm not sure if it's relevant."

"Okay, but you're angry at Pam now, so let's see how we can use that for personal growth. This will give you first-hand experience on what to do should you ever happen to get angry again."

We took Amanda on a trip around the Wheel and explained Radical Acceptance in general. She initially argued that this wasn't what she'd learned in social work school and was somewhat sceptical to proceed, but after a short discussion, she agreed to give it a try.

The Event was her husband leaving. Next was Feel & Accept - Amanda was swimming in her feelings. She was overwhelmed, and wasn't sleeping or eating. She said, "I feel so hurt and betrayed. Pam was my friend; I can't believe that she would do this to me! The bitch ruined my family – she has no morals or values. I hate her". Amanda went on at length about her lousy friend. Her anger was no longer something she could deny. To work with this, we suggested that she do some anger processing using the Projection Tool.

As we explained, the first step of the Projection Tool is to describe the event. Amanda had already done this in some detail. The next step is to list any judgements made. She had no problem in describing the many judgements she had against Pam: the woman was a family-wrecking bitch who cared for no one but herself. The next step, condensing those many judgements into a single one, took her a little longer. Eventually, she settled on 'bitch'. When we moved to the final step – discovering how

Amanda was similar to Pam. There was dead silence…and then an abrupt denial:

"I'm not the bitch here. I didn't sleep with someone's husband and ruin their marriage. I'm a good and compassionate person. I'm a social worker!"

"Hmm, you're sounding pretty bitchy right now," Ronna observed.

"I'm upset. It's her fault that I'm feeling so angry now."

Chris added with a hint of sarcasm, "Yes, and your judgements of Pam are not at all bitchy."

Amanda started to cry, "All right, so I'm feeling bitchy. But…"

Ronna cut her off, "Let's just pause here and breathe that in, 'I'm a bitch.'"

Amanda reluctantly took a breath, and we had her repeat the phrase a couple of times.

"So you're no different from Pam."

"I am. I didn't wreck a marriage. I may get angry and judgemental, but I don't wreck marriages."

Chris said, "Oh, so in your mind there are levels of being a bitch? It's okay to be an angry and judgemental bitch, but it's not okay to be an adulteress?"

Amanda smirked and said, "Well, if you put it that way, then I guess I can see your point."

We encouraged her to take home what she'd learned. As homework, we asked her to watch for the bitch acting out in her life. She could then use the Scoring Tool to record how good at being a bitch she was.

* * *

Amanda returned the following week. After settling in, Ronna asked, "So, tell us how your homework went: what did you discover about your bitch?"

"Well, this is kind of embarrassing and amazing at the same time – I scored a general 8.5 for the week. I thought some pretty hateful thoughts toward Pam. I can give the cold shoulder pretty well too, and I can hold a grudge. At work I demand a lot from my co-workers, and I know that they don't appreciate it. Also, when I don't get my own way, I go quiet, barely saying a word to anyone. I had no idea what I was doing and the effect I was having." Tears were now rolling down her face.

We paused, handed her a tissue and allowed her time to take in the full impact of her awareness.

"Okay, well this is good," she eventually continued. "This week was really hard, but now I know what I have to change. Can you help me do whatever it takes to get rid of that side of me?"

We chuckled, and Chris said, "That side of you is called the bitch – and why would you want to get rid of her?"

"Well, look at all the problems she causes! Of course I need to change."

Ronna asked, "Before deciding to get rid of her, ask yourself, 'How does the bitch serve me?'"

"Serve me?! She serves me by causing problems in my relationships with my children and my co-workers."

"Yep, she certainly can do those things when she acts in the midst of heated feelings. Then she's reacting instead of consciously choosing her actions."

Amanda agreed, "Yeah, when she's angry she comes out swinging."

Chris asked, "Oh, so she fights to protect you?"

"Protect me?"

Ronna took up Amanda's question, "Yes, she sees something that you won't deal with and so she comes out swinging and screaming. That distracts you from having to confront the issue at hand."

We could see the wheels turning, so we waited. Amanda finally said, "I get angry or bitchy when I'm feeling out of control or overwhelmed. So you're saying that she comes in to protect me from that?"

"Yes, she protects you by being bitchy so you can focus on what a terrible person you are. That's much safer than confronting the issues which had you feeling out of control and overwhelmed – in this case relating to your marriage."

"Wow, I can see how she moves in when I don't deal with things, but I don't want her dealing with things in the way that she does. She's too destructive."

Ronna responded, "Well, imagine being ignored, unappreciated and stuffed down. How refined would you be?"

Amanda laughed, "Okay, okay, I get it. So if I get to know her more and let her out more, she'll become more refined."

Chris responded, "The bitch is very powerful: the more you get to know her, the more choices you'll have in your bitchy behaviour. There will be times when your bitch will be a gift to you, and there will be times when she's destructive. The choice is yours. That brings us back to principles, actually. Remember, the principle I gave last week? Its intention was to use your feelings to bring about awareness. Reluctantly, you've done that – you've discovered your bitch. You might now wish to consider another principle, one that says, 'When I have a feeling, I'll feel it but not act in the heat of my emotions. I'll first wait until they've been discharged with the discovery step tools. Once the feeling is discharged, I'll make a plan and only then will I act. When I do react, I'll apologise for things which have been said and done in the heat of the moment."

"Run that one by me again, please?"

"You'll feel the emotion without acting on it. In other words, you'll get angry without yelling and without stuffing it down. You'll just feel it."

"I don't understand – feeling my anger is to get bitchy."

"You've merged two very different things into one. Anger is just a feeling – an entirely inward experience. Getting bitchy, on the other hand, is an outward action which is based on choices that you've made."

"It doesn't feel like a choice."

"That's the feeling. When you get angry at your children, do you lock them in a closet and leave them there for hours on end?"

"Of course not, that would be cruel."

"So you choose not to lock them in a closet." It was a statement, not a question. We watched as understanding dawned on her.

"Since I'm choosing not to lock them in a closet," she said slowly, "I can choose not to yell."

"Yes, except yelling is your normal response, so choosing an alternative response will be more difficult than not locking your children in a closet. You need a principle and the self-discipline to follow that principle. Notice that the principle doesn't say 'Don't get angry', as well. Its intention is that you not act in the heat of feelings, and that when you do, to go back and apologise."

Ronna added, "Not acting isn't about getting rid of the bitch. You need a powerful bitch, as she gets things done, is able to set boundaries, and protects when you're feeling unsafe – like a she-bear. Being powerful, though, doesn't mean that she gets to spew angry actions all over the place. Over time, you'll learn how to speak firmly and compassionately instead of flying off the handle. Additionally, the more you accept your bitch, the less you'll judge bitchiness when you see it in others."

Amanda agreed, "Even as you say that I'm starting to feel less judgemental – but I'm not all the way there yet."

"It's too soon, but Pam's a good enemy, and some day you will thank her for what she has given you."

"I'm going to thank her for sleeping with my husband and ruining my marriage? I don't think so."

Chris replied, "If you continue your work, you will undoubtedly come to that place – but as Ronna said, it's too soon for that."

Ronna concluded, "You've made good progress this week. Let's continue with the same theme next week. In the meantime, remember the two principles and watch for opportunities to practice them."

* * *

Amanda arrived next week fuming at her husband. She'd barely sat down before she started speaking. "I can't believe the nerve of that man: he's asking me to sign a bank loan! I originally said no, but then he started his sweet talking and I can see myself beginning to cave. The bitch came out a couple of times – you're right that I need her in my life – but I couldn't sustain it. That man is a conniving manipulator. He knows how to push my buttons, and when he does, it's like my bitch just deflates: I can't sustain the anger, and then he gets what he wants from me. I was able to delay the decision, but I'll sign the loan unless you two can save me from myself."

Chris jumped in, "Well done. You brought out the bitch to help you in standing firm. However, I notice that you're not using the first principle that we gave you." Amanda looked questioningly. "You're judging Joe for being manipulative, but you're not doing the processing work."

"Yeah, you're right. In fact, I don't want to let go of the judgement If I do, then I may not have the anger to stand up to him."

"But as you said, the anger isn't enough. recognise the manipulator in yourself, and you're less likely to be manipulated. We can then help you stand firm."

We spent some time helping Amanda to claim her manipulator by using the tools of the Discovery and Integrate & Accept steps. Then we moved on to the Plan step.

Ronna asked, "What are you going to do about the loan?"

"Knowing that I'm a manipulator doesn't change my decision. I'm not going to get involved."

Chris asked, "Based on what principle?"

"No principle. I just don't want to do it."

"Without a principle, how do you know if this choice is in alignment with how you wish to live your life?"

She looked puzzled. "I've never given much thought to how I want to run my life."

"Sure you have: we helped you to list your rules when we first met you. If you're going to follow those rules, then you'll sign the loan – after all, one of your rules was to avoid conflict."

"That's a dumb rule, so it's time to throw that one out. From now on, I'm going to take on conflict. I'm going to put the bitch to use!"

Ronna jumped in, "Is that consistent with who you are? Are you the type of person who welcomes conflict?"

"When I feel all angry and pumped, it feels like I'd welcome conflict – but when I step back from that, then no, I'm not that type of person. Actually, conflict terrifies me."

"Nice noticing. So your principle will need to address both the bitch and the part of yourself that's scared of conflict."

Amanda suggested with a grin, "How about I take on conflict when I'm angry and avoid it when I feel terrified?" We waited. "I know – that's based on feelings and not what's the right thing to do." She sighed. "Having a principle means thinking about the situation and making a decision. Rules are much simpler. With a rule, you don't have to think or decide what's appropriate. You just follow the rule or find some way around it if following it's too scary. Either way, it doesn't require a decision – you just let the Child take over." We waited again as she thought about the principle. "I won't seek conflict, but when there's an issue that needs me to take a stand, then I won't avoid conflict, either."

Chris said, "Nice one. That honours who you are and the times when conflict may be necessary. What's the rest of your principle?" Amanda looked confused, so Chris continued. "A principle has two parts: the intention, which you've covered, and the plan for when you miss, because you're not going to get the principle right every time."

"This is really hard."

"It's not that hard, but it's new. What would 'missing' look like?"

"It could be when I should have taken a stand but didn't."

" 'Should'? You're shoulding on yourself."

"Shoulding?"

"It's a play on words to suggest the shit you dump on yourself when using the word should."

"What's wrong with 'should'?"

"There are no 'shoulds'. You're perfectly free to act any which way, except for the inner restrictions that you place on yourself. We're talking about a process of moving from those inner, unconscious restrictions to a life lived by conscious outcomes and principles – which is very different from letting 'shoulds' dominate. How would the outcome differ between taking a stand and avoiding the conflict?"

She thought for a bit, "If I take a stand, then I'm able to get my point heard. When I avoid conflict, I tend to agree – even when I don't really agree."

Ronna asked, "How does it feel to agree when you don't really agree?"

"I end up feeling violated."

"Returning to Chris' point, then, the difference is feeling violated versus being heard. So how would you express that in your principle?"

"When I feel violated, I can ask myself what I agreed to when I didn't really agree. Then, if it's a point that I wish to be heard on, I'll return and make my point."

"Excellent. How does that feel?"

"Freeing, incredibly freeing. It gives me something to work with without being another heavy rule that I have to try and follow. It also gives me a way of knowing when I've missed."

"Yes, now feeling violated is a gift. It tells you that you've missed on the principle."

"Wow," Amanda said shaking her head, "I'd always hated that feeling."

Chris then spoke, "Where does the loan fit? Is it something that you want to take a stand on?"

With a firm voice, Amanda said, "Yes!"

"What would taking a stand look like for you?"

Her shoulders fell, "I don't know. That's the problem. He knows how to push my buttons and I end up agreeing even when I try to take a stand."

We spent some time leading Amanda through the Broken Record exercise – helping her to script the one, simple sentence to repeat and then teaching her to sit up and deliver it firmly. When she successfully stood up to Joe in the role play, she was amazed, "Wow! That was amazing. I didn't know that my posture changed when I'm caving in. Once I sat up straight and spoke louder, it was like I was serious and he wasn't going to move me. I felt really strong. I think the bitch helps out here. Is this the gift that you were talking about?"

"Yes, this is how the bitch can be powerful." Ronna paused and then added, "Now, to get back to not wanting to make your husband angry or upset."

"I know, I know, Social Work 101 – you're not responsible for other people's feelings. His reactions are his, and his feelings are his."

Chris said, "Good!"

"This wouldn't be happening if my so-called friend, Pam, didn't mess everything up."

Chris said reflectively, "Amanda, we find it interesting that all the blame is on Pam. Did she seduce Joe by holding a gun to his head?"

"No, but he said that he probably wouldn't have had the affair if she hadn't kept coming on to him."

"Oh, so he had no choice but to say yes to her advances?"

Amanda reflected, "Well, I don't know... I didn't think about that. He's always so nice and easy going."

"So nice and easy going that he couldn't put up a boundary or walk away?"

"Hmm, well... Geeze this is hard! I just don't know."

Ronna responded, "'I don't know' means 'I don't want to know'. So what don't you want to know?"

"I don't want to know that my husband is to blame too."

Chris asked, "Why would that be difficult for you?"

"Then I'd have to have a really serious look at my marriage. It's easier to blame her."

"Good awareness. I want you to think about that. Your homework is to have a look at the marriage."

"Damn, I knew that you were going to say that."

* * *

When Amanda came for her next session, she was very excited, "I did The Broken Record with Joe. I was able to keep my focus and speak clearly, and boy did he react all over the place! When he was yelling at me, I just kept remembering Ronna and he left in a huff and…"

Ronna interrupted, "Amanda, Amanda, take a breath."

"Oh yeah, breathe!" Amanda took one short breath and then motored on, "And not only that, but for the first time, I could see how he's to blame for our marriage not working. I'm so angry at him for what he's done. How dare he do this to me? He broke our marriage vows and humiliated me with family and friends. Now everyone knows: we had plans and dreams and he broke them all. What really pisses me off is that I can see what a jerk and an asshole he is – and those things bring me back to me seeing my bitch and arrrrgh I can't even have the satisfaction of being angry at him!"

We said in unison, "BREATHE, Amanda!!!"

Amanda took a couple of longer breaths, and eventually her energy calmed down. Finally she said, "As I was thinking over this past week – thinking about being angry – I was wondering: what are my principles? I don't know what they are. I know what my parents' are and that Joe doesn't have any, but I don't have a clue what mine are!"

"So, let's talk about your principles. Tell us which ones you have."

"I guess one of my principles is that I treat each person with dignity and respect."

Chris asked, "And when you fall down on that?"

A little defensively, Amanda said, "I don't. I treat everyone that way because that's the way I'd like to be treated." We sat in silence. "Come on! I do! God damn it. Now I suppose that you're going to ask me how and when I don't treat people with respect and dignity?"

Ronna turned to Chris and said, "Hey, she catches on quickly!"

Amanda slumped. "Man I hate this work – it just takes everything away." We again sat quietly waiting. "Great! Just great! You didn't deny it. Okay, I see where I can be disrespectful, especially with some of my co-workers. So it's not a principle if I fall down? Then what is a principle? I don't understand."

Chris asked, "Where did you get that idea? In fact, we said exactly the opposite: a principle knows that you will miss. That's why I asked what your plans are for when you fall down."

"So you mean that I don't have to use my principles perfectly?"

"Not only do you not have to use them perfectly, you can't use them perfectly because you're human and in your humanness, you make mistakes. Thank goodness for that."

"Oh okay, I can see that. I can breathe now." She paused to collect her thoughts, "So one of my principles is that I treat each person with dignity and respect. And when I mess up I apologise?"

Ronna agreed, "Sounds like a good place to start."

Amanda took a breath. Then she switched topics. "When I was thinking about my principles and my recent discoveries, I realised that I've blamed Pam and Joe for my marriage falling apart. Now I'm beginning to see that I too had a part in it not working."

Chris said, "Okay, continue pondering that. Your homework is to continue to explore your principles as well as having a look at how you also contributed to your marriage's failure."

* * *

Amanda arrived for her next session looking down. She sat quietly for a bit, and then tears started rolling down her cheeks as she said, "No wonder he left me for another woman. I was a cold, distant, angry bitch. I was either screaming at him or screaming at the kids. I hardly ever wanted to make love. I was so tired all the time with work, running the kids all over the place, taking care of the house, getting meals, lunches, laundry and shopping. I just took everything for granted. I let the one most important thing slide – my relationship. It was so much easier to blame Pam and Joe. Blaming them means that confronting my role doesn't hurt as badly. I can now see how I controlled so much that I had no energy left for him. I really betrayed him sexually. There just wasn't enough of me to go around. My to-do lists just kept growing so that I wouldn't have to be sexual or be in a relationship. I was cold and in my own world. I now see clearly that I'm a betrayer."

Ronna said calmly, "That's quite the discovery. It must have been very painful."

Amanda nodded, "This is very painful to accept. I was much happier blaming them for the problems. Now it I see that the affair was my fault."

"Hmm, it's gone from 100% their fault to 100% your fault?"

"Well, wouldn't you leave me too if I did all those things?"

"So the marriage failing is 100% your fault – and your husband has no responsibility in it?"

"That's what I'm working to accept."

Chris responded, "Yes, we see that – but you can only accept what's yours. You can't accept what belongs to Joe."

"Okay, but if I drove him away, then I see that as my fault."

Seeming to change the subject, Chris asked, "You've been doing work on your principles. What are they?"

"I've been writing them down here in my journal." Amanda opened her journal and started to read, "Well, my first one still stands:

1. I treat people with dignity and respect

2. I work hard and am responsible

3. I don't seek conflict, and when I need to take a stand, I won't avoid conflict

4. I won't be in another relationship with someone who isn't going to do their own individual work and take ownership of their own issues"

Ronna asked, "How does it feel to have a set of principles to guide your life?"

"It feels clear, because if – I mean when – I fall down, then I have something to come back to."

Chris asked thoughtfully, "So I'm curious: where does it say, 'I'm responsible for my husband's actions'?"

"I guess it doesn't." She paused and then added, "No, nowhere is that in my principles. I don't ever want it in my principles, either."

Ronna agreed, "Being responsible for your own actions will keep you busy enough. Let others be responsible for what they do."

* * *

We continued to meet Amanda on and off over the next several months. She grew in so many areas of her life, adding new principles as new situations arose. She also explored what it meant to be a strong independent woman – and even started dating, having first developed a nice set of principles about a possible partner. As part of this principle development, she explored her sexuality; she eventually realised that her lack of sexual energy in her marriage had more to do with the marriage than it did with her natural sexuality. She realised that she was a strong, sexual woman and that being fulfilled sexually was an important aspect of who she was. She arrived at one session telling us that she she'd met a man who had introduced her to 'sacred sexuality'. They were exploring the idea of spiritual sex.

Chris asked, "Please tell me more about this spiritual sex."

"Well, we have rituals which we perform before making love so as to bring the sacred into our sexuality."

"Oh, now I understand. You say 'Om' and then fuck."

Amanda was so angry that she turned red, collected her bag and walked out.

She came back the following week looking a little ashamed, "I apologise for walking out on you last week."

Chris nodded and said, "Apology accepted."

Amanda continued, "You were right. I think I knew it then, but didn't want to see it. He had me convinced that he was so spiritual, when really he was just justifying his need for sex. When I really looked at what he was doing, it was clear that he felt guilty about being sexual – somehow sex for him wasn't spiritual. That's what made him add all of the nonsense: to justify his sexual needs. I guess sexuality and spirituality just don't mix."

"Absolutely not," exclaimed Chris. "The two very much go together, in fact I'm not sure how to separate them. That's why I said what I did last week. When you need to ritualise and bring 'spirituality' into sexuality, then it's not spiritual. When you've fully accepted yourself as a sexual being, then sex is always spiritual. While some may express that link through ritual, what you described felt too contrived and rigid to be that kind of expression."

"I think that's why I was so angry. I knew something was off and was ignoring my gut. The relationship had become more important than honouring my intuition. Another principle for me now is 'I intend to trust my instincts when it comes to relationships'."

Ronna asked, "And when you miss?"

"When I realise that I've missed, I check out what wasn't feeling right and decide whether or not I can live with it. If I can't, then I leave."

* * *

On one of her later visits, she told us again that she had a new man in her life. "I met this guy, Brad, and I really think that it's going to work. He's great in bed and I ran the relationship by my principles and everything checks out."

Chris said, "Ah, the perfect man."

Defensively Amanda replied, "Now stop. I didn't mean perfect. He does have faults. He used to be an addict, but he isn't any more, and now he's into personal growth. Did I mention that he's good in bed?"

We laughed as Ronna said, "It's wonderful to see you applying your newly-acquired principles and skills in this new relationship."

A few months later, she came for another visit. "Well, the honeymoon is over and I'm struggling. I suppose you expected this since you teach it, but I thought that either I was different or that this relationship was different. But I'm not, and it isn't. This relationship, in fact all relationships, are bloody hard work."

In response, Ronna asked, "What principles do you use to guide your relationships?"

Looking confused, Amanda asked, "What do you mean?"

"I'll get to that, but first, what are your principles or goals for a relationship?"

"Common values, good sex, both partners doing their personal growth work – those sorts of things."

"That's what you want in a relationship, but what's the basis of a relationship?"

More confidently, Amanda said, "To love and be loved."

"What does that mean?"

Now Amanda looked really confused. She thought for a bit, and then said, "To meet each other's needs."

"And this is where that principle will land you: right here in the middle of disappointment. Now that's fine – if your goal is to spend your life being disappointed."

Amanda was starting to get frustrated. "Of course I don't want to be disappointed. All I want is a relationship that makes..." she paused, realizing where she was headed, "...me happy. Damn, damn, damn. What I've been seeking is a relationship according to the Child." She was truly angry now. "Then what the hell's the point in a relationship – to be miserable? To put up with endless frustration and disappointment?"

We let her calm down before Ronna said quietly, "In a way, yes. That's the point of a relationship." Amanda looked at us pleadingly, hoping for a punch line. "For us, life is about growth. Growth happens, and not when we're happy or even content – after all, why change when things are going well? Growth happens when we're miserable – when life is providing events that have a charge, especially a charge that makes us uncomfortable."

"Okay," Amanda said slowly, "But what does that have to do with a relationship?"

"Live day in and day out with someone, and they will push your buttons better than anyone else." Amanda nodded. "So the point of a relationship is to get your buttons pushed to inspire growth – to send the Radical Acceptance Wheel spinning."

"So, no matter what my partner does, I just accept it? If he beats me, then I just accept it? If he has endless affairs, then I just accept it? If he gambles away all of my money, then I just accept it? That sounds pretty stupid to me."

Chris asked, "Why does that sound stupid?"

Looking at him as if he was a total idiot, she replied, "Because I've no intention of staying in a relationship with a man who beats me, has affairs and gambles away all of my money."

"Oh, so you think that acceptance means becoming a doormat? Nothing could be further from the truth. Acceptance demands action. When we work with people in abusive relationships or people whose partners have affairs or addictions, nothing, and I mean nothing, can happen until there is acceptance. You have addictions experience: what's the first step of the twelve steps?"

Amanda looked at him with amazement. "Of course, it's acceptance. That also explains why I hear the abused women I work with making all kinds of excuses for their partners. They haven't accepted that their partner is an abuser: they're still clinging to the illusion that their partner really loves them." She started winding up again. "Why isn't this being taught in social work school?"

Before she could get too wound up, Ronna cut in, "Let's not try to fix the entire social work system right now. Instead, let's return to your principle on relationships."

"That feels really clear now. I'll use the feelings generated by my relationship to drive the Radical Acceptance Wheel. That includes processing the feeling to Discover and Integrate & Accept, but also to plan and act based on what I discover and in response to the original event. What's more, when the event isn't something that I wish to live with, I'll end the relationship."

"And when you miss?"

"You mean when I blame my partner for my anger? I'll go back and apologise. If, however, I've ended the relationship only to discover that the behaviour was something I could have lived with, then I'm not sure what to do. It seems a bit late then."

"For some people that would be a concern, but you give your all to these relationships; it's unlikely that that would occur for you. If it does, then it depends on how much time has gone by. In some cases you could go back and try again. In others, you'll just have to chalk it up to experience."

"The whole principle makes a lot of sense, but it also makes relationships hard work."

Chris said, "The hardest work next to raising kids."

Ronna then asked, "When you arrived, you said that there were problems in the relationship. What are the problems?"

"Well, things are still great sexually – Brad and I really connect on that level. That's so different from my marriage."

"And?"

"Well, his problem with money is a concern for me. He's in therapy and is doing his own work, but he's also really jealous and insecure. I don't want to be constantly reassuring someone: I feel like his mother. I did that with Joe, and I don't want to take on that role again."

Ronna agreed, saying, "It's not a good idea to become a reassuring mother. The partnership is lost when we take on a parenting role with our partner."

"I want him to change and become stronger and less jealous. How can I help him to do that?"

Chris spoke, "I want to have all my hair grow back."

Amanda laughed and said, "I know what that means: I need to accept him as he is, not who I want him to be. But I don't know if I can accept this."

"Let's separate a couple of things. Brad is jealous, insecure and doesn't manage finances well."

"Yes, I can see that, and I know that he has to change if this relationship is to last."

"I hear that. It sounds like his behaviour has come up against a principle."

"More damn principles!" She reflected a bit and added, "I hadn't thought about it in terms of principles. I know that from the place of Radical Acceptance, he is who he is and that's not going to change. But I want it to change, because I want this to work! Aaaarrrghhhh! This is so frustrating! I really love this guy!"

Ronna said gently, "It's not going to happen. If this relationship is to work, then it has to be from a place of acceptance. This means that you have to be prepared to live with the stress and tension of who he is, not who you want him to be. With this awareness, you can now run the relationship by your principles and see what you see."

"I see the need for a new principle: I'll be in a relationship with who the person is, not the fantasy of who I want them to be."

"Hmm, how does that feel?"

"Like shit. I want this relationship to work."

"We hear that, and sometimes there are show stoppers."

"Show stoppers?"

"A show stopper is a behaviour we choose not to live with for the long term. For some it's affairs, for some it's lying, for some it's anger, and in your case it sounds like jealousy might be one. Being aware of your show stoppers is important, because if we're in a relationship that has show stoppers and we're expecting the other person to change, then the relationship will generally end in disaster. We can either accept those patterns as something that we can live with long term, or we can end things. Once I accepted that Chris was disorganised, I could then decide whether it was a show stopper or whether the disorganization was something that would cause stress, but that I could live with. To ask him to be organised would be akin to asking for a fish to ride down the street on a bicycle. He can't do it: it's not part of who he is."

Amanda chuckled at the image of Chris being organised and said, "Okay, I get that. So my job is to have a look at this relationship and my principles and come up with my show stoppers."

"Sounds like a plan."

"Why do I have a feeling that this relationship is doomed?"

"I suggest that you do the work before you make any decisions," Ronna came back with.

A few weeks later, we met with Amanda again. She said. "Well, I looked at my principles and realised that a show stopper for me is having to parent my partner. Things began to fall apart even more when I wouldn't give Brad all the reassurance he wanted. He'd get angry and sulk, and sometimes he wouldn't call me for several days, thinking that I'd then be glad to hear from him and drop my plans when he did call. My growth and his growth are different – I can see that now. I'll grieve the loss of our lovemaking because it was great, but I've told him that I can't be in a relationship with him any longer."

Chris asked, "Are you grieving?"

"Yes, for what couldn't be. There was so much potential, but he couldn't step up. I also chose not to step down and repeat a relationship pattern similar to my marriage. I absolutely refuse to go there."

Ronna added, "Grieving and fantasies go together."

"Yes, I realised that I'd built a fantasy around this relationship. I knew what I didn't want, but I didn't see the fantasies that I'd built around my new partner. This was going to be the relationship where we would journey together, work out our issues together and have great sex together. We would each be what the other needed."

Chris smiled and said, "Yes, that's a great fantasy."

"It sure was until it all came crashing down."

Ronna then asked, "Amanda, where's the drama?"

"Drama?"

Flailing her arms around Ronna said, "Yeah, drama! When we met you a couple of years ago, everything was big: everything was chaos and drama. Your world was ending."

"I guess I'm growing up." She laughed and added, "And these principles are really guiding my life now. I run most of my decisions by them so I know whether or not I'm on track. Joe and I are actually mapping out a new friendship. He's respecting me more because I'm respecting myself more. When I say no, he knows that I mean no. The kids and I are doing much better: I've given them permission to call me on my bitch and my controller, and we have some fun with that. They're not so tense, and that's really nice." Her eyes got teary as she said, "I guess I'm really starting to love myself for the first time in 40 years. Two years ago I'd never have imagined myself saying, 'I'm a hateful, spiteful, betraying, controlling, judgemental, sexual, loving woman with a wicked bitch who has principles!'"

"Wow! That's quite an accomplishment!"

Amanda said reflectively, "Ronna, I can now say thank you to Pam, as well. It still hurts, but if it hadn't been for her, then I wouldn't be where I am today.

"No one recognises me any more Work is a totally different place, and I'm even starting to use Radical Acceptance with my clients. Co-workers are dropping by just to say hi and chat. I listen to what people are saying and don't put my two cents' worth in as often as before. I'm comfortable putting out suggestions, but I don't get upset when they aren't taken. At first, people would just stop and wait for me to say something sarcastic or get angry. They really didn't know what to do with the new me. Now when I'm in a bad mood I say, 'Okay ladies, my bitch is out today, so watch out,' and everyone laughs and we go about our jobs. It's even given permission for others to do the same, making the office a friendlier place to work in. All this has happened because I accepted and gave permission to the unthinkable – I gave my bitch room to play and the recognition that she doesn't need to be destructive. I gave her some principles, and she knows when she needs to protect me."

* * *

Amanda kept in contact with us on and off over the next few years. Sometimes she was in a relationship, and sometimes not. She now knew exactly what she wanted from her relationships, and when she became aware of show stoppers, she would end the relationship rather than keeping it going. She became quite confident in being alone and would now enter relationships not out of a fear of being alone, but because it was nice to share her journey with someone.

A couple of years ago, she met someone and decided to move in with them. This was new for her.

"I've been dating this guy, Phil, for about a year. He's an accountant. He's been divorced for a couple of years and has four grown children. We seem well-suited. He's not done a lot of personal growth work, but isn't opposed to doing it and supports my efforts. We're going to sell my house and buy a house together. My kids are almost done living at home – the last one leaves next year. Life is good."

Chris asked, "What else do you know about him?"

"He can get angry like my dad, but he's good at talking things through. He knows he has trouble with his anger, and I'm pleased that he's aware."

"It sounds like he's willing to explore things with you."

"Yeah, he likes to cook – and although my control issues in the kitchen are huge, we're working things out and trying to use humour to have some fun with it. I'm using the struggle to grow: when one of his characteristics is annoying – even really annoying (but not a show-stopper) – it becomes a vehicle for a lot of growth."

"Sounds like you've looked at things, used some critical thinking, run things by your principles and are ready to set out on a new adventure."

Amanda kept in touch on and off over the next little while. She sold her house and bought a new one together with Phil. They had too much furniture and had to negotiate who was getting rid of what and whose pictures they would hang on the walls. These issues created tension and struggle, but they worked through the difficulties together. They even took couple of trips together. Then the phone call came. Ronna took the call.

Amanda said, "I've broken off with Phil."

"That's surprising. What caused you to make that decision?"

"Things over the past year were getting challenging because he wasn't really into personal growth and kept blaming me for everything. I wouldn't accept the blame, and that made him sulk. Sexually things were slowing down as he became less and less interested. The final piece was when I discovered that much of what he told me at the beginning of the relationship was a lie."

"That must be very hard."

"Yes and no."

"Tell me more."

"Why I'm calling isn't because I've broken off with Phil, but because of my lack of emotion. I don't feel guilty and I don't feel all that sad, although it can come and go. I don't seem to have very much feeling at all."

"Hmm, keep going."

"Originally the relationship was in agreement with my principles. Then one by one, it started slipping. I kept an eye on things, and the issues were annoyances rather than show stoppers. His tendency to blame rather than own his anger, for example, let me practice my principle of not accepting blame. I grew a lot from that. When I wouldn't take the blame, he started to sulk, but I didn't rush in to rescue him. When things started slowing down sexually, I lived with the tension between his sexual needs and mine. Those were all things that I decided to continue to use for growth. Having the principle that relationships are a vehicle for growth helped me to be clear about the issues, and I've grown a great deal. The show stopper was discovering the lies. It was at that point that I decided to leave. The decision was clear and unemotional. It was like a fact. What's wrong with me?"

"I'm not sure that there's anything wrong with you, Amanda. From what I hear you saying, you started noticing – and that's the Observer. She just notices and doesn't have feelings. Events are neither good nor bad: she just observes. The more you live your life from this place, the more it'll seem like you don't feel. That's actually false. You feel very deeply, but you don't emote..."

"Yeah, but why do I not feel much around the relationship ending – or his lying or his anger? My God, that's what brought me to see you all those years ago!"

"Amanda, how much work have you done on your liar, your blamer and your anger? How much work have you done to apply your principle of discovering, integrating and accepting your subconscious?"

"I've worked damn hard. It's my whole life now."

"Once you've accepted these aspects of yourself, they have very little charge left when they're seen in others. After all: what is there to judge?"

"You're right. I've hardly made any judgement of Phil. Phil is Phil, just doing his Phil thing. For me, the relationship was just about knowing when to stay and then recognizing when it was over."

"Yes, and I'd like to suggest that you're a very deep feeler – that you now feel more deeply now than you did all those years ago when you came into our office crying and screaming. The difference is that you don't emote all over the place any more Instead, you feel, make plans and act."

"On good hair days."

Ronna and Amanda shared a laugh.

14 Tara: Responsibility

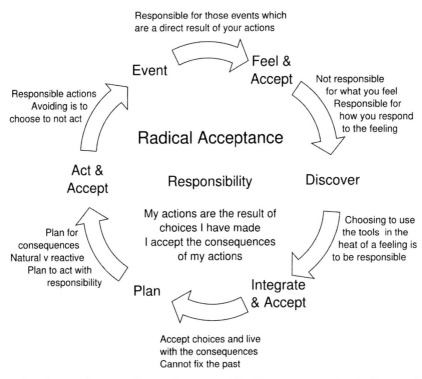

Tara first met us when she was 18. Her parents had divorced when she was young, and both had since remarried – her mother going on to have more children in her new relationship. She now had two younger half-sisters as well as her one younger brother. Her father was an engineer and her mother was a massage therapist, and Tara grew up struggling between the rationalism of her father and the New Age idealism of her mother. She now wasn't sure what she wanted to do with her life: she'd just left high school and didn't have any fixed academic goals for the future. As a way of helping her to find more direction, her friend, Penny, brought her to a Radical Acceptance group that we facilitate. After the group had checked in and gone over some of the general struggles and issues that they were facing, they decided that they wanted to talk about responsibility.

Chris opened the discussion by asking, "Everyone talks about responsibility, but what does the word mean?" People offered suggestions, but each attempt used the word responsibility in the definition. Chris rejected each of these, "If you use a word to define itself, then all you get is a circular definition – and that doesn't say anything." He continued, "All I'm hearing are vague guesses which suggest that responsibility is heavy and hard to do – but NO ONE can tell me what the term means!"

The room became silent. Ronna then joined in, "Radical Acceptance defines responsibility in two parts. Firstly, it's an acknowledgement that each of your actions is the result of a choice you've made. Secondly, it's an acknowledgement that the consequences of your actions are yours to accept. Let's focus on the first part tonight – the choices that you make."

Tara immediately beamed and started the ball rolling, ""I like that idea of choices, because I choose to love everyone. If we all made that same choice, then there'd be far less pain and destruction in the world." A couple of people smirked as they looked expectantly at us.

Ronna stood up and grabbed the flip chart while Chris grabbed the markers. Chris then said, "Ah yes, the old 'I'm dedicating my life to loving everyone' routine."

Ronna inserted, "Now, dear, be gentle – she's a newcomer and we don't want to scare her off!"

Tara began to squirm in her seat. Turning to Penny, she asked, "What did I say wrong?"

Penny, who'd been coming to our sessions for a while, whispered, "Nothing much, you've just opened up Pandora's Box." The members of the group around them laughed.

Ronna turned to Tara, "Are you okay with us putting you in the hot seat on your first night?"

"Yeah, sure, I think so… I mean, I was really looking forward to this – Penny has really changed since meeting the two of you. I'm a little nervous, though. Can I back out later?"

"Absolutely, just let us know if the experience is too much. We've been known to get onto a roll from time to time, but if you tell us to stop, then we'll honour that."

Tara nodded.

Chris then asked, "So you love everyone?"

"Yes, I do. I love meeting people in their uniqueness, and I love this planet; I'm very much into environmentalism. I believe in people."

"Okay, and what about your family? Do you love them?"

"Sure."

"Your friends and your animals as well?"

"Yep, all of them – especially the animals," she replied.

"And of course you love all the major polluting companies out there, too?"

Tara's reaction was immediate and forceful, "Of course not. I hate them. They're destroying the earth, and they don't care about anyone or anything – except lining their own pockets."

Ronna responded, "Ah, so your love is conditional?"

"But they're companies, not people."

"Companies run without people?"

"Well no, someone is making the decisions."

"Then I guess you don't love everyone!"

Tara sat for a moment before asking, "But no one loves those people, right Penny?"

Penny replied, "I'm sure they have family and friends who love them very much."

Chris added, "I'm sure the shareholders love them a lot, too."

"Wow, I never thought of it that way." She paused, before smiling and adding, "Then I guess I love them too."

Ronna reached down for a bell which was sitting on the floor beside her chair. She then lifted it up and started to ring it loudly. Tara turned to Penny and asked, "Is it break-time already?"

Penny laughed and said, "No, that's the bullshit bell. They use it in their addiction recovery groups when we're spewing bullshit. I guess they brought it along tonight – lucky us!"

"What did I say that was bullshit?"

Ralph, another member of the group, stepped in and said, "I think they have a hard time believing that you love the executives of polluting companies."

"Oh, well... Yes, you're right: I don't love them! But that's because what they're doing is wrong! I can't believe anyone would say otherwise!" She turned and addressed the group, "What those companies do is destructive. Do all of you here see this differently?"

Chris re-stated, "You're not always loving; in fact, you have a passionate hateful side."

Tara sputtered, "B-but..."

Ronna rang the bell again.

Tara glared at Ronna and said, "I didn't say anything!"

Ronna answered, "You didn't have to. It was going to be bullshit, because you passionately hate – and all the 'buts', rationalizations, blame and excuses in the world wouldn't erase that truth."

Suddenly, Tara started to cry. Another member of the group, Pat, reached over and handed her a tissue before adding, "Like Penny said, you opened up Pandora's Box. Don't worry, you'll get used to it. Well, maybe not used to it – but we keep coming back." The group laughed and put a few more digs our way. We kibitzed back and forth, giving Tara some time to settle in with her newly-discovered truth.

When she'd collected herself, Tara said, "This isn't good: I hate myself for hating. Hate is so destructive."

"Really?" asked Chris emphatically. "So all the environmentalists and activists should just close the doors on what they're doing? I'm sure they hate what's happening to our beautiful planet – but you're saying that nothing good has ever come from their interventions or endeavours?"

"Well, no. There are good things happening out there, and legislation is slowly changing. How will you bring about change if no one challenges what's happening in the world?"

"Right, so there is a place for hate and anger. We're not saying that there isn't destructive stuff happening out there. What we are challenging is the black and white thinking – the compartmentalizing which we do with our beliefs. Love is a good example: we often find it easy to say that we're loving, but then we never look at our thoughts and behaviours which are in complete contradiction to that belief. All the projections, the hypocrisies and the double standards we accuse others of…"

Interrupting, Ronna smiled and said, "Now dear, you can back off your soap box."

Ronna then turned to Tara and asked, "How are you doing?"

Sniffling, Tara replied, "Yeah, I'm okay. Is it always like this? I feel like I was hit by a bus. Hating is a difficult aspect of myself to see. I always believed that I was a loving person, but now I see that I'm not like that at all. I can really be quite nasty and judgemental"

"Yes, those things generally go together with hating. It's important to know that this discovery doesn't mean that you're not also a loving person, though. What this awareness does is open you up to another piece of being human – one that's known to others but not to yourself."

Tara shook her head, "I don't think anyone who knows me would say that I was hateful, nasty or judgemental, but…"

Penny faked a cough and laughed, "Ah, Tara, I hate burst your bubble – but all those times we get together and you gossip about people and…"

Tara threw up her hands, "Okay, okay, so it's not so hidden! I guess I really do have the blinders on!"

Ronna brought the discussion back on topic, "Tonight we're talking about responsibility and choices." She looked at the group and asked, "What would it mean for you all to acknowledge – to fully embrace – the idea that each and every thing you do is the result of a choice that you've made?"

"What about accidents?" asked Penny.

"Be specific."

"Okay – I'm in a store, and when I turn around, my knapsack knocks something off a shelf and it breaks."

"Who chose to wear the knapsack into a crowded store?"

"Hmm, I see your point."

Ralph then asked, "What if someone runs a stop sign and hits me when I'm driving?"

"That's a good example: no choice of yours produced that event. Life does happen to all of us from time to time. I'm not suggesting the New Age idea that you 'create your own reality' or that you're so powerful that you're creating all of life's events. In this context, all I'm speaking about are actions which are the result of choices."

Tara spoke, "Hold on a moment. Going back to those New Age ideas, I've always believed that if I think in a certain way, then things will happen to that effect. Thoughts can become your reality."

Chris responded, "Can they?" Tara nodded defiantly. "Then you must be thinking it's wonderful to have a polluted planet."

She sputtered, "No, of course not!"

"Well, you've wanted a healthy planet for some time now; how come your thoughts didn't make that happen? Did all nations sign the Kyoto Protocol? Has there been a decrease in emissions?"

Dejectedly Tara replied, "No. Things are worse despite more people being aware. It's the corporations – they use so much more than all the people put together. They don't care about anything but making money. The executives should be forced to live in the filth they create…"

Ronna cut her off, "Tara, I see your enthusiasm. Now I'd like you to be responsible."

"Responsible?" Tara was so angry that she could barely speak. After opening and closing her mouth a few times, she found her voice, "It's not me being irresponsible! It's those damn..."

Ronna cut her off again. "Tara, what are you feeling?"

"Outrage at..."

Ronna held up her hand, "Just the feeling. Now what are you doing with this feeling?" Tara looked confused. "Are you choosing to feel the feeling, allowing it to guide you into inner growth – or are you stoking the feeling?"

"You said earlier that anger can be good."

"And it can be destructive. The choice is yours. What choice are you making in this moment?"

"Choice? I'm angry! I didn't choose to be angry, it's just there when I see what the..."

One again, Ronna stopped her, saying, "I agree that the anger is just happening. I asked what you're choosing to do with it."

"I don't choose. When I see what's happening, I want it to stop."

"Then get a rifle and start shooting company executives."

Looking horrified, Tara said, "I'm a pacifist: I wouldn't kill. Then I'd be just as bad as they are."

"So you're choosing not to shoot them? See, you're making a choice."

All the fight left Tara, leaving her slumped in her chair. She wearily replied, "But look at what they're doing to our planet..."

Chris took over from Ronna, "Tara, we're not debating what's happening to our planet. We're talking about being responsible."

"They're the ones being irresponsible."

"They're not here tonight. You are, though, and you're not taking responsibility for your actions."

"I'm not the one..."

"You are the one – the one spewing your angry rhetoric all over the people who agree with you. What use is that? You talk a good line, but frankly, my dear, you're doing damn little about it. Instead of taking responsibility for your feelings, you blame them on the big, bad companies. This isn't being responsible."

"What do you mean? I thought responsibility had to do with working hard and doing what's right…"

"That's a common belief, but a fairly useless definition. After all, what's 'right'? You think 'right' is reducing pollution; the executives think that it's providing employment. Another group thinks that ramming fishing boats at sea and killing the crew is the 'right' way to stop overfishing. In contrast, the fishing company thinks that it's right to use bigger catches to reduce the cost of sea products for everyone. You're not the only one declaring what's moral and right."

"What do you think? Surely you agree with me?"

"Whether I agree or not is immaterial to this discussion. We're talking about responsibility being the acknowledgement that your actions are the result of your choices. That's a much more specific and measurable definition of responsibility than your rather vague one."

"I see," Tara paused while she absorbed this. "But that makes responsibility a personal issue. How do I know if someone else is being responsible?"

Ronna asked, "Why do you want to know that? Have you set yourself up as judge and jury? Are you the one to award 'The Tara Decree of Acceptable Responsibility'?"

Tara blushed before making one last attempt, "Yeah, but some people are just out for themselves. If no one can check that they're being responsible, then what?"

"Tara, I'd like to suggest that what you're really struggling with is your own inner powerlessness. Since you lack power in your life, you project this externally onto big business. Then you snarl and growl like a tiny dog threatening a statue of an elephant. Come to terms with your lack of inner power first, and only then begin to look outside. As things stand right now, you're of no benefit to yourself or the planet."

Tara looked like Ronna had slapped her. Then she broke down and cried once again. Penny handed her more tissues and put an arm around her for comfort. After a while, Tara said, "You're right, you know. I do feel powerless, and not just environmentally. I feel it in all of my life. What do I do?"

"How about forgiving big business?"

Her tears stopped immediately. A shocked Tara replied, "Forgive them? But they're still polluting and plundering the Earth! Besides, they're not seeking my forgiveness. As you said, I'm nothing to them."

"True, but they're not nothing to you."

Ronna paused and Chris took over, "People tend to think of forgiveness as somehow making what happened 'good' and 'right'. That's the view of the Child. The Adult knows that there's no 'good' or 'right' just as there's no 'bad' or 'wrong'."

Tara interrupted, "If there's no 'good' or 'bad', then what is there to forgive? Let's just have a party and kiss their asses."

"Their actions may not be 'good' or 'bad' from the Adult's point of view, but your Child has different feelings on the matter. She's latched onto this issue and is pouring her energy into it while, at the same time, accomplishing nothing. Forgiveness is not for their benefit, but for yours. It's the process of withdrawing your energy from the event – in your case the event of big business polluting the Earth."

"So it is a big ass kissing party?"

Chris laughed. Ronna stepped in, "Let me try and explain. As long as you have your energy wrapped up in you being 'right' and them being 'wrong', you're useless and ineffectual. Forgive them – withdraw your energy – and then you can see the situation with fresh eyes. You'll be able to appreciate their point of view as well as your own."

Chris added, "A few years back, a new kind of light bulb was developed. These bulbs used much less energy, but they sat on the shelves with only a few people using them. Then a creative environmentalist began to see the situation from the point of view of big business. This person approached companies and told them how using the light bulb would save the companies money. Now most companies have switched." He paused and then added, "Tara, what was more effective? Ranting and condemning, or a sound business plan that made sense to the companies?"

"I see what you mean," answered Tara, sheepishly.

Ronna continued, "But that's not the main reason for forgiving them." She went on to explain the concept of the 100 units of energy and how spending all her energy on worry and powerlessness had costs in terms of health, dreams and creativity. "So forgiving them would actually by useful for you. That's the main reason for doing this."

After making sure that the group was willing to continue, she then introduced the cord cutting exercise as an act of responsibility. "As you'll recall, responsibility is accepting that your actions are the result of your choices. Energy is no different; what happens with your energy is the result of what you choose to do with it. The Cord Cutting Tool is a meditative process for releasing the energies of the past in a conscious and deliberate manner.

"This is a good tool to use when you're having judgemental, angry or resentful thoughts about something or someone else. It's also useful when your thoughts and feelings are caught up in your past, especially in past traumas. You can even use it toward those nasty polluting companies. I like using it at the end of my day, personally. I'll look at all the energy that I've put out toward family, friends, co-workers, my boss, people budding in lines, people cutting me off on the highway – anything that hasn't been neutral. I'll then recall the energy from all the events of my day. Any questions thus far?"

Ralph spoke up and implored, "If this is a meditation exercise, then I'm afraid I'm a lost cause. I've tried for years to visualise waterfalls and flowers, but I can't do it."

Ronna responded, "Ralph, I'm glad that you mentioned that. You don't need to visualise. This can be done with thoughts: instead of 'seeing' the image, allow your thoughts to describe the image.

Not everyone is a visual person, but that doesn't mean that you can't meditate or do these kinds of exercises."

She continued, "To ensure that you all understand the Cord Cutting Tool, we'd like to talk you through it – step by step." She then turned to Tara, "Do you have someone or something to use as a point of focus for tonight's exercise?"

"There is a person that I think of when I think of the polluting companies. I could use him."

Chris said, "Yes - the exercise works best when you personalise it." He turned to the rest of the group and asked them to think of an event or person that they needed to forgive; something or someone that was still holding energy. Then he turned out the lights and Ronna began to speak in a quiet, gentle voice.

"Okay, let's begin by closing your eyes. Take some deep breaths, breathing deeply into yourself…deeply into yourself. Now picture the event or person. See them clearly – the sights, the sounds and the smells. It may be about someone who cut you off while you were driving or the fight you had with your sister 10 years ago. It doesn't matter what the event is or when it took place: what matters is that you're still spending time ruminating about it – still thinking about what happened. Imagine all the energy that's going into the event." Ronna gave the group a moment to gather the information.

"While picturing the person, see the cords of energy that link you to this person. Sometimes these cords will be small like threads, and sometimes they'll be as big and thick as redwood trees." She paused once again, allowing the images to collect and take form.

"Begin by offering an apology – an apology for the judgements, the anger and the resentment that you've carried and sent their way. Breathe deeply…breathe deeply into yourself. When you can see all of the cords clearly, it's now time to cut them. You can use whatever you need for this: scissors, axes or dynamite – whatever it takes to cut them. Once they're cut, see black ooze spilling out from them onto the ground – and then watch as the cord dries up and blows away in the wind. Now pull out any remaining roots that are still embedded in you." Ronna waited for the group to follow the instructions.

"Breathing deeply still, allow your body to fill with healing light. Pay special attention to filling the places that you've emptied when pulling out the cords. Maybe even apply some energetic cream to ensure complete healing."

"When all the cords are cut and the holes are filled, re-imagine the event. How does it feel now? How much energy are you now spending on it? If there's still energy flowing out, then you'll need to repeat the exercise – either now or later. For some people, complete forgiveness can take a long time. You'll know you're done when you can imagine the event or the person without feelings of any kind – when the event is fully neutral." Pausing for a moment, she began again, "Breathe deeply. It's now time to give thanks – thanks to those who have journeyed with you in your meditation. Give thanks for growth, awareness and the opportunity to be responsible to yourself."

After a few more moments, she added, "It's now time to return – to return to this room and to the sound of my voice. When you're ready, you can open your eyes –feeling relaxed and energised."

Chris turned the lights back on and suggested that the group gather their thoughts by writing in their journals. After they were finished, Ronna asked if anyone wanted to share what they're written down.

Ralph began, "I'm so glad that you told me this sort of thing can be done through thinking and thoughts." He looked down at his journal to and then said, "Last night, my wife and I argued about the kids – and I was still steamed about it today. This exercise allowed me to cut the cords of resentment. I can now see her point of view instead of being locked in the thoughts of the Child, still holding a grudge and wanting to be right no matter what the cost. Later tonight, I can go back and have that conversation again – this time with an open heart. I'm sure it'll bring about a very different result."

Tara spoke next, "Well, needless to say my cords were like the redwood trees – and I used dynamite to blow them up. The idea that I'm a pacifist is just another illusion about myself: I used dynamite! Some pacifist I am!"

She continued, "That awareness hit when I was filling my body with healing light. When I cut – I mean blew up – the cords, all this black, tarry shit just began seeping out of me. I guess I had more hate in me than I thought. But I was able to tell the person that I was forgiving them, since I saw the hard choices that they had to make – and even though I didn't agree with their choices, I understood that they'd been hard choices and that I couldn't judge them for coming to the that conclusions they did."

Nodding, Chris asked, "How does it feel to say that?"

"It feels like, for the first time, I'm being responsible for my shit. NO excuses, NO blaming, NO rationalizing – just saying 'YES, I'm hateful and judgemental sometimes...' Okay, maybe more than sometimes!" She laughed.

The group ended with everyone getting homework. Tara's was to observe her hatred and judgements

* * *

A few days later, Tara called us to set up a private session for the following week. When the appointment arrived, she came in and plopped herself down in a chair. "This responsibility thing has hit me pretty hard. I'm looking at a lot of areas of my life, and in general, I'm not very responsible. Penny says that my Child is on some kind of stand making a lot of decisions – is that right?"

Chris replied, "Yes, the 'stand' is a podium: your Child is on the podium."

"Yeah, that's right. That's what she said."

We spent some time with the flip chart going through the orchestra metaphor and the Child and Adult archetypes in detail. When we'd finished, she sat in shock and said, "I've always thought of myself as an older, more mature 18 year old. I've been told all my life how old and wise I am. But looking at this, I just shake my head."

* * *

Tara came back the following week, starting the session by saying, "This time, I'd like to talk about my mother. She's decided that she wants my step-sister, Rita, to move out of the house because her drug use is making her behaviour pretty bad. The only thing is, she wants me to tell Rita that she has to move out. Mom thinks that because I have drug use in my history, I'm the best person to tell her. I don't see it as my responsibility; the Radical Acceptance definition of responsibility says that my actions are the result of my choices, but it's my Mom choosing to ask Rita to leave. She feels differently, and says that it's my choice whether I talk to my sister or not. I have to admit, that's left me confused. Besides, I don't want to hurt my mother's feelings."

Ronna responded, "I'd say that you're both right. Your mother is making a choice to ask your sister to move out, so you have no responsibility there. Your mother's request for you to speak to your sister also belongs to her. In that regard, you're absolutely right: responsibility doesn't extend to the actions of others." Tara nodded. "However, your mother has now asked you to speak to your sister. How you respond to that request is your choice."

"But I'm not responsible for my mother or my sister."

"No, but you are responsible for the choice that you make in response to your mother's request."

With frustration, Tara responded, "I can see that, but I don't like it. I want to stay out of the situation, but I also don't want to hurt my mother's feelings."

Chris jumped in, "That's impossible." Tara looked confused. He continued, "It's impossible for you to hurt your mother's feelings." Tara now looked even more confused. "You're not that powerful. You can't control her feelings: whatever feeling arises in her belongs to her and her alone."

Tara responded, "I can see that: her response is her responsibility. But she'll still punish me by going silent if I don't speak to Rita."

"Now we've moved from the choice side of responsibility to the consequence side. Her punishing you would be a consequence of your actions – but not your responsibility. That difference is important."

"Can you explain the difference?"

"I'd love to. When someone responds to something that you've done, the response belongs to them. This applies to any emotional or physical response they may have to your action; since your action is a neutral event to them, their response is entirely their own. Clear so far?" Tara nodded. "While their response belongs to them, however, you're going to have to live with it. This makes their response a consequence of your action. You won't have to take responsibility for this response, but you will have to cope with it as a consequence."

Chris paused, and Ronna took up the explanation. "There are different kinds of consequences. Firstly, there are natural consequences – such as when you hit a wall and you hurt your hand, or when you throw an object and it breaks. No one else is involved, and the outcome is a natural consequence of your action. In the situation with your mother, you're facing the second type: a reactive consequence. This is when the consequence comes from another person – someone reacting to an action that you've taken.

"Here's an example that will help to make things clearer. Imagine that Chris does something and I feel angry as a result. In my anger, I throw a book onto my dresser – and as it lands, it knocks my favourite pig figurine onto the floor and smashes it into a million pieces. Chris gave this figurine to me, and when he finds out what's happened, he's upset that I broke it. In response, he refuses to talk to me for two days. Which of my consequences are the result of my actions and which are the result of Chris' actions? Which are natural and which are reactive?"

Tara thought for a moment before saying, "Losing your figurine seems like just an accident."

"Was it the result of my actions?"

"Yes."

"Then who else could it belong to?"

"I see," she said reflectively. "That would be a natural consequence. If it was me in that situation, I'd want to say that it was just an accident to avoid accepting my role in breaking it – but under the Radical Acceptance definition of responsibility, the consequence would belong entirely to me. That makes sense, even though I wouldn't like it in the moment." She thought for a while and then continued, "Chris refusing to talk to you is his choice: it's a decision that he's responsible for. How is it your consequence?"

"I have to live with it."

"True enough – so that's a reactive consequence. You said in our first meeting that you need to accept the consequences of your actions, though. I can see how that works with the pig, but how does it work with Chris? He's the one choosing to be silent. How can you accept that?"

"I don't take it personally: I see his silence as his reaction and his choice."

"Then what do you do?"

"I could do nothing – or I could apologise."

"apologise? What for? He's the one giving you the silent treatment."

"I would apologise because I acted in anger. Period."

"What if he refuses to accept your apology?"

"I've apologised. As far as I'm concerned, the event is now closed. If Chris chooses to keep it going, then that belongs to him, not me."

"Wow, have you ever done that?"

"Yes."

"And what does Chris do?"

"He'll come around soon enough. It's part of the agreement we honour as the basis of our relationship."

"Will he apologise for what made you angry? Hold it – he didn't make you angry. Will he apologise for his actions?"

Chris replied, "Only if I acted in the heat of my feelings or if my action was hurtful – either intentionally or unintentionally. In this example, my going silent would have been an action done in anger and would warrant an apology."

"Do you apologise as often as Ronna?"

"I don't have to: I rarely act in the heat of feelings." He then burst out laughing and added, "Of course I do."

"Wow, I've never seen a relationship like this."

"It's called a relationship based on principles and the Adult – with responsibility at its core."

Ronna said, "Now let's return to you and your mother. If you refuse to speak to your step-sister, then your mother might punish you. What kind of consequence would that be?"

"It'd be a reactive one. Even though I know it's her choice to punish me, it's not fun and I really don't like it."

"Part of planning is about factoring in the consequences of any potential actions. Sometimes the consequences won't dictate your course of action, but at other times, they will. If I see a mugging, for example, then I may choose not to try and stop it as I'll fear that I'll only get injured or killed for my efforts. Instead, I'll call 911 and keep walking – even though the 'socially right' thing to do might be making an attempt to intervene."

"Yes, but in my case it's not so serious. Giving in to my mother feels like I'm being manipulated by her – but it's not life or death."

"You're being manipulated. Is there a problem with that?"

"You guys turn everything upside down. I want to say that it's wrong to manipulate, but then I remember that there's no 'right' or 'wrong'."

Chris added, "And there are times when manipulation is the appropriate action for a situation."

"Hmm – like I said, everything I used to believe I now have to chuck out of the window."

"Good. If that's the case, then you're making terrific progress." Tara groaned. "So what choice are you going to make about your mother?"

"I don't know," she wailed.

"There's a tool that you can use to assist in your planning. It's called the Child Adult Worksheet. In this tool, you give voice to the Child's wants and fears and then respond from the Adult's perspective. It gives a new insight into your possible choices."

We took her through the worksheet and her decision became clear. She didn't like either choice, but came to the conclusion that getting involved with her mother's decision and asking Rita to move out was the wrong thing for her to do at that time.

* * *

Over the next few months, we continued to see Tara on and off. As with all of our clients, we didn't push her to come back – instead allowing her to set the pace of her therapy. Over this time, she made some important steps forward – not only in her personal growth, but in the rest of her life as well. She went back to school to get a firm foundation in environmental studies, for instance, and also started a new relationship.

"When Jake and I get together, we always have a lot of fun. I've enjoyed that, but as we're moving deeper, I'm growing more concerned. Jake is still in love with his old girlfriend, and I'll never be first in his life. I'm struggling to accept that."

"What are you struggling to accept?" asked Ronna, wanting confirmation.

"I have trouble accepting that I'll never be the most important person in his life – and that if she asked him back, he'd return to her."

"Why is that difficult to accept? It seems straightforward to me."

We watched Tara's frustration grow, "That's not right... That's not how relationships should... Argh! I can't use 'right' or 'wrong', and I can't use 'should', either. I don't know – I just don't like it."

Chris said, "Let's look at the situation again. In this case, acceptance has two components. The first is in seeing Jake for who he is, and you've managed that. The second is to see his actions without judgement – when his actions are neutral instead of being 'good' or 'bad', 'right' or 'wrong'. When you can say,

'Jake's ex-girlfriend will always be more important than me and that's just a fact', then you've accepted the situation."

"I don't see a lot of judgement, and I still don't want that in a relationship. It means that there's no safety – no chance to become more intimate. I feel that I need to hold back because he may leave at any time."

"Okay, have you told him how you feel?"

"No, I'm trying to practice Radical Acceptance first. I'm trying to think of how to tell him without blaming him."

Ronna suggested, "Let's set up a role play. Chris, you play the role of Jake."

After Ronna had explained the role play a little further, Tara began, "When you make your ex-girlfriend more important than me, you make the relationship unsafe."

"It's perfectly safe for me," replied Chris as Jake.

"But not for me. I need you to make this relationship safe."

Ronna stepped in, "Congratulations, you did a wonderful job of putting it all on Jake!"

"I know, that's why I haven't said anything to the real Jake yet."

Ronna explained the I Statements Tool to her, and Tara worked at speaking in this way. Her first I Statement was, "I feel unsafe because you keep hanging on to your ex-girlfriend."

Ronna cut in, "You started out with an I Statement, but then you went back to putting the responsibility for your feeling on Jake. Where did you go off track?"

Tara thought it over, and then said, "When I used the word, 'Because'. I do feel unsafe because of Jake hanging on to his ex."

Ronna spoke quietly, "Jake isn't the reason. The lack of safety you feel is caused by events from your past – by things that may have been said and done by your family, friends or teachers. It may be from something you read, or maybe you were just born that way. That's what causes you to feel unsafe: Jake is just a trigger back into those older events."

We watched as understanding dawned on her, "You've been talking about events being neutral and how the charge from an event belongs to me, but I didn't really understand what you meant until now. Jake's hanging on to his ex really is neutral. I can see it now without any kind of judgement." She looked in awe as she said, "This is incredible – it really does belong to me. I really understand this Radical Acceptance now!"

We let that sink in for a while, and then Chris said, "Don't worry, this too shall pass."

"What? I understand it now. How can that pass?"

"Radical Acceptance is a journey, not a destination. Understanding happens, and then it passes – an event comes along and all the understanding jumps out of the nearest window. Then you go back to work and 'get it' again, maybe at a deeper level. Like everything else in life, you won't do Radical Acceptance perfectly."

Ronna then brought the subject back to the I Statements, and Tara, with her new insight, was able to speak clearly about what she was feeling. "Jake, I see that your ex-girlfriend is more important than I am. Your feeling that way belongs to you, and I accept that. For me, it's triggering lots of unpleasant memories and I'm doing a lot of healing work as a result."

Ronna added, "That was good. You might also want to speak about the impact of the relationship of your feelings."

Tara turned back to Chris (who was still in the role of Jake) and said, "Jake, because I see that you could leave the relationship at any time, I'm choosing to keep this relationship superficial. However, I want to go deeper – and I want to do that with you."

"Very good, Tara," said Ronna, "You've spoken about yourself and have given Jake a choice as to whether he wants to go deeper or not."

"But what if he doesn't want to go deeper?"

"Then you'll have to choose whether to stay or go based on the facts of the relationship – not based on feelings."

"My mother always told me to listen to my heart, because my heart wouldn't lead me astray. Now you're telling me to ignore my heart and operate on thoughts alone?"

"No, that's not correct. Operating exclusively on the basis of feelings leads to inconsistency, because feelings come and go. There are also times when your feelings give you wrong information." Tara looked questioningly. "Either you or someone you know has surely felt attraction for an inappropriate person. Acting on the feeling alone means ending up in a bad situation."

Tara nodded knowingly, "So the heart's out – but isn't that what I said earlier?"

Chris picked up the dialogue, saying, "We didn't say the heart was out. Working on the basis of thinking alone is just as problematic. Firstly, people who claim to be purely rational thinkers are only ignoring their feelings. In fact, I've seen some of the most irrational, feeling-based decisions coming from people who claim to be acting on thinking alone." He paused, "Secondly, operating on the basis of thinking alone leaves people feeling disconnected and flat. The key is to bring input from both your head (thoughts) and your heart (feelings). The two work best together."

"What about intuition?"

"Sure, throw it in as well – find a balance between all three. What's key is to see that you're responsible for the decision that you're making."

Ronna said, "Coming back to you and Jake, your feelings aren't in question: you have strong feelings for him. Now it's time to add your thinking and your intuition."

"So what do I do?"

"You wanted to talk with him first, so start there. Then you'll have more information on which to base your decision."

Tara agreed, and left planning to speak with Jake using the I Statements Tool.

* * *

Tara had her conversation, and when Jake wouldn't put her first, she left the relationship. She later described this to us as a painfully clear decision.

We didn't see her for a while after that – not until her next major event came up some months later. She'd decided to go to India as part of her schooling, and had started to put these plans into action. About two months before she was due to leave, she booked a session with us.

"I'm in a new relationship – and I'm also going to India. That's a problem: this new relationship is really calling me, but I've planned to leave in two months. I don't see any way of resolving the situation, and the whole thing is really stressing me out."

Ronna asked, "What's his name?"

"Robert."

"Will Robert wait until you get back?"

"We're not really that far along."

"Then what choice are you going to make?"

After a few moments of silence, Tara relaxed and said, "Wow! I planned this trip to India and it's taken on a life of its own. When you asked what choice I'm going to make, I realised that I have a choice; I didn't see that before. I can choose to go or not to go." She paused with a look of wonder on her face, "It's amazing. I'd really forgotten that I had a choice. I feel so much lighter now." She reflected further, "I can see that I was trying to act based on rationality only – my feelings and intuition were saying 'Don't go', but I was ignoring them. The more I ignored them, the louder they spoke and the higher my stress levels. Now I can relax, listen to all of myself and make a decision."

Chris replied, "And it'll be a responsible decision – a choice made consciously, based on input from your thoughts, feelings and intuition. Nice work."

* * *

In the end, Tara didn't go to India and instead moved in with Robert. We started seeing both of them as they began to build a conscious relationship – a relationship based on the Radical Acceptance definition of responsibility, in which each partner takes ownership of their feelings and choices. As with all relationships, theirs moved from the romantic, 'in love' phase into the angry, power-struggle phase. We worked with them and gave them tools to aid in navigating the treacherous waters of their power struggle – and they caught on quickly. Over time, they both grew a great deal and only occasionally called on us to help them with particularly difficult issues.

On one such occasion, Tara stated her problem as soon as she came in, "Robert's a slob."

Ronna responded, "Is that a problem?"

"Well, yes… Yes it is. If we're going to eventually get married and have children, then I need him to keep a cleaner house."

"So either Robert becomes neater or the relationship is off because of the children you'll have one day?" Tara looked uncertain. Ronna said to Robert, "Well, there's your choice: become neater or take a hike. So what are you going to do? Are you going to promise to work harder at keeping the place neat?"

Robert was a wise man, and by the time we'd this conversation, he'd worked with us for long enough and knew himself well enough to know the answers to Ronna's questions. "No, I can't promise that. Even if I try, I know it won't last very long. I'm just not a neat person."

Ronna announced, "Okay, it's over. Tara will only be in relationship with a neat person and Robert, you're messy person. Will the two of you need help negotiating a separation?"

Shocked, Tara responded, "Wait a minute! I'm not ready to talk about separation yet!"

"But if being neat is a requirement and Robert isn't a neat person, then why hang on to a relationship that's clearly over? If this is a show stopper, then cut this now. If it's an annoyance, then work with it as a vehicle for growth."

"I'm not sure that it's a show stopper. I just think that if he really cared for me, he'd make the effort."

Chris then spoke, "There's a wonderful book by Gary Chapman called 'The Five Love Languages'. In it, Gary suggests that different people hear 'I love you' in different ways. For example, I hear it through physical touch: I truly know Ronna loves me when she gives me a hug, a massage or when we make love. Ronna, on the other hand, hears 'I love you' when I do things for her and with her. She feels loved when I offer to help make dinner or run an errand for her. While touch is nice for Ronna, she doesn't see it as being as loving as when I do things for her.

"What you're describing, Tara, is your love language. Try to give us more details: is it Robert doing the work that makes you feel loved?"

"I don't think so," she answered reflectively, "It's just that when I see the house messy, the dishes in the sink and clothes on the floor, I feel unloved and lonely."

"What are your options? Robert isn't going to become Mr. Clean. Is there anything you can do to take care of this on your own?"

"I guess I could try doing the tidying and dishes myself? As I said, it isn't so much who does those things as that they get done."

"So we can stop planning for separation?" Chris asked.

Tara laughed, "Yes – and you can stop being so dramatic and trying to push my panic buttons."

Chris looked innocent and replied, "Would we do that?"

Tara laughed, "Absolutely you would!"

* * *

[When we were putting this book together, we asked 'Tara' for her current thoughts on what she'd achieved. The following passages are an edited version of what she wrote.]

"I have an ongoing struggle with my house. If the house isn't clean, I feel unloved. I recently began some healing work in which I specifically focused on 'How can I meet my own needs better?' The question and some of its answers were seemingly simple: by making sure that the dishes are done every day, I can better meet my own need to feel loved. By folding my clothes and putting them away, I can better meet my own need to feel loved. By making sure that my living room stays tidy, I can better meet my own need to feel loved. Taking up these actions is a simple way of taking responsibility for my own feelings. In short, I can make choices which result in a healthier relationship with myself.

"My most major life decisions generally relate in some way to the theme of responsibility. My birth control method is no exception, for example. Having spent several years with no regular sexual partner and for the most part alone, I'd given up formal methods of birth control and had taken to regularly charting my menstrual cycle. I became used to watching the subtle rhythms of my body and was confident in my knowledge of them. When I finally did enter into a relationship, this knowledge eventually became the basis for our birth control. After several months of successfully using condoms and spermicide during my fertile times and abstinence and body wisdom for the rest, however, we eventually found out that I was pregnant. While this may have been due to the particular insanity of the two weeks in which we conceived, we could no longer deny that as two people who were not prepared to have children yet, we were being irresponsible. The decision to have an abortion was painful for both me and Robert; we plan to have children together one day when we're better established in our careers. Choosing the abortion was something we did with careful consideration. We made a decision, and we stand by it as the best for both us and the baby. In the wake of this painful experience, we had to reconsider our birth control method. With no option being ideal, I chose to get an IUD. This choice offers me the security I need with a minimal amount of change to my hormones. I made the choice, and I know that I can live with its consequences.

"Since responsibility is about consciously choosing, it lies at the base of my relationship with Robert. Choosing the relationship which I'm in today is a decision that I've made over and over again. At times it's a choice which I make on a weekly or even a daily basis. Right now, I've been sitting easily with this choice for a few weeks without questioning it. I can be hard on Robert when I go through periods of doubting the relationship – but we've learned that these times are both an indicator of some deeper issue that we need to deal with and an opportunity to move further into intimacy. The choice to be in this relationship carries with it deep pain, but also deep joy. Robert and I continually call on each other to test our boundaries, to push our limits, and to examine the validity of our core values and beliefs. Some of this happens in the day-to-day mundane, and some of it in challenges which strike at the very foundation of our relationship. Whatever the scenario, though, we try to meet it consciously. For two such intellectual people, this often means hours of conversation – but also includes crying and laughing together."

15 Kathy: The Observer

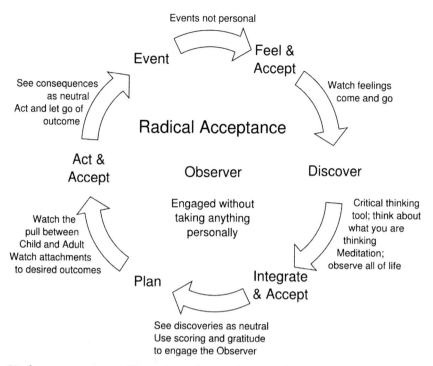

Kathy was a well-respected professional accountant who'd married young. Over the past 20 years of her marriage to Ken, she'd had three miscarriages but never any children, and her intimate relationships had become a mess. She now lived in chaos – at the mercy of her feelings, with fear and perfection driving her life. She seldom felt safe, and constantly moved from one drama right into the next. Her relationship with Ken had also become verbally abusive, but despite how he sometimes scared her, she wasn't prepared to leave.

After working with us for several months, she'd become painfully aware of how the Child affected her life. Although she was able to call on the Adult in some situations, however, her marriage was still driven by her Child. During one session, we started looking once more at how her feelings were driving her behaviour. This had been prompted by yet another incident with Ken: he'd been critical and verbally abusive again, which had left Kathy feeling overwhelmed with feelings.

After the situation had been explained to us, Ronna responded by saying, "Kathy, what do you think about Ken's behaviour?"

"I feel just terrible. Sometimes I'm angry at the way he treats me and…"

Cutting her off, Ronna said, "Kathy, I didn't ask you how you felt: I asked you what you think."

"Umm I think… What? What do you mean, 'think'?"

Chris joined in, "You're at the mercy of all these feelings. You have no ability to think about these dramas; get some distance from them."

"Well, I did get through university, you know! So I do have the ability to think!"

"I don't debate your intelligence, but where is it in your interpersonal relationships?"

Kathy didn't have a clue what he was talking about, "Okay, just a minute: I do think critically at work, because that's how I'm successful. I really draw a blank on how to think critically about my feelings, though. Can you really do that?"

Chris grabbed the flip chart, "Before we begin the exercise, I want to introduce you to a new archetype: it's called the Observer." He began to write, and Kathy brought out her journal – now filled with notes from previous sessions. Chris continued, "The Observer is the archetype which observes all of life. The Observer notices all thoughts, feelings, behaviour and events. It doesn't engage in emoting or reacting, it just notices. That's the role of the Observer – she just notices." He paused and asked excitedly, "Kathy, do you see our walls? They're beige. Isn't that incredible?"

Kathy looked confused and said, "I guess…"

Chris suddenly looked angry and continued, almost yelling, "Damn these beige walls! They make me so angry! Don't you agree?"

Looking more confused, she said uncertainly, "No, not really."

Chris looked totally devastated – as if he was on the verge of tears. "Kathy," he lamented, "these walls make me feel so sad. I want to cry just looking at them. You know what I mean, right?"

Kathy was now completely stumped. "Chris, I have no idea what you're talking about. Frankly, I don't care what colour your walls are. They don't make me feel much of anything."

Chris jumped up excitedly and yelled, "Write this down, it's profound – and make sure that my name is beside the information!" Kathy opened a new page in her journal, not sure what she was supposed to have discovered. Chris then continued, "The Observer watches life with the same emotional intensity that you have about the colour of my walls!"

Ronna added with a bemused grin, impressed by Chris' antics, "Any time there's a charge to an event, feeling or thought, then the walls aren't beige; you're not in your Observer and you're caught up in the drama of life."

The relief was visible on Kathy's face as she realised that Chris was making a point and not going slightly crazy – although she had to admit to herself that the distinction with these two was somewhat arbitrary. After a few moments of writing, she then said, "So the Observer only notices – it doesn't feel? I understand that you want me to observe my feelings, but I don't have a clue how to do that. I don't even know if it's possible."

Noticing Kathy's panic mounting, Ronna interjected, "Imagine that you're at a movie theatre. You're watching a movie about a woman named Kathy, and Kathy is in a dysfunctional relationship and feeling big emotions. How would that be for you?"

"When I go to a movie, I get so wrapped up in what's on the screen. I feel just what the characters are feeling."

"Okay, now imagine that you're sitting in the projection room and, instead of watching the screen, you're watching the Kathy who's in the seats – the Kathy who's watching the Kathy in the movie. How would that be?"

She thought for a moment, "From the projection room, I'd notice a woman getting all caught up in a movie. It's like she forgot that it was just a movie. I think I'd see her as being a bit over the top."

She paused. "Is that what I look like? Do you guys see me as being over the top?"

Chris said playfully, "No, not over the top – more like over the whole mountain!"

"Oh my God, I feel so ridiculous," Kathy replied, clearly affected by this revelation.

"See?" Chris pointed out, "You're doing it again. You're now caught up in feelings about being caught up in feelings. Stop and breathe."

Kathy paused for just long enough to take a breath, "It's like I do it automatically."

Ronna added, "Yes, without thinking. But let's stop here because you've just made a huge breakthrough."

"I did?" She grabbed her journal and started to write, but as soon as her pen hit the page, she paused and asked, "What was my breakthrough?"

Ronna laughed and said, "Sometimes you're so busy writing that you forget what to write about! Your breakthrough was noticing that you get caught up in feelings automatically."

"Oh yeah, that makes sense."

"Also note down that you came to this realisation by thinking about your feelings."

Kathy put down her journal and looked at Ronna, "Yes, and thinking does give me more control than feeling. It was a thought which noticed that I get caught up automatically. Maybe it is possible for me to think about my feelings."

Chris interrupted her musings to add, "That's right – you can. We've already seen that you can, in fact. The next step is to begin thinking about your feelings more consciously. To help with this, I want you to focus on how much you work to avoid thinking and how often you choose to become overwhelmed by your feelings. You're homework is to score how well you take emotional situations, ignore your thoughts and turn them into dramas. If the walls are beige, then score a 1 – and if your performance is worthy of an Oscar, then score a 10."

"How do I do that if I'm caught up in the moment?"

"At the end of the day, return to the projection room. Score how well Kathy – the one watching the movie – built up a huge drama."

* * *

She came back two weeks later and straight away began the session by saying, "How does anyone put up with me? I'm such a drama queen: I'm exhausted just thinking about all the drama that I create! I began to think about all the dramas that I've played out in the past, and then started to think about what people must have thought of me when that happened. I worried…"

Chris cut her off, saying, "Kathy, Kathy, Kathy – I hear that you're noticing your feelings, but listen to what you're saying about your thoughts. Your thoughts aren't beige."

"Shit – but I thought you wanted me to think? That's what I'm doing!"

"The Observer sees both feelings and thoughts as beige. It's all there in your notes," he chuckled.

Kathy paused, "This is really hard. I guess that making drama out of thoughts is no different from making drama out of feelings. "

Ronna said, "Sometimes it helps to see some of the underlying sources of your need for drama."

"Are you saying that I need this drama? I hate it."

"If it wasn't serving you at some level of consciousness, then you wouldn't continue doing it. That's a rule of life." She paused before resuming, "Let's begin by having you tell us about yourself. Tell us the behaviours that you wish you could change – the ones which keep reoccurring no matter what you do."

"I'm insecure; I lack confidence in who I am. I spend a large amount of time feeling worried and anxious. I work endlessly to make sure that others like me." Tears formed in her eyes, "And the worst of it is, the intense amount of energy which I exert trying to make everything okay comes at the expense of my integrity. I know that my relationship with Ken is unhealthy, and yet I stay in it.

"I've sexually rejected Ken, and now turn to other people to meet my sexual needs. I want him to touch me less and less as my resentment builds. I know that he's having sex with others too, but I just don't care! I hate kissing him: I know that he'd love it if I would, but I just can't. There's this huge underlying tension between us – an anger which is making an insurmountable wall." She paused, took a breath and then added, "I've never had the love from him that I've wanted."

Ronna asked, "Who's on the podium at the moment and what's the score on the drama scale?"

"The Child is on the podium with some Observer thrown in. I'd say the drama score is about 4 or 5."

Chris asked, "Have you ever received the love that you want from anyone?"

Kathy said, pondering, "Well, that's the confusing part. I know that my parents loved me... so I don't know why I feel this way."

Chris clarified, "So you have felt loved in the past?"

"Yes, but there's something else going on here – I can feel it."

"Let's keep going deeper: we're making a good start into the Systems that drive your behaviour."

Kathy opened her journal and began to write as she said, "My mother was very anxious and my father was dismissive. It took a lot to get my father's attention. I always did what I was told – kept my room tidy, didn't fight and had good grades. But I was the last one of their children, and I don't think that they had the energy for me which they'd had for the others. There's no baby book with my name on it, for instance, and I didn't get baptised, while the others did. I was even left behind when the family took trips, as I was a runner and they were afraid that I'd get lost."

Ronna inserted, "Were you praised for your good efforts – held up in front of your siblings as someone to aspire to?"

"Hmm no, I wasn't. Maybe once in a while when report cards came out there would be a general comment, but that would be it. I just did my thing and no one really noticed my achievements."

Ronna said, "So you were invisible – unimportant?"

Kathy stared at her page, her face suddenly pale, and then burst into tears, "That's it... Oh my God, that's it... I'm unimportant!"

Kathy sat for a while, allowing the new information to settle into her consciousness. This was a pivotal awareness in her journey, as it began to make sense of all her crazy behaviours.

Ronna said softly, "I'm unimportant."

Kathy nodded and repeated the words while wiping tears from the pages of her journal, "I'm unimportant. Yep, that's it. I thought it was about love, but love never really fitted. This fits. In fact," she said with more tears running down her face, "I'm so unimportant that I can't even have a child. I've had three miscarriages and no babies. I'm the one who always wanted children, the one who dreamed of a family and being a Mom – and I can't even have a child."

We watched as she integrated this new awareness – as she saw how her unimportance System had influenced so many things in her life. She then said, "I now realise that I was madly rushing around, not knowing what I was seeking or why I wanted it. I can finally see how I've used drama to help me get attention and to feel important. Wow. I suddenly see that as a Mom, I'd have been important." She looked dazed as this new information hit her.

Chris said, "Just keep breathing."

Kathy took another deep breath, tears still gently rolling down her face, "I take a large number of photographs. I use them to try and stay connected with other people. I keep them all over the house, especially on my fridge. I look at them to remind me that I'm important and connected to something or someone else."

Ronna repeated, "I'm unimportant."

Kathy nodded, still looking stunned, "I'll need to be with this for a while and to work with it."

"Where does this realisation score on the acceptance scale?"

"On the acceptance scale, it feels pretty high right now: probably an 8. It's just such a close fit." She spent a few moments finishing her writing.

Chris ended the session by saying, "For homework, I want you to observe how your unimportance System plays out in your day to day life."

* * *

Kathy came back the following week, "It seems that my drama and unimportance play off each other. The drama gives me the illusion of being important – so the greater the drama, the more important I must be. I can see that this is all nonsense, but it keeps playing out. I try to Observe – try to make all these dramas as neutral as beige walls – but as soon as I've done that, I'm caught up in another dramatic incident."

Chris asked, "What do you do to ensure that you're unimportant?" Kathy looked confused, so Chris continued, "Your inner Child developed the System to make sense of the chaos in her life. In that moment of discovery – that moment when the rule made sense of all the chaos – the Child felt a huge sense of relief. Now the Child is trying to re-experience that moment – to re-establish the context, re-make the rule and feel the deep sense of relief again."

Kathy said reflectively, "It's like being an addict. The first high is incredible, but then you spend the rest of your life trying, but never quite succeeding, to recapture that high."

"Yes, it's just like an addiction. Given that new insight, I'll re-ask my question: how do you contribute to your experience of being unimportant?"

"I don't know. I'll have to watch for that."

"Yes, you'll need a strong Observer to watch your actions from this new perspective."

"I don't think that my Observer is developed enough to do that. It's hard to watch if you're caught up in a drama."

Pausing for a moment, Ronna asked, "Are you up for trying something new?"

Kathy nodded, and looking at Chris, said, "I'm not going to like this, am I?"

Chris chuckled, "No, probably not. Are you up for it anyway?"

Kathy took some deep breaths and then said, "Okay, I'm ready. What do you want me to do?"

Ronna began, "This is something that we call Directing. It's an eclectic blend of bits and pieces from other therapies that we've mangled into our own process. In this tool, we're going to use pillows to represent the various parts of you. We'll ask you to place the pillows around the room – the location in the room representing how you see each part within your psyche and how it relates to the other parts." She paused, "Kathy, pick up a pillow. This pillow will represent your need for drama. I want you to place it anywhere in the room – for this first one it really doesn't matter where." Kathy moved to the corner of the carpet and placed the pillow there. "Now choose a place to represent 'I'm unimportant'." After thinking for a moment, she put another pillow fairly close to the drama pillow. "Where's the thinker?"

Kathy asked, "The part of me that thinks about my feelings, or the part that gets caught up in worrying?"

"Take two pillows – we have lots – and place one for the worrier and the other for the thinker." Kathy placed the worrier pillow alongside the other two, and then placed the thinker pillow in the middle of the room. "Now, for your last pillow, where's the Observer?" Kathy placed a pillow completely across the room, as far away as possible from the other pillows.

"Good, now where are you in this room?"

Kathy stepped into the centre of the three pillows which represented unimportance, drama and the worrier and then said, "Here I am."

Chris asked Ronna to stand where Kathy was standing, and then Kathy went over to join Chris. When she could see where she'd placed herself, Chris asked, "What do you notice?"

"I see that my unimportance, drama and worrier are close to each other. The part of me that thinks about my feelings is further away, and the Observer is as far away as possible. In fact, I was tempted to open the door and throw the pillow out onto the lawn."

Chris walked over, picked up the pillow, opened the front door and threw the pillow outside, right onto the lawn. He returned to Kathy and asked, "Is that better?"

Kathy shook her head, "I can't believe you just did that. But yes, that's better."

"So what else do you notice?"

"It seems rather crowded over there," she said pointing to where Ronna and the pillows were situated. She pondered that for a few moments and then added, "And the Observer is nowhere to be seen."

"Well, what do you expect? You keep her out on the lawn where she can't see what's going on – while unimportance, drama and worry have your full attention."

"No wonder I get so overwhelmed," she said. She then looked at Chris and asked, "What do I do now?"

"'Do'? This is an exercise in becoming aware. This is your life. There's nothing to do but notice." He led Kathy over to the cluster of pillows and asked her, "We're now going to give each of these parts of you a voice so that you can see externally what's going on internally. Let's begin with drama: what does it have to say to you about its role in your life?"

"She doesn't say much – she just takes any feeling and blows it up to huge proportions."

"How about worry?"

"Oh, she has lots to say. 'You're not doing this right.' 'That person doesn't like you.' 'You'd better stay in touch or people will forget about you.'"

"How about unimportance?"

"She has a lot to say too. 'You don't matter.' 'You don't deserve to be loved.' 'You'd better work harder to be someone.'"

Chris asked Kathy's unimportance, "What do you have to say to Ken?"

Kathy answered, speaking on behalf of unimportance, "Kathy tried to talk to Ken, but he wouldn't listen. Mind you, she doesn't try too hard – she's too afraid to push Ken away in case he stops loving her. She's given up trying to talk to him."

Chris looked toward the pillows with Ronna, representing Kathy, standing in the middle of them, and said, "I see. And you're standing in the middle of this – looking a little like a whipped puppy just taking all this from drama, worry and unimportance. It's like you don't know any better."

"It's pretty pathetic," Kathy said with disgust.

"Who's saying that?"

"Unimportance."

"Okay, then stand on the pillow and say it."

Kathy walked over to the pillow, looked at Ronna (who was still pretending to be Kathy), and said, "You're pathetic. You're an unimportant loser. No wonder no one wants you: you disgust me. You can't even have a child. Now you hide and get angry when you see a pregnant woman. You'd better stay with Ken; no one else would have you." She stopped and paled. "I didn't know that. I stay with Ken because I believe that no one else would have me."

Kathy and Chris talked for a while longer, exploring the relationships between the various parts of Kathy's psyche and getting more information from the thinker - the one who thinks about her feelings. When this was done, they both walked outside to the pillow lying on the grass. Chris then asked, "What does the Observer have to say?"

"It's a nice day and the sun is shining," said Kathy as the Observer.

Chris asked, "How do you feel out here on the grass?"

The Observer responded, "I just notice that the sun is shining. There are no beige walls out here, but that's how I feel about what's going on inside the house."

Kathy looked amazed and said as herself, "That's incredible. I throw her out here on the lawn and she just watches the sunshine."

"That's the Observer. She just watches what there is to see. Let's head inside." Chris picked up the discarded Observer and the two of them returned to the house.

After everyone had sat down again, Ronna said, "When I was standing amongst the pillows as Kathy, I felt overwhelmed."

Kathy replied, "Yes, that's how I feel a lot of the time. Give me a minute, I want to record this before I forget." She began writing down the experience as a way of integrating the work.

When she was done, Chris said, "Earlier in the session, I asked how you were helping to create situations in which you're unimportant. I'd like to come back to that the next time we're together. In the meantime, score how far away your Observer is during events. Is she out on the lawn or a little closer?"

* * *

Kathy returned a couple of weeks later. When she was settled in, Ronna asked, "How have you been doing with scoring your Observer?"

She responded, "I couldn't forget the final thing that Chris said to me at the last session – about how I work to create situations where I'm unimportant. He was right: it seems like everything I do is about craving attention, but much of what I do actually makes me less important, not more. My sex life is a good example: I've tried to get attention through sex: I've tried being a swinger, being with women, being promiscuous etc. I've always been looking for connection, but in places where connection wasn't being offered. Instead of getting what I was seeking, I was left feeling ashamed.

"I'm seeing it all so clearly now, as if asking the question removed the blinders from my eyes. The question pushed me into the

Observer, and that gave me the perspective to see how unimportance drives the need for attention – but in ways that bring more shame than attention.

"I also made some other discoveries. I realised that sex gives me a sense of power over men, as it's the only time that I feel powerful. I've heard that promiscuous women actually dislike the men they're with – that the sex is more about anger and punishment than love and attention. In a moment of brutal honesty, I realised that I was one of those women – seeking to punish the men I was with. Instead of getting what I thought I wanted, I was working hard to get the opposite. I was seeking to punish them while they sought to punish me in the same way."

Chris said, "So how does this fit into your relationship with Ken?"

Kathy smirked and replied, "I knew you were going to ask me that. I'm already beginning the process of leaving. I told him last week that it's over and he's moved out to a friend's place. I knew I couldn't continue after getting these insights into what I was doing and why. It's pretty scary being on my own, though: I've never been on my own before, and the fear is very intense."

Ronna asked, "How are you managing that?"

With her head down, Kathy said, "Ah, well... I'm in a new relationship. His name is Brian." Her words were barely audible.

Ronna asked, "I see your shame: you think we're going to judge you?"

"Most people are judging me. Unimportance, worry and drama are having a field day. I'm torturing myself and being extremely critical, but I've been doing my homework. That means that I'm also watching things from the Observer. In the moments when the Observer isn't on the front lawn, I can see that it's all bullshit – that the criticisms have little basis in reality. Choosing a new relationship is my choice to make, not anyone else's. Too often, though, unimportance has the upper hand."

Chris said, "Hmm, hence the shame."

Ronna added with sarcasm, "Well, unimportant people should hide in shame, right?"

Kathy chuckled and then sat up, "I feel ashamed and weak about needing a man in my life to leave Ken…but having a man was the only way I could do it!"

Ronna asked, "What's the drama scoring, based on the shame?"

"It's a good 8."

Chris changed the topic slightly and said, "So this is bad? It's bad to feel shameful and weak, and bad that you've had to have a new man so you can leave Ken?"

"Yes, that's how I feel. In my head I know it's neither good nor bad – I've grown enough to know that. But this is how I'm feeling."

Ronna stated, "So if you feel it, it's reality? It's the truth?'

"No, but my feelings are so powerful."

"So are your thoughts, but neither your thoughts nor your feelings are the Observer. What does the Observer see?"

"She sees the feelings – and also sees the Child being caught up in them."

"Nice noticing. The Observer is good at identifying who's on the podium. What's your drama score now?"

"Actually much less – maybe a 3? That's strange: just asking the Observer reduces the score. Why is that?"

Chris answered, "When you ask the Observer a question, you've already taken back the podium from the Child. Then you can call on the Observer to act, which in turn helps to reduce the drama score."

"That's incredible! So what do I do now?"

"When you're caught up in your feelings of shame and guilt or are feeling weak because you needed another man to leave Ken, you call on the Observer. All of these events, from the Observer's viewpoint, are like beige walls."

"The idea that I just watch seems so strange. I'm used to doing things – trying to get things right."

"Yes, you're used to doing – doing drama. You're used to taking a feeling and making it into an Oscar-winning performance. But earlier, when you moved from the Child to the Observer, the drama score moved from an 8 to a 3. Which serves you better?"

"You ask that like I have a choice!"

Chris looked surprised and asked, "Don't you? When Ronna asked you about the Observer, you called on her and the drama moved from an 8 to a 3. You chose, when asked, to be in the Observer."

"Yeah, actually you're right. I think I'm getting this: I can choose to bring in the Observer as another archetype and lower my drama scale." She laughed and stated, "I've been a little slow here. I now see that I can bring the Observer in just like I bring in my Adult."

"Right, excellent parallel," Ronna said. She then added, "Let's change the subject for a moment. Tell us about Brian."

"Well, he works as clerical staff for one of my clients. One look and there was an immediate click. He's so different from Ken: he's gentler, more compassionate – really Ken's opposite. And," she paused, blushing slightly, "he's great in bed. Sex is like nothing I've ever had before. We make love with our souls and it's mind blowing."

She looked at Chris and said, "Don't bother saying 'This too shall pass.' I think it's the real thing; it's just too different from with Ken."

As the session came to an end, Chris smiled and said, "Okay, I won't say it."

* * *

Kathy cancelled the next appointments, saying that she was using her Observer and that everything was going fine. She finally returned about ten months later. After arriving, she sat down and immediately said to Chris, "Okay, you can have your 'I told you so' moment now. Things with Brian aren't going very well. The sex is still great – better than great – but he can be so mean. He's often critical and, when I confront him about it, he just walks out. Then I get scared, go over to his house and manipulate him back into the relationship with sex. It's become clear that the relationship is about attention more than love, although love is there. I confuse sex and love: I always have. It's a big part of me. Touch, especially sexual touch, feeds a place inside which longs for love and connection...and with Brian the sex is so great. It confuses me."

"How is your Observer in this? Is she still out on the front lawn?"

"She's better. I know that I'm being driven by my fears and the insecurities of the Child, but knowing those things doesn't stop me from repeating the same pattern over and over again. Brian knows how to push my buttons – how to get me feeling insecure. Jealousy is the worst: he knows that all he has to do is look at another woman and make a comment about how sexy she is. I get hooked, even though I know that he's doing it just to be cruel. Why would someone be like this? I keep trying to get him to change and then he's okay for a while, but soon something happens and he does it again. It can be something small which sets him off, like me asking him to help out with something.

"When I get caught up in the drama of the relationship, I can see what I'm doing. I know it's not what I want to do, and yet I keep doing it. Although," she added, "I'm less extreme than I used to be. Even in the confusion between sex and love, I still try to get love through sex – but I now observe myself doing it. It's funny how I watch it, knowing that it's false and yet still strong enough to draw me back to Brian over and over again."

Ronna said, "Kathy, the Observer gives you the ability to see – even if what you're watching isn't what you want. However, the observing is leading to changes, big changes, in your behaviour. We're seeing them, even if you can't."

"Really? That's encouraging to hear. Sometimes it feels like I'm doing all this work just to stand still."

"Thinking that generally means that you've made progress and are at a new layer of your journey. Old patterns are still there, but your awareness is different and there's less of an extreme to what you're doing. This is common for those patterns of behaviour which sit at the root of who you are. Everyone has some behaviours like this, whether it's eating, spending, co-dependency, substance abuse, over-working or something else. These behaviours repeat over and over again regardless of the amount of work that you do or the successes that you have in other areas of your life. All you can do is continue to observe these patterns and, on good days, make different choices. This is very true in your case: you've made all kinds of shifts personally and professionally, but your core personality hasn't changed."

Kathy nodded. "Yes, you're right. I certainly feel different and, in many areas, I see that I'm acting differently. I just sometimes get focused on this one area and lose sight of the rest."

Chris suggested, "Let's go back to Brian. You're going to continue this pattern of getting jealous, angry and fearful before calling him back into the relationship through sex. Your Observer is watching this: she sees the pattern and is as excited about it as you are with the colour of the walls in our office."

"Yes – and at times, I can be the Observer and know that. Then…"

Ronna interrupted saying, "Just be with that: sometimes you can be the Observer. No one lives there permanently."

"They don't? I was trying to do it perfectly and be there all the time."

"Kathy, there's no such thing as perfectly. Now take a breath."

She visibly relaxed. "Right, breathe."

Moving the discussion on, Chris said, "You said that you keep trying to get Brian to change?"

"I know," Kathy said with a sigh. "I know that I can't get him to change, but I want him to. The sex is so great and I'm afraid that I'll lose it all."

"Okay, I just wanted to check." We spent the rest of the session working through some additional issues. The homework was unchanged: continue to call upon the Observer.

* * *

It was some time before Kathy returned. The first thing she said as she arrived was, "I feel exhausted."

Ronna responded, "There's a contradiction here. You look so vibrant – so much more alive than I've ever seen you – and yet you also look tired. What's that about?"

Kathy sighed, "I've just fought so much with myself and my issues that I've become exhausted by the whole thing. It's all left me cracked wide open, and in the openness, I'm seeing a sense of nothingness." We asked her to explain what she meant. "I realised that my Systems, drama and worry have muddled my thinking process and kept me locked in a pattern which isn't really focused on anything. The purpose has been to keep me away from the sense of nothingness and emptiness that I'm feeling now."

Chris added, "So, the war is over. Now you see what all the fighting has been about. It's just a distraction to keep you out of the nothingness and emptiness. That doesn't mean that your life is now easy: all of the old Systems are still there and will still play out. There will be times of drama, frustration, fear and struggle – but now you'll know that these are only distractions. In the midst of it all, you can return to the Observer and know times of nothingness, equanimity and peace."

With gentle tears, Kathy said, "It's over?" She breathed for a moment, "Yes, it's really over… I know that. But the emptiness…"

"Kathy, look at yourself. You're calm – almost serene. You're quietly observing the emptiness in your life. What's there left to fight about?"

"Even though my drama and worrier are making lots of noise, I know that you're right. I see what you mean about both the struggle and the Observer co-existing."

She opened her journal and said, "I'd like to share some discoveries that I've made recently. What I've written is rather long, but I'm so grateful to you two and so proud of what I've accomplished that I'd like to share it with you."

[The remainder of the chapter is made up of edited writings which have been taken directly from Kathy's journal.]

"My relationships have served me and helped me to grow, even while they've been abusive, critical and lacking in support. Over the years, I've settled for less because it's familiar. I've completely depended on these relationships emotionally, and not realised that there wasn't a whole lot there for me. The support didn't really happen, as my partners weren't there for me emotionally. It's been a process of muddling through, year after year, episode after episode – staying and trying again until I'm completely busted open and woken up a little bit more. Then I have a slightly improved ability to see without attachment – to be the Observer of my thoughts, my pain and my own bullshit.

"It's been a process of awakening. When I was with Ken, I was completely asleep, unaware of why certain things made me feel certain ways and without the insight or ability to make other choices. Through experiences, pain, heartache, reflection, support and the teachers that came into my life, I slowly began to wake up to what I really am, getting insight into the core Systems which have served me as well as the bullshit stories that I've told myself. Seeing through my own bullshit, therein lies the truth... and it's beige walls.

"I still wonder why I stay with Brian. I see how mean he can be and I see how dark he can be when he's triggered, angered or called on his shit. If I don't call him on his issues then he's there to help out and to do Brian stuff, but when challenged or called upon to really be there in a way that I need, he's quickly gone. I've been living in an illusion of depending on him as if he was supporting me – and yet all along I've really been there for myself, picking up my own pieces and not giving myself any credit for doing so."

"Since last month I'm not as driven by the sex: I observe it a bit more. I don't feel the same need, which is unbelievable – I often shake my head in wonder, knowing that it used to completely control me. I know that I've changed, because the last time I challenged Brian on something, I didn't run back in the middle of the night to manipulate him with sex. Instead, I told him that if sex is going to happen, it'll be because we decide to have sex. I did the right thing for me – I gave myself value and self-respect. Doing that felt right – and Brian was shocked. More recently, I've watched him have sex with my body. It wasn't really sex with me.

I felt disconnected, but not antagonistic toward him; I just watched.

"There's still a lot that centres around my being with him. If he wasn't there, then I wouldn't be able to use him as the 'excuse'; the fall guy. I'd end up taking even more responsibility for myself on this journey. Brian is just being Brian. Seeing the same thing repeated over and over again tells me that he is who he is. I see that – while also seeing myself wanting it otherwise. I can now recognise how skilled he is at manipulating a conversation, for instance: I used to think it was me at fault. Now I see his strategy to knock me down verbally. I'm taking responsibility for my own stuff, and realising that how I choose to react or respond is up to me.

"I feel the familiar feeling of being trapped – like I was with Ken for those last few years. Being trapped in an illusion of bullshit that I know in one sense isn't real...but it feels so real at times.

"I'm now more likely to remove myself from a situation in which I'm not comfortable. I don't feel as compelled to see people so often.

"I realise how much my Observer has grown. I used to be snarled up in life and not able to see it at all. Now I can allow life to happen without trying to control it – just watching it, instead. This is a step forward. Where it goes from here, I don't know. I'll just continue to watch and find out.

"I watch myself when I'm tired or in physical pain. I see myself complain to certain people and, depending on their reactions, feel like I have them hooked and feed on this a bit. With others it goes nowhere, so I diffuse the pain myself. The Observer sees how I can get caught up in the drama of an illness as a way of serving and bringing attention to myself.

"I watch myself being more open, loving and caring and notice how this opens up channels and paths of vitality, life and true existence. It isn't the manipulating with drama, but real, true kindness and caring that opens me up more and often lands more deeply with other people.

"Now I get attention by doing workshops. I get a thrill from that and see how it's a more positive and healthy direction for the drama to get channelled in. I see that, but don't let it go to my head. I know that I'm not more important than others.

"I'm now feeling more and more awake – in the midst of a transformation. I finally have some tools to navigate around my own insanity. I can be caught up in the story one moment...but then I'll look up past the storm above my head and get some glimpses beyond into nothing. At the same time, I'm learning how to move more consciously through the world. I want people in my life who will call me on my shit as well as people I can call on theirs! I'm bringing humour into the insanity to help transcend situations – to make this journey a 'joy-ney' (ha ha, that's really corny!)"

16 Conclusion

As a conclusion to this book, we've decided to do something a little different. Instead of reviewing what was covered in the previous chapters, we'll instead tell a couple of stories. These are stories from our lives: stories of how Radical Acceptance has influenced our journeys. They're also stories about archetypes – specifically the Martyr and the Control Freak. As we said in the introduction chapter, there are many different archetypes. We covered the Child, the Adult and the Observer back then, and these are two more. In our next book, we'll explore these and other common archetypes in more detail – so as well as summarizing this book and giving you some more details about our personal lives, we'll also be making a shameless plug for our next publication. Start looking out for it sometime over the next year.

I, Christopher, am writing on the Martyr. I'll refer to the Martyr as masculine simply because I'm male – not because this archetype is inherently masculine or is found more often in men. In fact, we see the Martyr equally in men and women. What defines this archetype is how much it suffers: oh how the Martyr suffers! People with an active Martyr archetype identify themselves as caring, loving people who feel unloved, misunderstood, unappreciated, laden with demands, and saddled with responsibilities beyond those given to others. More generally, Martyrs believe that they suffer without cause – that they're innocent of the wrongs that they're punished for having committed. Because Martyrs believe that they're innocent, they constantly look to the future: a future where wrongs will be righted and the guilty punished. The origins of the archetype are wrapped in the shadows of childhood. Its exact causes aren't clear, but it likely stems from a longing to be loved that seems to never get met.

I discovered my Martyr while listening to a tape recording back in the early 1990s. The tape was of a man who claimed that he channelled an entity called 'Lazarus', and the recording was entitled Ending the Crisis of Martyrhood (yes, it was one of the many 'fix' teachings that I went through during my earlier searching). The first time I said, "Yes, I'm a Martyr" was when I listened to this tape, but looking back, it wasn't my first big encounter with my Martyr archetype. For that, I need to go back further. In some form, I can trace the archetype back to my early childhood – but since we're looking for big encounters, I'll talk about an incident that stands out for me from the late 1980s.

In 1985, I went on a weekend retreat called a 'Shalom Retreat'. At this event, I was invited to really feel my feelings. Using a deep breathing exercise, the particular feeling I explored was anger. Before the retreat, I wouldn't have said that I was an essentially angry person, but during my work with the deep breathing, I exploded into a huge rage. The sense of relief and freedom I felt from going through this process removed the emotional chains that bound me, and I broke free. It was a freedom that I immediately relished and celebrated. Interestingly, however, the retreat didn't change my image of myself as a non-angry person. Instead, I still saw myself as the same caring, sensitive person – but recognised that I'd built up some anger and so had needed to blow off some steam. When I left the retreat, I was happy to be able to feel my anger fully for the first time, but my innocent self-image hadn't altered.

After such a powerful weekend, I started attending retreats regularly. At one weekend session, I had an interaction with another participant – the details of which are now long lost to me. The interaction didn't go well, and she told me that I'd done something very insensitive. In saying this, she broke the bubble of my innocent self-image; she challenged my Martyr. This made me get angry – really angry. In a rage, I left the group and began thinking irrational thoughts. I felt the woman had been overly-critical and incorrect in her assessment of me. I blamed the retreat leaders and the circumstances for her 'mistake' – anyone and everyone except for myself. This is a very typical response for the Martyr in such a situation. Another typical response came next: in an unconscious attempt to balance the injustices done to him, the Martyr punishes those around him. As I walked away into the forest that surrounded the retreat property, I began thinking about how I might get hurt, lost, injured or even killed – each option punishing the other people at the retreat for what had been said more than the last. That sure showed them for criticizing me! Of course, I actually left during a break in the activities, so no one even missed me – and certainly no one was aware of my vicious thoughts. I'm not saying that the processes of the Martyr make any sense, but there it is.

Withdrawal, like I did from the group, is a common punishment for the Martyr. I'd particularly enjoy waiting for someone to come and find me and attempt to make me feel better – and then quickly rebuffing them because I was angry and wanted others to be punished. No matter what they said, I'd then continue the punishing by telling them that they weren't saying the right things, that they didn't say them in the right way, or that they just didn't understand what was going on. As I've observed over the years, other Martyrs withdraw by just going silent and not speaking to anyone. I've seen men and women who'll punish each other in this way by going silent for anywhere from hours to months (the record holder for me was a person who didn't speak to their partner for three months!).

When I took myself away from the group, the withdrawal seemed justified and appropriate to the situation: the other people at the retreat were to blame, and my anger was directed firmly toward them. All Martyrs who withdraw in some way see themselves as innocent in this regard. For me, though, the situation wasn't quite as simple. Before the incident happened, I'd done extensive reading about projection – so when I'd calmed down, I knew that my anger was really directed at myself. I knew that the woman was right and that I had been insensitive. Looking at the broader picture, I knew that I was often insensitive and that my innocent self-image needed serious revision. This was a difficult and painful discovery, and one I quickly set about trying to fix – by attending more retreats, reading book after book and going for countless therapy sessions. Nothing worked.

When I discovered the Ending the Crisis of Martyrhood tape a few years later, I could finally put a name to this part of me that loved to suffer. Better yet, the tape offered a fix of its own – a way to 'cure' me of being a Martyr. Just like the other fix therapies, though, it didn't work. Instead of being free from this horrid character flaw, the tape only helped me to see how frequently the Martyr was active in my life; I could suddenly recognise how often I was punishing others and how very often I felt unloved, unappreciated and burdened. Once I could see these aspects of myself, I started talking to others about the Martyr, and we'd often all find the experience quite funny. As I laughed, I felt a sense of relief and release. This was an early clue that aided in both my and Ronna's eventual move toward acceptance. At that point, however, I hadn't yet moved from fixing to acceptance, and so the work to fix continued.

I'm a firm believer in the philosophy that anything worth doing is worth over-doing, and fixing my Martyr was no exception. As such, I read, studied, meditated and went on countless retreats to remove this part of who I am. For books, I became especially interested in those on Jungian psychology, which at one point led me to study fairy tales as clues to healing the psyche. My studies then took me back to university to study Religion and Culture: courses included Philosophy, Native Studies, Biblical Studies and even the Sociology of Witchcraft. My meditation covered Hindu and various Buddhist traditions, including a nine-day Silent Retreat. Of the many other retreats I went on, I experienced Shalom Retreats, Native Sweat Lodges, a Drumming Retreat and several more.

Whatever I tried, though, nothing worked. I still felt the familiar feelings of the Martyr, and when I was under stress, I'd strike out in ways that were punishing to others. With all the work I'd done, I was certainly more comfortable with the Martyr's feelings and my frequency of striking out was reduced – but the basic patterns remained present. It was around this time that both Ronna and I started exploring how feelings could drive growth, which led to an early incarnation of the Radical Acceptance Wheel. Using this, I began to see the Martyr's feelings as my guides and teachers: aides to helping me know myself better. The Martyr was still a problem for me, though, so I continued working to get rid of it.

As I carried on, the self-discovery tools that we used helped me to work with my feelings. This allowed me become more mature. From there, I was able to work with the Child (a great friend of the Martyr) and could call upon the Adult. I knew who was on the podium, and could often even take the podium back from whoever had taken charge. I was also making great discoveries, defining my principles, becoming more responsible and learning how to move into the Observer.

Finally, as I continued to grow, I saw the light: no amount of work can fix who I am. From here, we developed the Wheel and made acceptance key throughout the circle. This changed my focus on the Martyr from fixing to accepting. Now I worked hard to score how well I punished others and myself and how well I suffered. I also began to look for how the Martyr serves me and to seek out reasons that I can be grateful for its presence in my life. With time, I began to see how important it was for me to suffer – and how if life didn't provide sufficient suffering, I'd act to ensure that there was enough to keep my Martyr happy.

This last discovery was a crucial one: I was an expert at creating suffering in my life, and would often satisfy my Martyr in the subtlest of ways. A typical example centred on my birthday. Growing up, my birthday was the most important day of the year – even more important than Christmas. It was the day where I was special: where the focus was on me. This attention is important to the Martyr, as it often feels unloved and that it's not special in anyone's life – no matter how much evidence there is to the contrary. Ronna is a Christmas person, however, and birthdays don't mean that much to her. This created a wonderful situation for my Martyr: Ronna wouldn't make as big a deal over my birthday as I'd want her to, proving to me that I wasn't loved. This would then cause me to get angry and withdraw. Was the problem with Ronna? Was she failing to honour my need for a special birthday? No. Ronna was just being Ronna. It was my hanging on to the Child's need to be special that created the suffering in my life: a job well done by my Martyr.

Another example of my expert ability to create suffering for myself concerns the idea that Ronna doesn't love me. Whenever I wouldn't get my way with – or what my Martyr felt that I deserved from – Ronna, I would immediately start thinking that she didn't love me. Then, one day, I used the Critical Thinking Tool to ask myself, "Is it true that Ronna doesn't love me? What evidence/facts do I have to show that Ronna doesn't love me?" Before long, I realised that I couldn't come up with any supporting facts – and what's more, anyone who has seen Ronna and me together knows one thing for certain: Ronna loves me very much. In that moment of Critical Thinking, I could see that Ronna loved me. She loves me in big and little ways: she loves me even when I'm deep into my Martyr and acting in ways that aren't very nice. She even manages to love me when she finds my dirty socks on the floor – again. The thought that she didn't love me had no basis in truth, but it did feed my Martyr.

That was many years ago, and since then my Martyr has continued to be a constant companion. I'm still discovering new tricks and areas of my life into which he enjoys jumping. How do I feel about the archetype now, though? I've accepted him. For the most part, he's just a fact in my life. Over the years, he's taught me a great deal: I've learned compassion for those who suffer, I've recognised the importance of the Critical Thinking Tool, and I've also deepened my ability to separate love from neediness. All in all, I'm grateful and give thanks to him.

I, Ronna, am writing about an archetype that plays a big role in my life: the Control Freak. As with Chris' writing about the Martyr, I'll refer to the Control Freak as female only because I'm female – it appears equally in both men and women. What defines this archetype is her need to feel in control of at least some areas of my life. Regardless of how small these areas might be, if I'm able to successfully manage them, then my Control Freak feels a sense of relief. However, as with many archetypes, the Control Freak seeks to do one thing but actually achieves the opposite: instead of controlling my life, in the long run she creates chaos. This is similar to the Martyr who, while seeking love, creates suffering.

My Control Freak has been a part of my life for a long time. Looking back, for instance, I can see times in my teens when it was active – although it really played out in my first marriage. In that marriage I controlled everything: the money, the children, the house repairs, the cooking, the cleaning – and I even took a course in car repair. I controlled my feelings (or at least thought that I did) only by allowing myself to feel depressed when everyone else's needs had been addressed. This didn't happen often, though: I was married to an alcoholic and drug addict, which meant that my life was always spinning wildly out of control.

As Chris mentioned in his story, his first experience of serious personal growth came through attending a Shalom Retreat in 1985. I also attended that retreat: it was where we first met. The event was my first Shalom Retreat, but I'd been involved in personal growth for a couple of years prior to attending, and had already left my husband and was working hard to become a better person (which was just one more thing for the Control Freak to grab hold of!). When Chris and I became a couple, I saw him as a healthy, together man and looked forward to letting go of the heavy burden of control that I'd been carrying.

A few words about my specific Control Freak: what she particularly likes is a sense of constancy. Change is chaos for her, so it makes her uncomfortable and fearful. I lived quite happily in one house from my birth until I moved out as a young adult, for example. When I first married, we bought a house and stayed there until the separation – at which point I was forced to move into a smaller home. Even though that last move hadn't been an enjoyable one, I was planning on settling down in my new place for a long stay.

Then I fell in love with Chris. Constancy, for Chris, is a word that generates a high level of stress. Since the day he moved out of his home, he'd never lived for two years or more at any one address. Since we became a couple twenty-three years ago, we've lived at fifteen addresses in eight cities and towns across four different countries. We've moved so much, in fact, that moving and the chaos associated with it has almost become a constant in my life itself. Similarly, in terms of work and money, I'd always envisioned the kind of life that my father had: he worked one job for most of his life and retired with a comfortable pension. Doing the same is hard when you don't live in the same city for more than a few years at a time.

I also made another mistake – perhaps the biggest mistake – for someone wanting control and constancy: I had children. Oh, I didn't have one or two: that would have been too simple. By the time Chris and I were done, there were five of them – two from my first marriage, two from Chris' first marriage and one together. I'm not saying that I regret having them, as I love them all dearly. The point is just that children will drive a Control Freak crazy, which is how the archetype keeps chaos present while you work so hard for control. A big part of the problem is that children each have their own individual personalities that, as a parent, you have very little control over. Oh, you learn effective parenting techniques – but ultimately the more your child grows, the less control you have over their individual actions and decisions. The worry associated with this gives the Control Freak even more ammunition to feed the chaos.

Given how my lifestyle has played to the Control Freak's influence, learning to accept her has been difficult. Initially, I was on a mission to fix this aspect of myself, because she would often express herself angrily. Finally, as I learned to accept her, she didn't need to be so angry any more She could relax and not need to work so hard to be heard; I knew and saw benefits in how I'm a controlling person. An example of this realization came from housework.

I like to live in a clean, organised and tidy house. Chris is comfortable in a house that's much more chaotic. When it came to housework, therefore, we had very different ideas of what was a clean room. I'd ask Chris to tidy a room, for instance, and after a while he'd say that he was done. When I'd walk in, I'd see many things not done – at least according to my standards. This led us into arguments, as I felt like he was being deliberately lazy to force me into doing all of the work. I didn't want to control the housework: I just wanted it done 'properly'. One day, we sat down to talk about the situation. Chris explained that it wasn't laziness that was causing the problem, but rather that what he saw after he'd tidied a room was a tidy room. He didn't see what I saw. I then explained that I didn't want to be controlling and a nag. He asked me why not: after all, he said, you are controlling around the housework.

I wasn't very happy about that accusation. Instead, I felt that he'd insulted me – when all he'd actually done was to state a fact. It was a fact that was clear to both of us, but a fact that I wanted to keep hidden. Control Freaks aren't nice people, after all: no one loves a Control Freak. Chris continued by saying, "I've seen you as controlling when it comes to housework and I love you. Why would the love change just because you acknowledge that you're controlling?" I was speechless. I watched as my Child wanted to deny what Chris was saying – to call him a liar. It took a real effort to take back the podium, call on the Adult, and use the Critical Thinking Tool. From that perspective I couldn't deny the truth of his statement – even though the idea that I could be loveable and controlling just didn't fit. This was one of my big acceptance breakthroughs. I could finally accept my Control Freak and know that Chris wouldn't leave. When I talked to my oldest daughter about this breakthrough several years later and said that I'd never seen myself as controlling around the housework, she simply burst out laughing. After she'd stopped, she said pretty much the same thing as Chris. The only one who hadn't know that I was controlling was me.

Having accepted my Control Freak, Chris and I renegotiated the housework. We would now share the workload, but I'd be in charge of setting out what needed to get done and what it meant for a room to be done. The arguments stopped, and we both relaxed. In time, it turned out that I liked to control the kitchen as well. Once more, I became the manager while Chris was my assistant. Now, instead of arguing, we often shared a laugh – and Chris would often tell folks that I was the Control Freak and he was the galley slave. Instead of being a struggle, the situation became a source of amusement, connection and intimacy. We sat back, looked at the relationship as a whole, and realised that there were areas where I was in charge and areas where he was in charge. This awareness brought humour into our struggles and greatly improved our relationship.

The more I could say 'yes' to my Control Freak, the less she needed to create chaos. When I denied her need to manage the housework, I created arguments with Chris. When I accepted her need and worked with it, the arguing stopped. The Control Freak's desire for control didn't go away – after all, it's a part of who she is. Instead, I learnt to live with her tendency as a part of myself. In many ways, coping with her desire for chaos has been the harder journey for me, as it was the chaos that I always fought against. I kept insisting that I really didn't want it, no matter how much of the chaos I kept creating. Like Chris, I started scoring it: tracking how much chaos I created in my desire for order. I began to explore the gifts in chaos – gifts like flexibility and strength. Only after a lot of work could I feel grateful for it. And now I am grateful: grateful for the ability to roll with life, grateful for the strength of character it has given me, and grateful for the inner knowledge that I can handle whatever life dishes out.

Am I in a state of complete acceptance? There's no such state – only the state of moving toward acceptance. This includes an ever-growing awareness of the Control Freak's role in my life, and an always-increasing gratitude for the gifts that she brings me.

* * *

17 Summary

The Wheel

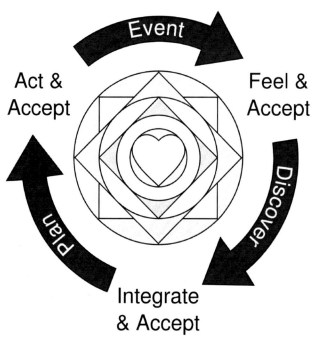

Use the Radical Acceptance Wheel to gain a deeper understanding of yourself by looking at how you respond to life. From this place of deeper understanding, you can choose to respond to life's events in new ways. You particularly need this theme when you respond to an event with an emotional response – when the event becomes 'charged'. Imagine that someone lies to you, for instance. In reality, the lying is what's termed a 'neutral' event – it's just something that's happened. If you respond to the lie by getting angry, tearful or afraid, however, then your emotional response means that you've 'charged' the event. This is where the Wheel comes in: its six spokes use the charge from the event as the energy which propels you through Radical Acceptance's other six themes.

Event

- Events are happening all the time, and events are neutral
- Most events aren't important to us and so are simply ignored
- Some events grab our attention and become 'charged' with an emotional response
- Charged events are really just invitations from our subconscious minds to take a deeper look within ourselves

Feel and Accept

- Do this every time you're feeling happy, sad, angry, powerful, fearful or excited etc.
- Step back from your emotional response – to be aware of the feeling without becoming caught up in it
- This can only happen when you fully feel and accept the feeling instead of judging it as either positive or negative

Discover

- To open the door to your unconscious world, Radical Acceptance uses a variety of tools – all driven by your feelings, your thoughts or events
- This opening leads you to discover parts of yourself that have been forgotten, suppressed or rejected
- These discoveries aren't flaws which needing fixing: they're integral parts of who you are
- Journey deep into your psyche to explore the amazing world which is you

Integrate and Accept

- Radical Acceptance prompts you to accept what you find – no matter how awful it may first appear
- This means seeing the gift in each discovery and being grateful for what you once despised
- Integrating and accepting what was once rejected is a process, and we teach you tools to aid in deepening the integration over time
- There will be discoveries where integration is a lifelong process - one at which you will never fully arrive - and there will be discoveries where the integration will be shorter and more solid

Plan

- It's now time to plan a response to the original event: if it was someone lying to you, for instance, then that event now needs some kind of response, even if the response is a decision to do nothing
- Stand back and plan an appropriate answer: make time to analyse your possible options and consider the potential consequences associated with those choices
- Planning is part of the Adult archetype; without this step you will perpetually live from the Child in a cycle of Feel-Act-Regret

Act & Accept

- Sometimes acting will be easy, at other times difficult
- Some responses will be internal and others external: if they're external and likely to affect others, then you'll need to remember that anyone else's response to your actions belongs to them and not you
- The acceptance of Act and Accept invites you to accept the consequences of your actions instead of blaming them on others

Systems

- Systems are one of the cornerstones of Radical Acceptance: rules made by a child to make sense of their world that then become unconscious, firmly-held beliefs
- A young child experiences many painful and traumatic events – some of which may be extremes such as sexual or physical abuse, but most often will be events that appear less traumatic to an adult but which were still significant to the child
- 'Insignificant' events may have come from parents, teachers, other children, siblings or the child's extended family
- The psyche needs to develop a way of managing the pain and trauma associated with such events
- Since the young child has limited cognitive ability at understanding why the events are happening, he or she compensates by believing that the problem lies within
- The child then creates a belief that gives order to this chaos – e.g. a child believing that he or she is unlovable as a result of receiving too little attention from a significant adult in their life
- Over time, the belief becomes re-enforced and deeply engrained into our psyche: Radical Acceptance calls this a System
- In life as an adult, all thoughts, feelings and events go through your Systems – giving them a powerful impact on your life
- Generally speaking, you have two to three major Systems which are the foundation to your personality
- Understanding the concept of Systems gives you an important awareness of why you make the choices you do as an adult
- You can't see a System directly, but you can see its influence through your actions and behaviour
- A System is active when what you're doing is in contradiction to your stated goals; Systems direct your actions into dysfunctional patterns to re-create the experiences which formed them

Archetypes

- Another cornerstone of Radical Acceptance is archetypes
- 'Archetype' suggests that the human psyche is structured in a way which helps us to interpret our experiences of life – a structuring which is inherent to being human and also personal based on your history
- This book focuses on the three archetypes which are most important to Radical Acceptance: the Child, the Adult and the Observer
- The Child archetype is the one everyone encounters first in life and is also carried into our adult lives
- The Child doesn't grow or mature, but remains as a child
- It's the Child which accumulates all of your hurts and traumas
- If the Child is left to run your life without the supervision of the Adult archetype, it can lead you to make dysfunctional choices
- The Adult archetype generally develops later in life as you physically and emotionally mature and begin to leave adolescence behind
- The Adult is the one that thinks about the world in a mature and responsible way
- The Adult acts based on principles, continuing to act even when that action hurts others, costs you money, makes you look bad or faces opposition
- Often there are areas of your life where the Child is in charge, regardless of how old you become – e.g. you may be an adult financially, but your personal relationships may remain more dysfunctional

- The Observer archetype also develops later, coming into play when we learn to step back from life and just notice what's going on
- The Observer is fully aware of all feelings, but doesn't act upon them – instead just standing back, seeing with awareness and knowing that all is neutral
- Calling on your Observer gives you space and time to call on either the Child or the Adult depending on the situation
- Each of the three archetypes mentioned has gifts to offer, and each can also cause problems
- All of the archetypes are available to us at any time, and each has its appropriate (and inappropriate) times and places in which to appear
- What many people don't realise is that you have a choice: you can choose which archetype to put in charge

Maturity

- Radical Acceptance defines Maturity as when both the Child and Adult archetypes are honoured and respected
- You're in charge of which archetype is appropriate in a given situation
- You can work on developing a strong Adult to act as an alternative choice in any given situation
- You can also learn to limit the Child, take charge of your life, and move both archetypes into balance

Self-Discovery

- The self-discovery theme makes you more aware of who you are, continually inviting you to go deeper into your subconscious mind
- The self-discovery process is vital to making the discoveries which play a key role in the Radical Acceptance Wheel, giving you some real insight into why you act in the way you do
- This step won't show you things to fix or a roadmap to change – but will instead give a view into your inner world and a glimpse of the forces that motivate your behaviour

Self-Acceptance

- This step involves accepting that your discoveries are both real and useful parts of who you are
- Acceptance allows you to be brutally honest with yourself – freeing up the significant amounts of energy that you'd otherwise use in repressing those unwanted personality traits
- The self-acceptance process also helps you to see and accept others for who and what they are; once you stop judging yourself, you'll be able to see the world around you with much more clarity and compassion

Principles

- Radical Acceptance defines principles as 'an intention to guide how I behave and a plan for when I miss'
- Your intentions and plans can cover anything, from how you'll treat others to how you'll treat yourself
- Principles offer a clear outline for what to do in any number of situations – both before events occur and in response to them
- By spending time working out in detail what principles you want to live by, you can increase your chances of living a life that develops in accordance with your goals
- Principles can only be established and adhered to from the place of the Adult

Responsibility

- Responsibility is the broadest theme in Radical Acceptance – defined both as 'everything you do comes as a result of choices that you've made' and 'the consequences of your actions are yours to accept'
- This step is about not blaming others for what you do or rationalizing behaviours
- You're also responsible for how others' reactions to the choices you make affect your life

Observer

- The Observer covers the third archetype introduced in this book; noticing all thoughts, feelings, behaviour and events without engaging in them in any way
- When you develop this archetype, you'll be able to set aside the relabelling and rationalising of your emotions which is associated with the Child and the Adult in certain situations – instead experiencing life from a more distanced and objective perspective
- Developing this archetype doesn't lead to detachment or apathy; it enables you to experience life more fully
- With the Observer, you'll be able to feel your feelings in their purest form – and to make the most rational decisions from that basis

Now that all of the key ideas have been recapped, we invite you to go forth and be Radical. Put aside your fixer, as he or she isn't useful. Instead, begin to see your life from a whole new light: the light of Radical Acceptance.

18 About the Authors

Ronna Smithrim

With over 25 years of personal growth and 18 years of being a psychotherapist I have a few tools and wise tidbits I can share.

As a child/teen, I never really felt I fit in; not in my family, school, social scene or work. After high school I decided to be a nurse and went into psychiatry. I was married at the age of 20 and had my daughter when I was 21.

I began exploring alternative health at the age of 22. It opened up areas to my life that I never knew existed. I learned about herbs, homeopathy, energy work and the connection between feelings and physical states such as pain. This challenged my beliefs and introduced me to people who became mentors and teachers.

At work I had just accepted a position in the Out Patient Department to provide group and one-on-one therapy. As a psychiatric nurse I began a group where staff would present a client and then we would look at our unconscious motives for what was happening or not happening in our sessions. I loved this weekly group. I had to look at some painful things, like why I took on clients' battles instead of letting them do it.

I came smack up against powerlessness and that is certainly what was happening in my personal life; powerless to stop a marriage from falling apart, powerless against feelings of shame, depression, grief and anger. I was just plain powerless. And here I was at age 25, married with two great kids, working full time and exploring alternative health with a marriage on the rocks and feeling depressed. I felt like a fraud by presenting myself as confident and self assured, but feeling like damaged goods.

At age 28 my marriage ended and I went into therapy. I was fortunate to meet a woman who knew just what to say to get me to explore myself. She invited me on an intensive retreat that she and her husband led. This was another major step in my life.

I attended many, many retreats trying to get my emotional world working for me or at a minimum to try and understand it. I met Chris at this first retreat and we began a friendship. The foundations of the relationship were that we challenged one another to grow and change. Over the 15 months of friendship our relationship grew and deepened until we entered a committed relationship and eventually married.

By age 31, Chris and I had 5 children; 2 were mine, 2 were his and 1 was ours. We were on a spiritual journey, but we had responsibilities and could not go off to an ashram for the next 15 years. However, I refused to put my journey on hold. It was too important to me and frankly, I couldn't even if I wanted to. Chris and I continued the painstaking journey of challenging, reading, constructing and deconstructing. Every time we thought we had arrived somewhere, we challenged each other to go deeper.

I went through many, long dark nights of the soul episodes. I worked with various models like Psycho synthesis, Gestalt, Creation Theology, Jungian, Archetypes, Carolyn Myss, and chakras. All assisted us in letting go of attachments.

Then one day while I was leading a retreat, I realised I had totally accepted myself and that I loved all aspects of myself. That included the hater and lover, the feelings of sadness and the joy, the bitch, Kali and Venus. There wasn't anything that I could not say yes to. I was all. I no longer had to get my self esteem met from others. I no longer had to look outside of myself for respect, or confidence. It was all right there. Radical Acceptance!!

Clients are angry asking me why they are spending thousands of dollars on therapists, workshops etc. and come to see me and their lives are transformed in a relatively short period of time. They complain that they can't find this in a book either!! They go away with the skills to begin radically accepting themselves. They no longer have to fight the wrong battles. The inner wars are easier to win when we know what tools to use and how to use them. Choosing wrong tools can lead to years and years of battles without going anywhere.

Now at 50 I teach my passion so others can have the tools to Radically Accept themselves and fully embrace life.

Christopher Oliphant

As a child I was curious in matters of spirituality, as a teen I was driven. I started as a staunch atheist and then became a part of the Christian Youth Movement. In a hurry to grow up, I was married with two wonderful children in a marriage that was clearly not working by the time I was twenty-five. I returned to Christianity as a way of saving my marriage. I was still driven and was quickly immersed into fundamentalism. It didn't work and at twenty-nine I started looking for alternatives.

My therapist had a unique way of getting me in touch with myself and invited me on an emotional intensive weekend. I blew my emotional world wide open. I worked for the next year and a half going to retreats, trying to figure out what was wrong with me. If I could only figure out what was wrong, then I knew I could fix it.

At 30 I began a new relationship with Ronna. This relationship would be different; without the problems of my first marriage. After all we were two aware people on a conscious journey and spiritual journey. By age 32 I was a father to 5 kids, working full time, often out of town, and 100% committed to my personal journey. The only trouble was, I was less and less sure of what that meant.

Ronna and I entered our power struggle years and all the old feelings came back. This wasn't the relationship of eternal love, happiness and never feeling damaged. More retreats, more books and more spirituality. I worked with all kinds of models and began looking at constructing a life that I could be proud of. I started leading my life by principles rather than rationalizations and feelings. I explored all aspects of the psyche celebrating each with new awareness; painful, angry, shameful and fearful parts of myself that needed to be integrated. Transforming them into light didn't work; every time I turned around they were still there. I began looking at these as gifts and strengths rather than damaged goods and weaknesses.

Ronna and I began our own psychotherapy practice and began leading retreats. It took various forms over the years depending on our lifestyle and the age of our children. I enjoyed teaching, reaching out, and watching people transform their lives. I celebrated their struggles, failures and successes.

At 39 the questions still begged to be answered. Where does God fit? Who is God? What is Love? What is the meaning of life? What is the meaning of death? Many questions, few answers and the answers I did have kept slipping away. I had to go deeper. Deconstructing and challenging with nowhere to go but deeper. No thought was left unturned. I watched all my walls, all my beliefs, all my security come crashing down, fade away and move beyond existence.

Now at 50 I teach my passion so others can have the tools to Radically Accept themselves and fully embrace life.

19 Bibliography

Anatomy of the Spirit, Caroline Myss

My Way, the Way of White Clouds, OSHO

Invisible Partners, John Sandford

The Dark Side of the Light Chasers, Debbie Ford

I Am That, Sri Nisargadatta Maharaj

Iron John, Robert Bly

When Bad Things Happen to Good People, Harold Kushner

The Five Love Languages, Gary Chapman

The Emotional Incest Syndrome, Dr. Patricia Love

Healing the Shame that Binds You, John Bradshaw

Facing Co-Dependence, Pia Mellody

Enneagrams, Variety

20 Contacting the Authors

The authors welcome questions and feedback using the following contact details.

Email Christopher Oliphant	ra.therapist@gmail.com

Website	www.radicalacceptance.com

FaceBook	www.facebook.com/RadAcc

Twitter	@RATherapist
	#radicalacceptance